Imago Dei

Beihefte zur Ökumenischen Rundschau Nr. 141

Ibolya Balla | Jaap Doedens (Eds.)

Imago Dei

The 12th Comenius Conference

EVANGELISCHE VERLAGSANSTALT
Leipzig

Bibliographische Information der Deutschen Nationalbibliothek
Die Deutsche Nationalbibliothek verzeichnet diese Publikation in der
Deutschen Nationalbibliographie; detaillierte bibliographische Daten
sind im Internet über http://dnb.dnb.de abrufbar.

This book is printed on ageing resistant paper.

Cover: Kai-Michael Gustmann, Leipzig
Cover image: Creation of Adam, Michelangelo, Public domain, via Wikimedia
Commons
Typesetting: Steffi Glauche, Leipzig
Printing and Binding: BELTZ Grafische Betriebe GmbH, Bad Langensalza
ISBN 978-3-374-07602-4 // eISBN (PDF) 978-3-374-07603-1
www.eva-leipzig.de

Table of Contents

NEW TESTAMENT

SYSTEMATIC THEOLOGY

PRACTICAL THEOLOGY

PHILOSOPHY, CULTURE, AND SCIENCE

The Kaleidoscope of *Imago Dei* An Introduction

Throughout the ages, human beings have been reflecting, talking, writing, philosophizing about what exactly makes them human. What is our task as humans, what is conscience, what goals should we set for ourselves, why do we suffer, in what do we differ from the animal world, with which we share our bodily existence? In an attempt to answer this kind of questions, the Judaeo-Christian tradition consistently referred to the conviction that humans are created in the image of God. This stance apparently provides a reassuringly brief answer. Yet, upon a closer look into this belief, it gives people a direction to look, but not all the answers. As a result of the secularization of what can be called rather loosely "western civilization," some would have expected that the whole concept formulated in this term *imago Dei* by the Judaeo-Christian tradition would become soon superfluous and obsolete. However, the opposite appears to be true in our age. The direction pointed to by this tradition not only has proved not to be outdated, but has actually gained in relevance.

The studies in this volume approach many of these questions beginning from the notion of humans as being created in the image of God. They provide insights from multifaceted fields of interests within human society. The texts presented here originate from the 12th Comenius Conference, held in Pápa, Hungary, 20–23 April 2022 at the Pápa Reformed Theological Seminary.

From a neo-Darwinian viewpoint, suffering, and specifically human suffering, is merely a built-in characteristic of nature. However, human experience usually does not concur which such an interpretation. A biblical-anthropological approach starting from humans created in the image of God does not allow for easy answers to the question of human suffering, but at least can search for answers in a deeper and more honest way. After all, if humans have intrinsic value in the eyes of God, how can this same

God allow so much suffering? *Ibolya Balla* deals with these questions by comparing the view on humans in Psalm 8 and in the Old Testament Book of Job. Another pressing question, if one accepts the *imago Dei* concept, is what to think about the way in which humans can dehumanize others. This question is treated by *Áron Németh* by analysing how the Old Testament displays the way in which humans do not accept the image of God in each other. Human sin, thus, appears to contradict the human existence as *imago Dei*. This is why *Marcin Zieliński* concentrates on how sin and perfection are presented and contrasted in the Book of Wisdom. It turns out that even if the *imago Dei* is not lost in humans, it is in dire need of restoration. When saying that humans are created in the image of God, this also implies certain limits. Being created in the image of God means that humans are no gods. *Francis Macatangay* approaches this human limitedness by studying how the Book of Tobit depicts the concept of male and female as limits imposed by God for life to flourish. When dealing with the restoration of the image of God in humans, the person of Christ Jesus is paramount within the New Testament. *Mirjam Piplica* provides a narrative-critical study about how the prologue of the Gospel of John depicts Christ as the Logos for its implied and real readers, in order to make them understand that Christ is both human and divine. Viewed from the image of Christ, the question can be iterated how humans have to view themselves and others in the light of still being affected by the brokenness of creation. It is this question that is addressed by *György Kustár*. When reflecting further on creation's fractured nature, *József Nagy* calls attention to the fact that the New Testament also has the notion of the *imago Diaboli*, as described in the Book of Revelation. *Gyopárka Köves* concentrates on how Karl Barth viewed the role of humans as created in the image of God viewed through the biblical and systematic-theological concept of God's covenant with people. When addressing humans' createdness, the question naturally arises as to what the task of people is. The question of work as an important dimension of the likeness of God is being dealt with by *Zoltán Balikó*. The concept of *imago Dei*, of course, has also implications for how Christian homiletics ought to reflect on how people should be addressed in sermons. *Enoh Šeba* demonstrates how this concept can give a more active role to listeners within communication. Moreover, it can hardly be otherwise that the restoration of the image of God will play an important part in pastoral care. *Theo Pleizier* reflects on whether or not the idea of "restoring the image of God" is a useful concept within pastoral care practices. Modern psychology raised the question as to what extent humans are only driven by their instincts and impulses. *Bernhard Kaiser* addresses this view on humans within the light of biblical anthropology. *Jaap Doedens* deals with this theme through the lens of Iain McGilchrist's view on how within western civilization a left-brain hemisphere dominated approach of reality has been deforming the way in which humans see themselves and their culture.

Ibolya Balla
Jaap Doedens

OLD TESTAMENT

"You Would Long for the Work of your Hands" Job as the Example of the Suffering *Imago Dei*

Ibolya Balla

Introduction[1]

The Book of Job is most often viewed as dealing with the question of theodicy or more specifically why the righteous suffer, where is the righteousness of God in the face of the suffering of the righteous. The book is also known as having a fair amount of vivid descriptions of Job's suffering. In other words, interpreters most often treat the questions of both why Job suffers, and how he suffers. This second aspect is very helpful in formulating questions regarding the topic of *imago Dei* in the Book of Job, for the work offers important insight into the attitude of the Creator towards his creatures, into what it means to be human. The book draws our attention to many important tenets regarding God's traits considering his relationship with humans. This relationship, or rather stance on God's part towards humans – represented here by the righteous and suffering Job – is described in the book by various concepts and motifs which express Job's understanding of the Creator, creation and humans' role in it. It is especially interesting how Job receives and in some cases inverts some of the most important traditions about creation in general, and human's place in it. There are especially relevant passages in this respect which, taken in the context of the book, can shed light on the above questions. Some of these passages will be highlighted in this paper.

Especially through the speech cycles the book challenges some of the traditional Israelite beliefs. One of them is the teaching about act and consequence, according to which every act has its consequences and on the day of retribution the righteous will be saved from judgment while

---

[1]   The English text of the biblical passages is taken from the NRSV.

the wicked will be punished by God.[2] This teaching is important for the wisdom writers but can also be traced back to the work of the Deuteronomists.[3] In wisdom the sentiment appears even among the godly that God is not able to carry out retribution or does not care about the faithful; he does not end the suffering sometimes caused by the wicked.[4] In Psalms and wisdom literature the authors declare that the acts of the humans are hidden before God (Ps 10:4–7). Moreover, in certain cases God seems not only indifferent but even hostile towards the faithful. It is especially the Book of Job that formulates the questions: what is the reason of the contradiction between belief in and traditions about God's nature and his righteousness and reality; why is it possible that the god fearing righteous suffer, while the godless prosper and seemingly get away with their wickedness.[5] In the speech cycles Job's friends argue in long dialogues using well known traditions about the fear of God, the fate of the godly and the godless, but do not want to hear Job's argument. They want Job to admit his guilt because – as they argue – that is the condition of his salvation (cf. Job 4:7–8). They even claim that Job is still able and permitted to contend because God did not punish him enough or at least not in proportion to his sins (35:15–16). Job is disappointed with them.[6] Even though the friends' observation – that "those who plow iniquity and sow trouble reap the same" (Job 4:8) – can be true generally and in certain cases, the arguments based on them are not always correct; they are not helpful or useful in Job's very specific situation of extreme suffering.

Another important belief that the book challenges is what it means to be human, how is human the image of God. In order to understand it we have to look at the Old Testament background of Job's teaching on creation and the role of humans in the order of creation. The most relevant body of literature is contained in the Priestly Document – more narrowly the

---

2   John J. Collins, *Introduction to the Hebrew Bible*, Minneapolis 2004, 505.
3   Moshe Weinfeld, *Deuteronomy and the Deuteronomic School*, Oxford 1972, 316–319 examines both biblical wisdom literature and Deuteronomy in terms of how these works account for suffering, the former in the case of the individual, the latter in the case of the community.
4   This concept is found in some of the prophetic works as well, see e.g. Mal 2:17; 3:15 in the context of 3:13–21. Both wisdom and prophetic literature affirm that God knows what happens in creation and Israel and there will be retribution.
5   See Job 21:7–34 but also Ps 34:16–23; 73:3–12; Prov 23:18; 24:14; Qoh 7:15; 8:11–13.
6   According to Job 6:14–30 he has no helper.

priestly creation account –, Deutero-Isaiah and a few psalms, and Job. Texts treating the question of creation of the world and man can be categorized as those that are theologically didactic and those that are hymnic. The former mainly presents theological tenets in order to give instruction on things which were not known or not known exactly, the latter have no didactic content. Their purpose is mainly to glorify the Creator and creation. In consequence, the style of these statements is different: the latter is enthusiastic and joyful, the former is restrained. Those which sing praises outnumber the others and can prevent us from over-estimating the didactic element. Direct theological statements about the creation in the form of extensive texts occur mainly in the two creation accounts, the first of which is contained in the Priestly Document (Gen 1:1–2:4a).[7] The texts in Deutero-Isaiah are mainly polemic against the Babylonian belief concerning worshipping the host of heaven (esp. 40:12–31), but can be understood in the context of deliverance from the exile. In many of the relevant psalms the psalmist also praises God both as Creator and saviour.[8] It is noteworthy that the doctrine of creation is relatively late in Israel which means that older, already existing beliefs about creation were formulated as statements and connected with the traditions about God as saviour fairly late.[9] In wisdom thought creation is a central topic, "an absolute basis for faith, and was referred to for its own sake altogether and not in the light of other factors of the faith" (see Job 38–41; Prov 3:19–20; 8:22–29).[10]

[7]   The other account is found in the so-called Jahwist source (Gen 2:4b–25); see Gerhard von Rad, *Old Testament Theology, 1. The Theology of Israel's Historical Traditions*, Edinburgh 1962, 139–140.
[8]   See, however Psalm 8 later.
[9]   Von Rad, *Old Testament Theology*, 1., 136–138: The soteriological understanding characterizes both Deutero-Isaiah and the relevant psalms. According to von Rad, the purpose of Ps 89 is to celebrate God's act of grace concerning the covenant with David, the establishment of the Messianic kingdom, connected with the topic of creation (see also Ps 74:12–17 where salvation and creation are also intertwined); cf. also Claus Westermann, *Az Ószövetség theológiájának vázlata*, Budapest 1993, 83–84.
[10]   Von Rad, *Old Testament Theology*, 1., 139.

The Most Important Elements of the Creation of Humans According to the Relevant Passages that Could Have Informed Job

First of all, God created man to have a relationship to him, a creature that corresponds to him, to whom he can speak, and who listens to him. Creation is an event that takes place between God and humans. Man is created so that something can happen between Creator and creature.[11] "The relationship to God is not something which is added to human existence; humans are created in such a way that their very existence is intended to be their relationship to God," and the dignity of all humans to which all are entitled are based on this.[12] The "image," and "likeness," or "something like" (Gen 1:26) together affirm that God has endowed humans with dignity, and exalted them above all other creatures. Ps 8:6 supplements the concept whit the expression "little lower."[13]

Human beings are created for a definite purpose or goal. In addition, there is a hierarchy of order established between humans and animals, in their relationship humans are entrusted with dominion over animals. This is a function committed to man, a status as lord in the world (cf. Ps 8:7). This rule, however, has its limits: man signifies God's rule on Earth, he is responsible for his actions. Dominion over the animals does not mean their exploitation by humans. The relationship between them is to be understood in a positive sense.[14] Gen 1:28 further adds to our understanding, since it has God addressing man and woman. Up until now the formula which introduces God's words in Genesis 1 is "and God said," or "saying." But 1:28 has "and God said to them." This difference implies that the "two can be addressed with the blessing because God has created them as his counterpart with whom he can speak."[15] The fact that creation is good – which includes its beauty – already entails its glorification and praise. This praise is contained in some of the psalms (cf. Psalm 148) and in this praise humans have a special role.[16] For the Israelites creation never be-

---

[11] This is true concerning both creation accounts, the difference is that Genesis 2 expresses it in story form and not in conceptual terms; cf. Claus Westermann, *Genesis 1–11. A Commentary*, Minneapolis 1984, 157.

[12] Westermann, *Genesis 1–11*, 158; Westermann, *Az Ószövetség theológiájának vázlata*, 94–95.

[13] Von Rad, *Old Testament Theology*, 1., 144–145.

[14] Westermann, *Genesis 1–11*, 158–159; Walter Brueggemann – William H. Bellinger, Jr., *Psalms*, Cambridge 2014, 59–60.

[15] Westermann, *Genesis 1–11*, 160.

[16] Westermann, *Az Ószövetség theológiájának vázlata*, 90.

comes nature that can be viewed independently of the Creator, the praise of the Creator and creation as his work is praised together (Psalm 104).[17] Finally, being the image of God is also connected with the protection of human life according to Gen 9:6, "Whoever sheds the blood of a human, by a human shall that person's blood be shed; for in his own image God made humankind." In summary, the environment in which man and woman will live is his and her dominion. God made humans in his own image, placed them in a unique position vis-à-vis himself; all creation is very good, but humans are created with a special dignity.[18]

Job as the Suffering Imago Dei Especially from the Viewpoint of the Similarities of Psalm 8 and Job

The most relevant passages for comparison are Ps 8:5 and Job 7:17–18. Their similarity is often noted but there are parallels between Psalm 8 and the Book of Job which has not been pointed out, as will be detailed below.[19] The Psalm has distinct hymnic elements to praise God as Creator by praising the glory of God (vv. 2–3), man as the crown of creation (vv. 4–9), and at the same time by contrasting the majesty of God with the insignificance of man.[20] The body of the psalm which praises God's majesty and glory in creation starts in verse 4, which depicts the psalmist as looking up to the sky with awe and seeing all the luminaries created by God.[21] The word "your heavens" with its singular 2nd person suffix emphasizes that the heavens are of God's, in it there can be no other God (cf. Ps 20:7; 115:16; 144:5; Lam 3:66). The psalmist also stresses that God created them by using the expression "the work of your fingers" (v. 4).[22] In this regard the psalm is closer to the priestly creation account than to Isa 40:18.21–26 which also emphasizes the createdness of the luminaries.[23] According to

---

[17] Westermann, *Az Ószövetség theológiájának vázlata*, 91–92.
[18] Dominic Robinson, *Understanding the "Imago Dei." The Thought of Barth, von Balthasar and Moltmann*, Farnham 2011, 7.
[19] We cannot treat in detail the question of relationship between the priestly creation account and Psalm 8.
[20] See also Brueggemann – Bellinger, *Psalms*, 58.
[21] Kustár Zoltán, *A Zsoltárok könyve válogatott fejezeteinek magyarázata (Zsolt 2, 8, 22, 30, 79).* (Egyetemi jegyzet), Debrecen 2016, 31;
[22] See Nancy deClaissé-Walford – Rolf A. Jacobson – Beth LaNeel Tanner, *The Book of Psalms*, Grand Rapids 2014, 122–123.
[23] Kustár Zoltán, *Zsoltárok könyve*, 31.

v. 5 the psalmist makes a statement on the basis of what he sees, and does so in poetic questions. He realizes the insignificance of humans: "what are human beings that you are mindful of them, mortals that you care for them?" What are human beings compared with these splendid creatures as the luminaries, but especially compared with God their Creator? The question itself is the answer which employs a term appropriate to emphasizing the smallness and transient nature of humans. The word אֱנוֹשׁ signifying "human being" is from the stem אנשׁ which means "to be sick/weak," or "to be incurable" (cf. 2 Sam 12:15). The term demonstrates that humans are weak, their life is fleeting, and as such they are mortal (cf. Deut 32:26; Isa 13:12; 24:6; 33:8, Ps 9:21; 90:3; 103:15; Job 10:4–5). In parallel with אֱנוֹשׁ stands בֶּן־אָדָם, translated variously as "son of man," "human being" or "mortal." The word אָדָם is related to אֲדָמָה ("ground," "land") and reflects that God formed man from the dust of the ground (Gen 2:7, cf. also Ps 144:3; Job 7:17).[24] As Allen notes, "[t]he psalmist is amazed that the majestic God of creation thinks of him in such a way as to do things for him, to meet his needs."[25]

According to Ps 8:6–7 God has endowed humans with special dignity, responsibility and tasks. This is expressed with various terms: "you have made them a little lower than God, and crowned them with glory and honor. You have given them dominion over the works of your hands; you have put all things under their feet." The interpretation of the term אֱלֹהִים in the expression "little lower than God" is a matter of debate. Some consider it to refer to "God," and the God-given role of dominion to be exercised by humans within creation,[26] while others understand it as a reference to the heavenly beings in the heavenly court of God (cf. Ps 29:1).[27] The Septuagint understands it this way and renders "angels." This would indicate that human beings' task is to praise and serve God just as much it is the task of the members of the heavenly court. What the word "little" means is not detailed, since the emphasis is on the similarity to heavenly beings, not on the difference. Perhaps it refers to mortality, or the abode of humans on earth.[28] Humans are crowned with glory and hon-

---

[24] Kustár Zoltán, Zsoltárok könyve, 31–32; Brueggemann – Bellinger, Psalms, 59.

[25] Allen P. Ross, A Commentary on the Psalms, 1. (1–41), Grand Rapids 2011, 295.

[26] See among others Brueggemann – Belliger, Psalms, 59; Ross, Commentary, 288, 296; Peter C. Craigie – Marvin E. Tate, Psalms 1–50, Grand Rapids 2004, 108.

[27] Cf. Kustár Zoltán, Zsoltárok könyve, 32; deClaissé-Walford – Jacobson – LaNeel Tanner, The Book of Psalms, 122, 124–125.

[28] Kustár Zoltán, Zsoltárok könyve, 32.

our which can be the epithets of God (Isa 32:5; Ps 29:1; 90:16; 145:5), the heavenly king (Ps 96:6; 104:1; 145:12), or the earthly king (Ps 21:6; 45:4). The rulership God endows humans with, is in accordance with Gen 1:27. God has given dominion to humans and put all things under their feet. However, it is noted that all these things are the works of God's hands. This shows that humans are stewards of creation, their rule is stewardship which – as noted above – comes with responsibility and limits. This is again in harmony with the two creation accounts in Genesis 1–2. Ps 8:4–9 also implies that human beings' dignity and value comes not from anything they have done for themselves, "but rather something that God has done for them. Our worth comes to us from outside of ourselves (*extra nos*). That which God confers upon us is the key to our status, not that which comes from inside of us."[29] The frame of the psalm in v. 2 and 10 shows that the entire creation, humans included, praise God, his majestic name.[30]

Ps 8:5

מָה־אֱנוֹשׁ כִּי־תִזְכְּרֶנּוּ וּבֶן־אָדָם כִּי תִפְקְדֶנּוּ׃

what are human beings that you are mindful of them, mortals that you care for them? (= v. 4 in NRSV)

Job 7:17–18

מָה־אֱנוֹשׁ כִּי תְגַדְּלֶנּוּ וְכִי־תָשִׁית אֵלָיו לִבֶּךָ׃
וַתִּפְקְדֶנּוּ לִבְקָרִים לִרְגָעִים תִּבְחָנֶנּוּ׃

What are human beings, that you make so much of them, that you set your mind on them, visit them every morning, test them every moment?

Job 7:17–18 not only alludes to this psalm, especially its fifth verse, but there is also a verbal correspondence between them. The term פקד ("to have concern for," "to care for," "to visit" etc.) of Ps 8:5 appears in Job 7:18; Job expands the thought of Ps 8:5 on humans in two verses. He employs the stem אנשׁ a number of times: with the meaning "mortal wound" (34:6), as a reference to simply man or as a demonstrative pronoun (5:17), people (28:4) or human being, mortal (4:17; 7:1.17; 9:2; 10:4.5; 13:9; 14:19; 15:14; 25:4.6; 28:13; 32:8; 33:12.26; 36:25). In most cases the

29   DeClaissé-Walford – Jacobson – LaNeel Tanner, *The Book of Psalms*, 124.
30   Kustár Zoltán *Zsoltárok könyve*, 32; Ross, *Commentary*, 296–297.

author stresses the mortality of people. Job also uses the stem פקד 6 times. While it appears in the sense "to inspect" in 5:24 (for instance to inspect one's home and to find everything in good order), it is mostly used in the sense "to visit," or "to care for" (7:18), "to make enquiry" (31:14), or to express that God did not punish Job enough according to Elihu: "And now, because his anger does not punish, and he does not greatly heed transgression" (Job 35:15). The noun form in 10:12 is part of a positive statement: "You have granted me life and steadfast love, and your care has preserved my spirit." However, the context of the sentence demonstrates that Job does not understand why God turned against his own creature.

In the passage under discussion (7:18) it is in parallel with "to test" (בחן). By using anthropomorphic concepts, the verse together with 7:17 emphasizes that God visits and tests Job. While the verb זכר ("to remember," cf. Ps 8:5) does not appear in 7:17–18, Job uses it frequently, sometimes in the sense that Job should consider well the content of his arguments (4:7; 36:24), in 7:7 and 10:9 in his plea to God to remember his mortality, and in 14:13 where he implores God with the following words: "Oh that you would hide me in Sheol, that you would conceal me until your wrath is past, that you would appoint me a set time, and remember me!"[31]

By the occurrences of the above terms Job on the one hand emphasizes the mortality and the weakness of humans, and on the other, expresses his anguish about God's concern for him. The fact that the Creator has concern for mortal beings inspired the psalmist to praise and glorify God. The mortality of humans causes Job to wish to be dead and out of concern and vigil of God, far from his watchful eyes. The context of 7:17–18 that contains the wish of Job to be left alone and be dead corroborates this:

Job 7:15–16.19–21:

so that I would choose strangling and death rather than this body.
I loathe my life; I would not live forever. Let me alone, for my days are
a breath.

---

[31] According to 24:20 the godless will not be remembered; 28:18 employs it concerning wisdom.

Will you not look away from me for a while, let me alone until I swallow my spittle?

If I sin, what do I do to you, you watcher of humanity? Why have you made me your target? Why have I become a burden to you?

Why do you not pardon my transgression and take away my iniquity? For now I shall lie in the earth; you will seek me, but I shall not be.

Every detail in creation is witness to God's power and care in a positive sense in Psalm 8. However, Job subverts this in his use of the topic of creation. Seen in the context of the book, Job 7:17–18 suggests that God's closeness is dangerous and is understood by Job as testing which will eventually result in punishing, since mortals cannot be just before God.[32] The positive assertion of the Psalmist in Psalm 8 that God is mindful of human beings and cares for mortals is not a comfort for Job but causes him despair.[33] Towards the friends he maintains his claim of integrity before God (Job 27:2–6) and insists on being innocent[34] while admitting that humans have flaws. From his arguments with God it becomes clear that he does not understand why God is punishing him. Under divine scrutiny Job wishes to be left alone, fearing that God can prove even him perverse. He wants to be far away from the watchful eyes of God. Moreover, he wishes to be dead, since one who is the target of God (6:4; 7:20) has no hope. His dignity seems lost before God and humans; he is objectified, he cannot lift up his head (10:15). In his descriptions of divine scrutiny there are images of himself as an object of vision and violence. Levinas notes similar connections of seeing and seizing, as "vision moves into grasp" in

---

[32] Even in the prologue Job points out that the affliction comes from God (2:10), see also Roger N. Whybray, "'Shall Not the Judge of All the Earth Do What Is Just?' God's Oppression of the Innocent in the Old Testament," in David Penchansky, Paul. L. Redditt (eds.), *"Shall Not the Judge of All the Earth Do What Is Just?" Studies on the Nature of God in Tribute to James L. Crenshaw*, Winona Lake 2000, 1–19, 14.

[33] See also John E. Hartley, *The Book of Job,* Grand Rapids 1988, 151–52. A number of other passages – employing vivid images – attest that the pain Job experiences is inflicted by God; e. g. Job 6:4: "For the arrows of the Almighty are in me; my spirit drinks their poison; the terrors of God are arrayed against me." Apart from the words "arrows," "poison," and "terrors," animal and food comparisons used in 6:5–7 express the gravity of his grief. According to Job 16:7–14 God surrendered him to his enemies.

[34] See especially ch. 31.

its apprehension of an object.[35] Apart from the question of God being mindful and having concern for humans, another parallel between Psalms 8 and Job concerns the dignity of humans expressed with the words "glory" and "honour." They express God's care for humans. Job 19:8–12 demonstrates not only that God is Job's enemy and the cause of his suffering, but also that He stripped him of his honour which had adorned him like a garment, and removed the crown form his head;[36] he deposed Job from his position as an elder statesman. Job ceased to be the head of his own family, he lost his dignity, his seat in the council, and sits on the ash heap in shame. This is also in contrast with the tradition of Psalm 8.[37]

If we consider all the accounts in Job that deal with the question of the suffering of the protagonist, it is apparent that there is a large number of vivid descriptions of the state of mind and of the bodily suffering of Job. He compares his condition to being dead. The language or symbolism of death, or near-death conditions is apparent, including accusations that God is Job's murdering foe (6:4; 7:14; 9:17.34; 10:8–9; 13:21.24; 16:7.17; 19:6–20) or declarations of God's injustice with regard to death (9:22–23).[38] Job 7:9 emphasizes that Sheol is the final destination for humans, who are mere shadows and do not return from there.[39] However, it is particular to Job to speak about Sheol as the place where he could be hidden from God as if he were safe again after God's wrath has passed. The so-called death wish is also characteristic of his book. Immediately after the prologue he curses the day he was born (3:1–9).[40] Human inability of understanding God's mysterious power and deeds is connected with God's hiddenness ("Look, he passes by me, and I do not see him; he moves on, but I do not perceive him," 9:11; cf. 23:8–9 in the context of 23:2–9).[41]

---

[35] Emmanuel Levinas, *Totality and Infinity. An Essay on Exteriority*, Pittsburgh 1969, 191.

[36] For similar language see Jer 13:18; Lam 5:16.

[37] Hartley, *The Book of Job*, 284–286.

[38] Dan Mathewson, *Death and Survival in the Book of Job. Desymbolization and Traumatic Experience*, New York 2006, treats in detail the symbolism of death in the Book of Job and characterizes the time before Job's affliction as life, full of joy, happiness, full of movement, while the time after the affliction as near-death or death experience.

[39] See also 21:13b; 24:19.

[40] Cf. 10:18–22. In 17:7 Job – mocked by others – confesses: "My eye has grown dim from grief."

[41] The theme of hiddenness, or of desiring God's presence frequently recurs in Job; see also 13:24; 24:1; 34:29; 37:19–24; cf Anathea Portier-Young, "'Eyes to the

The afflictions make him a shadow of his former self. Job reaches the point where he thinks that God wants to destroy him. This shows that he suffers from the conflicting views of the merciful and punishing God. On the one hand he praises the Creator in 9:6–11:

who shakes the earth out of its place, and its pillars tremble;
who commands the sun, and it does not rise; who seals up the stars;
who alone stretched out the heavens and trampled the waves of the Sea;
who made the Bear and Orion, the Pleiades and the chambers of the south;
who does great things beyond understanding, and marvelous things without number.
Look, he passes by me, and I do not see him; he moves on, but I do not perceive him.

He even declares that God formed him (10:10–12):

Did you not pour me out like milk and curdle me like cheese?
You clothed me with skin and flesh, and knit me together with bones and sinews.
You have granted me life and steadfast love, and your care has preserved my spirit.

On the other hand, the praise of the Creator is continued with a bitter complaint concerning Job's specific situation according to 9:17–35. While the confession that God made Job betray the care and love of God, Job experiences its opposite as the context of 10:10–12 (10:3–9.13–22) shows. Job feels like being a prey to God who attacks him and wants to break him. Considering passages which depict God as a potter, this is surprising since the potter takes care and time to fashion his product and is proud of it. Although it is in the potter's power to break the result and make a new product, and God is also sovereign in his dealings with humans, Job considers this as contradictory to the nature of God (cf. Jer 18:1–11).[42] The

---

Blind.' A Dialogue Between Tobit and Job," in Jeremy Corley, Vincent Skemp (eds.), *Intertextual Studies in Ben Sira and Tobit. Essays in Honour of Alexander A. di Lella, O.F.M.*, Washington 2005, 14–27, 17–19.

[42] Hartley, *The Book of Job*, 186.

Hebrew term in the background of the word "to destroy" (Job 10:8) also means "to swallow up"; they are both very strong terms.[43] As noted before, Psalm 8 emphasizes the creating process with the words "the work of your fingers" (Ps 8:4). Job also refers to the creating process of God with which he formed humans, including Job himself. However, in his view, God now turns against his own creation. This conflicting view leads him to think that the only explanation for God's actions is that He forgot the limits of his creatures, their vulnerability, mortality and weakness. In a series of rhetorical questions found in 10:4–7 Job calls God to task, reminding him of the shortness of human life and the weakness of humans. In other words, Job asks: is God also characterized by the limitations of humans? It seems that even human finitude cannot prompt God to have compassion.[44] Job concludes that God should not act in a way that humans do. He can choose, he has the power and opportunity to be merciful, even if the sufferer cannot prove his innocence. According to Job his friends' view of the complex question of God's mercy and righteousness is faulty. The fact that God created humans, including Job, means that he had a purpose with them, and this purpose should not be mere suffering.[45] He has no choice but to implore the same God who causes his suffering. But he cannot do otherwise, and since he is in a near-death condition he has nothing to lose. This is one of the motivations for his boldness in the face of God. Another one is the faith which characterizes not only his words, but also most of the lament psalms. The latter not only speak of the specific crises in which the community or the individual suffers, but also testify to God as saviour. He may have caused the suffering, but he is also the sufferer's only hope. In other words, the believer's purpose in lament points beyond lament itself. His aim is not simply to depict his deplorable situation. Even in near-death conditions the faithful places his case in the hands of God.[46] In prayer the love, responsibility and care of God is assumed.[47] Job also

---

43 Cf. Job 2:3.
44 Carol A. Newsom, *The Book of Job. A Contest of Moral Imaginations*, Oxford 2003, 141–142.
45 John Gray, *The Book of Job*, Sheffield 2010, 203.
46 Claus Westermann, *Lob und Klage in den Psalmen*, Göttingen 1977, 128; Claus Westermann, "The Role of Lament in the Theology of the Old Testament," *Interpretation* 28 (1974), 20–38, 32; Federico G. Villanueva, *The "Uncertainty of a Hearing." A Study of the Sudden Change of Mood in the Psalms of Lament*, Leiden 2008, 80; cf. also Psalm 22.
47 Newsom, *The Book of Job*, 157.

longs to lay his case before God (23:3–4: "Oh, that I knew where I might find him, that I might come even to his dwelling! I would lay my case before him, and fill my mouth with arguments"). At the same time, he also wishes to remain in darkness in fear of what God has decreed for him:

> For he will complete what he appoints for me; and many such things are in his mind.
> Therefore I am terrified at his presence; when I consider, I am in dread of him.
> God has made my heart faint; the Almighty has terrified me;
> If only I could vanish in darkness, and thick darkness would cover my face!
> 23:14–17

According to the canonical form of the book, Job does not stop arguing with God. He might not have health, might look like a shadow, but he still has God. Even extreme suffering cannot take away a human's being the image of God. Afflictions make him a shadow of his former self, a caricature of the human being depicted in Psalm 8. But God is with him all the way. Job may wish to be left alone and fears the closeness of God but he constantly talks to God. God does not leave Job, Job does not leave God alone. His faith remains despite his experiences. Job seeks God because his faith tells him that God can be found, God can be trusted. Job 38–39; 40:6–41:26 shows that even though God reproofs Job, he listens to him, teaches him with the patience of a master or a teacher. In the end God rebukes Job's friends: "for you have not spoken of me what is right, as my servant Job has" (42:7). Job is considered as speaking more wisely about God than his friends who keep repeating their theological tenets without sympathizing with Job. Kreeft even argues that "suffering can be hopeful. It was for Job. Job never lost his faith and his hope (which is faith directed at the future), and his suffering proved to be purifying, purgative, educational: it gave him eyes to see God."[48] God convinces Job that he is not his enemy, the purpose of creation is not its destruction. This is reflected where the author has Job saying: "Am I the Sea, or the Dragon, that you set a guard over me" (7:12). The aim of the author here is to demonstrate the hyper-

---

[48] Peter Kreeft, *Three Philosophies of Life*, San Francisco 1989, 9; cf. also Michael V. Fox, "God's Answer and Job's Response," *Biblica* 94 (2013), 1–23, 3.

bolic style of the sentence.[49] 42:2 ("I know that you can do all things, and that no purpose of yours can be thwarted") also implies that creation is ordered, it has a purpose. Job's sin is that he has hid this order with his speech, did not recognize it as he should have, or failed to speak of it as he should due to the afflictions and suffering. He was not present at creation, and God does not expect him to recognize his plan as if he were present. Job is also unaware of the bargain God made with Satan. His experiences of the Creator, and traditions he inherited and believed to be true are the basis of God's teaching. He is not talking to Job only in declaratory sentences. This would lead only to his self-praise. He involves Job in the dialogue using rhetorical questions through which Job can recognize the magnificence of creation.

Conclusions

The biblical background on creation and especially creation of humans that informed Job attests that creation and human beings are not only good but are also created for a purpose. Humans are not only given a place in creation spatially and temporally, but also have dignity and value before God. They can be called by God, they can answer him in words and in deeds, they have special responsibilities and tasks, they have the ability to praise God, to reason, to communicate. They are created not only *by*, but also *for* the word of God. Their special position is indicated already in Gen 1:28, according to which God addresses humans at the time he blesses them.[50] Genesis 1 has theological statements about creation, while Psalm 8 reflects humanity's response as a celebration of God. Closeness of God and humanity suggests an intimate proximity. This divine proximity is the foundation for the dominion of humankind in creation. Humanity's status as little lower than God is connected among others with God's being mindful of and caring for humans. This concern and care can be the basis of praise (Psalm 8) but also of fear (Job). However, in both cases it is clear that the question of *imago Dei* is a relational question. We may not only ask What is man (in creation), but also: Whose is man, to whom does he belong? A human being is neither individual, nor collective, but personal and relational at the same time. This relational aspect is present in his re-

[49]   Fox, "God's Answer," 5.
[50]   Westermann, *Az Ószövetség theológiájának vázlata*, 24.

lation to God, to creation, including other humans. Being the image of God is also connected with the protection of human life (Gen 9:6).[51] Job's experience, however, is the opposite. He feels that God is his enemy, wants to destroy him instead of protecting him. The suffering of Job means that God is testing his fidelity. While bodily suffering is extreme, and Job is in a near-death condition, the realization that God caused his suffering is an even greater test. Suffering is the direct result of God's watching over Job; there seems to be an inevitable connection between looking and harming. This test, however, is only secondarily the loss of all Job's earthly goods and his sickness. The test is fundamentally that Job has seemingly lost God. For almost forty chapters in the speech cycles he argues with his friends and in the end with God himself who is the only acceptable partner for him in the dialogue. This is reflected in 42:2–6.[52] All the afflictions Job suffers cannot take away his dignity. He may suffer boils, may sit in the dust scratching himself with a potsherd, but he is still able to communicate with God. His being as an image of God is not reflected in his physical body but in the fact that God calls him and he can answer. God justifies his words and not those of his friends. Speaking "truthfully" means that Job – despite all his laments suggesting otherwise – is standing in the presence of God, who is right there all the time. Job believes this fundamental truth and therefore speaks truthfully (that is, to the God who really is present), while the three friends act as if God were absent.[53] The most important difference between the communication of Job and that of the friends is that the three friends speak *about* God while Job speaks *to* God.[54] In other words, while Job describes his pitiful condition in his monologues and dialogues with God, he is in a constant relation with him. This relational aspect is important. He involves God into his speech, prays to him. The friends talk about God, but leave him out of the conversation.

Job in his extreme suffering subverts some of the Israelite tenets about creation, human dignity, God's relation to humans. However, there are also similarities between his work and the traditions he alludes to. The world is the place where God's and not human's glory is reflected. Humans need to acknowledge this and the fact that there are heavenly beings which are mysterious. Humans can still witness this glory and glorify the Creator.

---

51 Szűcs Ferenc, *Teológiai etika. Református Zsinati Iroda Tanulmányi Osztálya*, Budapest 1993, 29–31.
52 Kreeft, *Three Philosophies*, 78.
53 Kreeft, *Three Philosophies*, 90.
54 Kreeft, *Three Philosophies*, 90.

This is one of the most important elements in Job's speech. Despite his laments he acknowledges God as Creator and glorifies him in the end. Job as part of humanity is a creature that points beyond himself with his entire being.[55]

In our view the author of the Book of Job deliberately uses a large number of vivid descriptions of Job's condition, often referring to human frailty. Many of the terms are related to body, mortality, weakness, bodily suffering, brokenness, blindness. The role of speech is also very important. The book consists of a short narrative frame and extensive speech cycles containing the monologues and dialogues of Job and his three friends. The author probably aims at contrasting the fragility of Job's condition and his being the reasoning, communicating image of God, never leaving him alone, practicing the presence of God. As Kreeft argues, "the most practical lesson we can learn from Job [...] 'the practice of the presence of God,' the simplest and most fundamental exercise in realism and in sanctity. The two are identical, for both mean simply living in reality, not illusion, acting as if what is real is real. And the most fundamental reality is the God who is present."[56]

---

[55] Szűcs, *Etika*, 33.
[56] Kreeft, *Three Philosophies*, 91.

Homo homini lupus
Die pejorative Animalisierung des Menschen im Alten Testament

Áron Németh

Die dogmatische Konzeption über den Verlust der Gottebenbildlichkeit durch die (Ur-)Sünde lässt sich mit alttestamentlichen Texten nicht begründen. Nach dem Sündenfall beschließt Gott, die ganze Schöpfung auszulöschen, aber durch Noahs Familie überlebt nicht nur die Menschheit, sondern auch die Konzept der Gottebenbildlichkeit. Am Ende der Sintfluterzählung wird die Gottebenbildlichkeitsaussage nicht zurückgenommen, sondern gar wiederholt und bestätigt (Gen 9:6).[1]

Die beiden *imago Dei*-Erwähnungen in Gen 1:26–28 und Gen 9:1–7 bringen die Zwischenstellung des Menschen zum Ausdruck,[2] indem sich die *imago Dei*-Aussage stark mit der Repräsentation Gottes einerseits, und dem Herrschaftsauftrag (כבש; רדה) über die Tiere anderseits verknüpft (vgl. Ps 8). Die Gottebenbildlichkeit des Menschen geht mit dem Sündenfall nicht verloren, der Herrschaftsauftrag wird aber modifiziert. Nach dem Sündenfall und Sintflut geht es um eine Herrschaft über die Tiere, die auch die Tiertötung mit einschließt. In dem Mensch-Tier Verhältnis setzt Gott "eine Art Kriegszustand" ein, indem die Herrschaft des Menschen über die Tiere zu einer "Schreckensherrschaft" umwandelt.[3] Das Mensch-

---

[1] Gerhard von Rad, *Theologie des Alten Testaments. Band 1. Die Theologie der geschichtlichen Überlieferung Israels*, München 1987⁹, 160–161.

[2] Wolfgang Raible, "Zur Begriffsgeschichte von 'Mensch'. Skizze einer kognitiven Landkarte," in Justin Stagl – Wolfgang Reinhard (eds.), *Grenzen des Menschseins. Probleme einer Definition des Menschlichen*, Wien 2005, 171. Nach Raible gehört zur kognitiven Landkarte des Begriffs "Mensch" die Achse Gott – Mensch – Tier, die sich aus der doppelten Opposition (dh. Gott/Mensch, Mensch/Tier) ergibt, in der der Mensch steht.

[3] Zum verdorbenen und feindlichen Mensch-Tier Verhältniss siehe auch die nicht-priesterliche Tradition: "Und Feindschaft setze ich zwischen dir und der Frau,

Mensch Verhältnis steht in der priesterlichen Urgeschichte außerhalb dieses Herrschaftsauftrags, der Mensch wird dementsprechend nicht beauftragt über anderen Menschen zu herrschen. Und "wer das Blut eines Menschen vergießt, dessen Blut soll für den Wert des getöteten Menschen vergossen werden. Denn als Bild Gottes (צֶלֶם אֱלֹהִים) hat er den Menschen gemacht" (Gen 9:6).[4] Gewaltsame Herrschaft (רדה) über einen Volksgenossen ist in Lev 25:43.46.53 explizit verboten.

Mein Beitrag setzt sich mit dem Phänomen der Animalisierung des Menschen in alttestamentlichen Kontexten auseinander. Die pejorative Animalisierung der Mitmenschen ist m. E. das Schlupfloch, in dem die Gottebenbildlichkeit im Alten Testament implizit aberkannt und der Herrschaftsauftrag eigenmächtig ausgeweitet wird. Es geht also im Alten Testament nicht darum, dass wegen der Sünde Gott die Ebenbildlichkeit zurücknimmt, sondern darum, dass der sündige Mensch die Gottebenbildlichkeit des anderen nicht akzeptiert. Diese Nicht-Akzeptanz artikuliert sich in der Animalisierung des Menschen, in dem der Zusammenhang zwischen Gottebenbildlichkeit und Sünde – mindestens implizit und indirekt – auch im Alten Testament zu begreifen ist.

Animalisierung in sich muss selbstverständlich nicht unbedingt dehumanisierend und pejorativ sein. Tiervergleiche sind im Alten Testament häufig und vielfältig. Tiermetaphern, Tiervergleichen, Tiersymbolik werden also sowohl im positiven als auch im negativen Sinne verwendet. In der Liebeslyrik des Hohenliedes, im Jakobssegen, in der Weisheitsliteratur haben die Tierbilder beispielsweise sehr positive Konnotationen.

In dieser Studie möchte ich durch einige Beispiele aufweisen, wie sich eine implizite Aberkennung der Gottebenbildlichkeit durch pejorative (d. h. dehumanisierende) Animalisierung des Menschen im Alten Testament vollzieht. Dies zeigt sich besonders in den folgenden sechs Kontexten: Hofsprache und Hofpraxis (1); individuelle Klage (2); prophetische Kritik (3); göttliche Strafe (4); alttestamentliches Recht (5); extreme Notsituationen (6). In einem Ausblick untersuchen wir auch den zeitgenössischen Kontext, inwiefern eine pejorative Animalisierung in der westlichen postmodernen Kultur präsent ist (7).

---

zwischen deinem Nachwuchs und ihrem Nachwuchs: Er wird dir den Kopf zertreten, und du wirst ihm nach der Ferse schnappen" (Gen 3:15).

[4] Die nichtpriesterliche Urgeschichte erwähnt ein zwischenmenschliches Herrschaftsverhältnis im Kontext des Sündenfalls in den göttlichen Strafworten für die Frau: "Nach deinem Mann wirst du verlangen, und er wird über dich herrschen (משׁל)." (Gen 3:16).

1) Hofsprache und Hofpraxis

Im Hintergrund der priesterlichen Urgeschichte steht höchstwahrschein-
lich der altorientalische Gedanke, den König als das Bild der Gottheit
zu betrachten. Die Erschaffung des Menschen in Gen 1:26-28 ist eine
Adaptierung dieser *imago Dei*-Vorstellung, um das Menschenbild zu roya-
lisieren, beziehungsweise das Königsamt zu demokratisieren.[5] Eine Herrschaft von Menschen über Menschen nimmt der priesterliche Schöpfungs-
bericht nicht in den Blick, der Herrschaftsauftrag gilt nur in Bezug auf die
Tierwelt, nicht auf Menschen. Die Einführung des Königtums in Israel,
wie es in dem Deuteronomistischen Geschichtswerk vor uns liegt, wird
als Abkehr von Gott interpretiert, und die Geschichte der Monarchie ist
nach deuteronomistischer Darstellung eine Sündengeschichte.

Wenn wir die Animalisierung in der Hofsprache und in der Hofpraxis
betrachten, muss man unterscheiden, ob es um einen Untertanen aus dem
eigenen Volk, oder um den Feind geht.

Eine Dehumanisierung der Gefangenen als Teil der psychologischen
Kriegsführung war im Alten Orient ganz gewöhnlich.[6] Nicht jeder Art der
Entmenschlichung ist aber eine Animalisierung. Es sind institutionalisierte
politische Demütigungsakte wie z. B. die Entkleidung/Entblößung der
Rebellen,[7] oder das Abrasieren des Bartes (vgl. Jes 20:1-5; 2Sam 10:4).[8]
Diese Sanktionen gelten als Schande des Mannes, funktionieren als Dehu-
manisierung und Entwürdigung des Menschen, ohne aber eine direkte
Animalisierung zu verwirklichen.

Die Huldigung eines Vasallenkönigs vor seinem Herrn aber ruft die
negative Konnotation des kriechenden Hundes hervor. Eine solche Geste
der Proskynese ist auf dem schwarzen Obelisken zu sehen, wo der israe-
litische König Jehu vor dem assyrischen König Šulmānu-ašarēd (Salmassar)
III. auf allen Vieren liegt. Eine Steigerung dieser Haltung, nämlich die
Geste des Auf-dem-Boden-Liegens, ist Ausdruck völliger Wehrlosigkeit und

---

[5]   Bernd Janowski, *Anthropologie des Alten Testaments. Grundfragen – Kontexte –*
      Themenfelder, Tübingen 2019, 409–410; Andreas Wagner, Art. Gottesebenbild-
      lichkeit, in: WAM, 2013, 218.
[6]   Lyn M. Bechtel, "Shame as Sanction of Social Control in Biblical Israel: Judicial,
      Political and Social Shaming," *JSOT* 49 (1991), 63.
[7]   Auch ikonographisch belegt, siehe dazu Thomas Staubli, "Ikonographische Quel-
      len als Grundlagenmaterial für die Rekonstruktion anthropologischer Themen der
      Südlevante," in Jürgen van Oorschot, Andreas Wagner (Hg.), *Anthropologie(n)*
      des Alten Testaments, Leipzig 2018², 249–250.
[8]   Janowski, *Anthropologie*, 209.

Unterwerfung. Das Liegen auf dem Rücken oder auf dem Bauch ist in ihrem Ursprung ein (tierischer) Reflex, sich tot zu stellen, ein ängstliches Erstarren des Körpers angesichts des Stärkeren. Die erweiterte Metapher כֶּלֶב מֵת "toter Hund" (1Sam 24:15; 2Sam 16:9) weist darauf hin, dass die unterlegenen Gegner in der Sphäre des Todes aufhielt, und dieser Zustand nur durch die gnädige Zuwendung des Herrschers aufgehoben werden kann.[9] "Die Hund-Metapher hat einen festen Anhalt an der Hofsprache,"[10] was jeweils biblische und außerbiblische Texte bestätigen. Dies zeigt sich auch in der metaphorischen Verwendung von כֶּלֶב "Hund in den Samuelbüchern.[11] Die menschliche Herrschaftsausübung über anderen Menschen geschieht demnach zum Teil durch eine negative, und zwar protokollarische, zeremonielle Animalisierung. Ein Diener kann sich selbst – oder einen anderen Untertanen – als "Hund" bezeichnen, wie das z. B. in den Amarna- und Lachischbriefen der Fall ist. "Knecht" und "Hund" sind also in der Hofsprache Synonym verwendet.

In der Huldigungszene des Königspsalms 72 wird die Geste der feindlichen Völker vor dem König sehr plastisch ausgedrückt: "und seine Feinde sollen den Staub lecken" (vgl. Jes 49:23). In den Amarnabriefen finden wir einen Wunsch mit ganz ähnlicher Formulierung. Im Brief (EA 100) an den Pharao von der Stadt Irqata steht: "Es höre der König, unser Herr, auf die Worte seiner treuen Diener und gebe Geschenk an seinen Diener, während unsere Feinde zuschauen und Staub essen."[12] Aus den Büchern Genesis und Micha wissen wir, dass dieses Verhalten für die Schlange typisch ist: "Auf deinem Bauch wirst du kriechen, und Staub wirst du fressen dein Leben lang" (Gen 3:14) "Wie die Schlange lecken sie Staub, wie jene, die auf der Erde kriechen." (Micha 7:17a).

Denn die Redeformen der Hofsprache sollen die Status der Redenden eindeutig widerspiegeln, zielt die negative Animalisierung in der Hofsprache nicht die Entmenschlichung des Anderen, sondern eher eine Klassifizierung. Dies zeigt sich auch darin, dass die altorientalische Königsideologie auch eine positive Animalisierung kennt. Löwe oder Adler sind beliebte Metapher für Könige, der Untertan wird manchmal als Ga-

---

9   Peter Riede, *Im Spiegel der Tiere. Studien zum Verhältnis von Mensch und Tier im alten Israel*, Freiburg 2002, 73–89.

10 Riede, *Im Spiegel der Tiere*, 88.

11 1Sam 17:43; 24:15; 2Sam 3:8; 9,8; 16:9, vgl. 2Kön 8,13.

12 Jørgen Alexander Knudtzon, *Die El-Amarna-Tafeln mit Einleitung und Erläuterungen*, Band 1.: *Die Texte*, Leipzig 1915, 453.

zelle/Beutetier dargestellt, das durch den (menschlichen) König vor dem feindlichen Raubtier verteidigt wird.[13]

Auf der anderen Seite werden in den Königsinschriften die fremden und feindlichen Leute abwertend mit "junge Tauben," "fette Ochsen," Wildesel und Schweine verglichen. In manchen propagandistischen Königsinschriften aus Mesopotamien und Ägypten geht es auch um eine praktische Animalisierung des Feindes. Nach diesen Texten werden die Gegner nicht nur als Tier beschrieben, sondern als Tier behandelt. Aššur-bāni-apli (Assurbanipal) zum Beispiel tötet seine Feinde nicht nur "wie Schweine," sondern macht das "auf echten Schlachttischen."[14]

Es ist auch kein Zufall, dass nach dem Verlust des Königtums das eschatologische Bild des Tierfriedens sich im Kontext der messianischen Erwartungen entwickelt hat. Bernd Janowski sieht in den Bildern vom Tierfrieden "ein Modell für den Umgang mit dem Feind."[15]

2) Individuelle Klage

Die individuellen Klagen des Alten Testaments liefern einen weiteren Kontext. "Vor allem in den Feind- und Ichklagen der Psalmen begegnen häufig Tierbilder."[16]

Die Isolation und Exkommunikation wegen Krankheit oder Verfolgung führen manchmal dazu, dass man sich als Tier fühlt. In der metaphorischen Schilderung der eigenen (Not)Situation vollzieht sich ein Identitätswechsel (vgl. Ps 102:4-8), so das lyrische Ich empfindet sich nicht mehr als Mensch, sondern als Tier.[17] Der Vergleich mit Wüstentieren oder Saprophagen in

---

[13] Othmar Keel, *Die Welt der altorientalischen Bildsymbolik und das Alte Testament. Am Beispiel der Psalmen*, Zürich 1972, 49–50.

[14] Tracy M. Lemos, "Neither Mice nor Men: Dehumanization and Extermination in Mesopotamian Sources, Ḥerem Texts, and the War Scroll," in Tracy M. Lemos et al. (eds.), *With the Loyal You Show Yourself Loyal. Essays on Relationships in the Hebrew Bible in Honor of Saul M. Olyan*, Atlanta 2021, 251–252.

[15] Janowski, *Anthropologie*, 239.

[16] Peter Riede, Art. Tier, in: WiBiLex, https://www.bibelwissenschaft.de/de/stich-wort/35794/ (09.11.2023). Ausführlich zum Thema siehe noch Peter Riede, *Im Netz des Jägers. Studien zur Feindmetaphorik der Individualpsalmen*, Neukirchen-Vluyn 2000.

[17] Susanne Gillmayr-Bucher, "'Ich wachte und war wie ein einsamer Vogel auf dem Dach' (Ps 102,8). Ps 102 als exemplarischer Identitätsdiskurs," in Andreas Wagner, Jürgen van Oorschot (Hg.), *Individualität und Selbstreflexion in den Literaturen des Alten Testaments*, Leipzig 2017, 288.

den Ichklagen ist eine Art literarische Selbst-Animalisierung, welche die Aberkennung der Menschenwürde durch den Feind widerspiegelt. Dies können wir z. B. in der Bildsprache der Ichklagen von Ps 22 oder Hiob 30 gut beobachten.

In Ps 22:7 sieht sich das betende Ich nicht mehr als Mensch, bzw. Mann, sondern als Wurm. Eine Identifikation mit Tieren finden wir auch im Hiobbuch, wo der Klagende sich Angehörige von Wüstentiere nennt (Hi 30:29).

[...] וְאָנֹכִי תוֹלַעַת וְלֹא־אִישׁ	Ich aber bin ein Wurm und kein Mensch [...] (Ps 22:7a)
אָח הָיִיתִי לְתַנִּים וְרֵעַ לִבְנוֹת יַעֲנָה:	Ein Bruder der Schakale bin ich geworden und ein Gefährte der Strausse. (Hi 30:29)

In beiden Texten fühlt sich die redende Person isoliert, was einen nicht nur mit Tieren gleichsetzt, sondern auch zu einem "sozialen Tod" führt. Die Gemeinschaft mit Nekrophagen Lebewesen oder mit Tieren (Aasfresser) der gegenmenschlichen Wüste bedeutet Tod mitten im Leben (vgl. Ps 88:19).

Die Isolation geschieht vor allem durch Verhöhnung oder Verspottung in Form einer diskursiven und psychischen Dehumanisierung bzw. Animalisierung, manchmal kann man aber auch eine physische Aggression voraussetzen. In der Feindklage von Ps 22 geht es um lebensbedrohliche körperliche Gewalt, psychische und physische Aggression.[18]

In den Feindklagen wird letztendlich auch der Feind entmenschlicht.[19] Der Beter von Ps 22 animalisiert zwar seine Feinde, wenn er sie als Löwen und Stier bezeichnet (Ps 22:13–14.22), aber diese verbale Animalisierung ist im Grunde genommen nicht explizit negativ (S. noch z. B. Ps 17:12; 57:5).[20] Das Bild von Stier/Wildstier/Baschanbüffel und Löwe betonen die Bestialität der Feinde, drücken aber zugleich Stärke und Macht aus.

---

[18] Bester, *Körperbilder*, 235; Móricz, Nikolett, "Traumák a zsoltárokban. Az erőszak narratívájának poétikai feldolgozása a 22. zsoltár példáján," *Ókor* 18 (2019), 90.

[19] In der Feindklage kommen die folgenden fünf Tiere vor: Löwe (Ps 7:3; 10:9–10; 17:11–12; 22:14.22; 57:5; 58:7, vgl. 91:13); Stier (Ps 22:13.22); Hund (Ps 22:17.21; 59:7.15–16); Schlange (Ps 58:5; 140:4, vgl. 91:13); Biene (Ps 118:12). Die Feinde werden nie mit Haustieren verglichen, Bernd Janowski, *Konfliktgespräche mit Gott. Eine Anthropologie der Psalmen*, Neukirchen-Vluyn 2003, 117.

[20] Bester, *Körperbilder*, 222, vgl. Stiebert, Shame and the Body, 810–811.

Diese Eigenschaften der genannten Wildtiere stellen einen übermenschlichen Feind dar.[21] Gemein ist in den aufgezählten Tieren ihre Gefährlichkeit und die von ihnen ausgehende Bedrohung.[22] Diese Art der Animalisierung des Feindes ist darauf ausgerichtet, die normalen menschlichen Eigenschaften zu überbieten. Der Klagende benutzt aber Tiervergleiche auch im pejorativen Sinn. In Ps 22:17.21 werden die Feinde mit dem Bild der Hunde negativ charakterisiert (vgl. Ps 59:7–15).[23]

In Psalm 22 wird sowohl der Betende als auch der Feind gegenseitig entmenschlicht. Die gegenseitige Animalisierung wirkt, wie eine implizite Aberkennung der Gottebenbildlichkeit des anderen Menschen. Diese Redeweise wird aber im Alten Testament nicht abgelehnt, sondern wird als adäquates Stilelement der Klage behandelt. Ein dehumanisierter Mensch darf den Kontakt mit Gott aufnehmen, und das (Klage-)Gebet zu Gott funktioniert als legitimer Ort zum Verbalisieren der extremen Gefühlsäußerungen gegenüber anderen Menschen. Analog zu Rachepsalmen auch in diesem Fall ist zu bedenken, "dass Feind- und Vergeltungsaussagen in den Psalmen einen *beschreibenden* und keinen *vorschreibenden* Charakter haben."[24] Die Feindpsalmen – so Bernd Janowski – "setzten den Beter in ihrer schroffen und direkten Bildsprache instand, das Feindproblem zu bearbeiten, d.h. das Unbegreifliche der Feindschaft in seiner Abgründigkeit begreifbar und bearbeitbar zu machen."[25] So können diese Texte, und auch die verbale/literarische Animalisierung der Feinde als "sprachliche Ventile"[26] vor Gott benutzt werden. Letztendlich kann der Beter gerade in dieser Beziehung Mensch bleiben.

---

[21] Vgl. Janowski, *Konfliktgespräche*, 118; Szabolcs Ferencz, Kató, "'Örül az igaz, mikor látja a bosszút, mikor lábát a gonoszok vérében mossa' Az úgynevezett bosszúzsoltárok a נקם szemantikájának fényében," *Református Szemle* 107 (2014), 646. Das Motiv des feindlichen Gottes wird oft auch theriomorph dargestellt, siehe z.B. Jes 5:29; 31:4; Klgl 3:10; Hos 5:14; 11:10; 13:7–8; Hi 10,16; 16:9. Zum Vergleich mit Gott werden hauptsächlich mächtige Tiere (Wildstier, Raubtiere) herangezogen, die Gottes übermenschliche Macht hervorheben. Es geht im Ps 22 trotzdem um menschlichen Feinden, nicht etwa um Dämonen. Die feindlichen Menschen haben aber einen übermenschlichen Charakter.

[22] Christiane de Vos, *Klage als Gotteslob aus der Tiefe. Der Mensch vor Gott in den individuellen Klagepsalmen*, Tübingen 2005, 116

[23] Bester, *Körperbilder*, 222.

[24] Beat Weber, "Rachepsalmen: Sollen wir unsere Feinde hassen?", *Magazin INSIST* (2012), 29.

[25] Janowski, *Konfliktgespräche*, 132.

[26] Marianne Grohmann, "Ein Gott der Rache? Feindpsalmen in jüdischen und christlichen Auslegungen," in Nadja Rossmanith et al. (Hg.), *Sprachen heiliger Schriften*

Wie bereits erwähnt, stellt sich die berechtigte Frage, ob das eschatologische Bild des Tierfriedens (Jes 11) nicht ein alternatives Modell für den Umgang mit dem Feind sein könnte.[27]

3) Prophetische Kritik

Die prophetische Religions- und Sozialkritik verwendet auch Tierbilder, um das animalische Verhalten des Volksganzen bzw. der herrschenden Klassen oder die unterdrückte Stellung einer sozialen Gruppe zu veranschaulichen. Die Fürsten, Richter und Propheten, die ihr Amt missbrauchen, werden mit wilden Raubtieren verglichen,[28] die Unterdrückten mit schwachen Tieren. Manchmal wird das ganze Volk wegen seines gottlosen Verhaltens abwertend animalisiert.

In Zef 3:3 wird das gewalttätige Vorgehen der Führungsschicht durch Tiermetaphorik deutlich gemacht: "Ihre Fürsten in ihrer Mitte sind brüllende Löwen (אֲרָיוֹת שֹׁאֲגִים), ihre Richter sind Wölfe am Abend,[29] nichts lassen sie übrig bis zum Morgen." Die zweite Hälfte des Verses ist sprachlich problematisch, seine Bedeutung ist nicht ganz klar. Exegeten meinen in der Regel, dass die Wölfe keinen Knochen mehr haben, an dem sie am Morgen nagen können, oder dass sie am Morgen immer noch an dem Knochen nagen.[30] Wie in den oben genannten Psalmbeispielen stehen auch hier große und gefährliche Raubtiere für den Feind, hier sind diese Fleischfresser speziell die gewalttätigen städtischen Beamten. *Homo homini lupus*, ein Wolf ist der Mensch dem Menschen. Eine dem Zef 3:3 ähnliche Formulierung findet sich in Ez 22:25–27: Propheten sind wie brüllender Löwe, und Fürsten sind wie Wölfe, die Beute reissen, Blut vergießen und das Leben (נֶפֶשׁ) wegnehmen bzw. auffressen, um sich selbst bereichern und etwas zu profitieren.

---

und ihre Auslegung. Beiträge zur Veranstaltung "Sprachen heiliger Schriften und ihre Auslegung. Krieg und Gewalt – Recht und Frieden in Judentum, Christentum und Islam" am 30. Mai 2012 an der Landesverteidigungsakademie in Wien, Wien 2015, 46.

[27] Janowski, *Anthropologie*, 239.

[28] Riede, Tier, https://www.bibelwissenschaft.de/de/stichwort/35794/ (09.11. 2023).

[29] Die Septuaginta liest hier: λύκοι τῆς Ἀραβίας "Wölfe von Arabia / Wölfe der Wüste" (Text. em. עֲרָבָה; עֶרֶב?).

[30] Zu der philologischen Frage siehe Hubert Irsigler, *Zefanja*, Freiburg 2002, 319–320.

Gegenüber dieser Rhetorik, wo die Führenden explizit Raubtier genannt sind, werden in Micha 3:2–3 nur die Opfer der sozialen Unterdrückung animalisiert. Hans Walter Wolff macht darauf aufmerksam, dass Micha ein ungewöhnlich starkes Bild verwendet, um soziale Konflikte und strukturelle Gewalt zu beschreiben. Micha 3:2–3 enthält "eine solche Kette roher Handlungen, in denen der Mensch wie Schlachtvieh behandelt wird."[31]

שֹׂנְאֵי טֹוב וְאֹ֣הֲבֵי רָ֑ע[Q]	Sie hassen Gutes und lieben Böses,
גֹּזְלֵי עֹורָם֙ מֵֽעֲלֵיהֶ֔ם	sie reissen ihnen die Haut herunter,
וּשְׁאֵרָ֖ם מֵעַ֥ל עַצְמֹותָֽם׃	und das Fleisch von den Knochen!
וַאֲשֶׁ֣ר אָכְלוּ֮ שְׁאֵ֣ר עַמִּי֒	Und wenn sie das Fleisch meines Volkes gefressen
וְעֹורָם֙ מֵֽעֲלֵיהֶ֣ם הִפְשִׁ֔יטוּ	und ihnen die Haut abgezogen
וְאֶת־עַצְמֹֽתֵיהֶ֖ם פִּצֵּ֑חוּ	und ihre Knochen zertrümmert haben,
וּפָרְשׂוּ֙ כַּאֲשֶׁ֣ר בַּסִּ֔יר	dann zerstückeln sie es wie im Topf
וּכְבָשָׂ֖ר בְּתֹ֥וךְ קַלָּֽחַת׃	und wie Fleisch im Kessel!

Reiner Kessler geht davon aus, dass der Text die Hirtenmetapher verwendet, wenn er die Führer des Volkes als schändliche Hirten darstellt, die das Vieh schlachten und verzehren, anstatt die Herde zu hüten.[32] Der Text schildert die Phasen der Küchenvorbereitung, vom Häuten des geschlachteten Tieres über die Verarbeitung des Fleisches bis hin zum Kochen im Kessel. Es ist jedoch überraschend, dass in der Mitte der metaphorischen Rede (Micha 3:3a) eine klare Auflösung des zentralen Bildes zu finden ist. Die Formulierung שְׁאֵ֣ר עַמִּי "das Fleisch meines Volkes" rückt die Hirtenmetapher in die Nähe des Grauens des Kannibalismus[33] und macht deutlich, dass die Missbräuche der Führung nicht nur menschliche Existenzen (oder sogar Menschenleben) kosten, sondern dass die politische Elite sich

31 Hans Walter Wolff, *Dodekapropheton 4: Micha*, Neukirchen-Vluyn 1982, 69.
32 Rainer Kessler, *Micha*, Freiburg 2000², 149, vgl. Jörg Jeremias, *Die Propheten Joel, Obadja, Jona, Micha*, Göttingen 2007, 161; Björn Corzilius, *Michas Rätsel. Eine Untersuchung zur Kompositionsgeschichte des Michabuches*, Berlin 2016, 310.
33 Vgl. Manfred Oeming, "'Ich habe einen Greis gegessen'. Kannibalismus und Autophagie als Topos der Kriegsnotschilderung in der Kilamuwa-Inschrift, Z. 5–8, im Alten Orient und im Alten Testament," in Manfred Oeming, *Verstehen und Glauben. Exegetische Bausteine einer Theologie des Alten Testaments*, Berlin 2003, 160; Nicholas R. Werse, "Violence in the Minor Prophets," in Julia M. O'Brien (ed.), *The Oxford Handbook of the Minor Prophets*, Oxford, 2021, 175.

davon "ernährt," die Führer von ihrer Brutalität und Bestialität leben.[34] Herodot berichtet von einem Vorfall, bei dem Kambyses einen korrupten Richter häutete und die aus seiner Haut gefertigten Riemen zur Mahnung und Abschreckung an den Richterstuhl nagelte (*Hist.* V,25).[35] Micha 2:8 bereitet die metaphorische Häutung etwas vor, denn in dieser Vers ist das Herunterreißen der Kleidung als "zweite/soziale Haut" in der Tat eine "soziale Häutung."[36] Die hier verwendeten Begriffe wie Haut (עוֹר), Fleisch (בָּשָׂר ;שְׁאֵר) und Knochen (עֶצֶם) sind keine exklusiven anthropologischen Begriffe; wir teilen diese Aspekte der Leibsphäre mit Tieren.

Tierbilder werden auch im Buch Jeremia verwendet, um Israel in ihrem verdorbensten und schändlichsten Wesenszustand darzustellen. Die als Frau angeredete Gemeinschaft wird einer Kamelstute und Wildesel(in) verglichen, um die Ziellosigkeit, Unbesonnenheit und Triebhaftigkeit auszudrücken (Jer 2:23-24). In Jer 5:8 kommt das Bild des Hengstes vor, das sich als eine Anklage geschlechtlichen Fehlverhaltens interpretieren lässt.[37]

In der Verkündigung von Deuterojesaja findet man auch die Metapher des Wurms. Wegen ihrer Kleinheit und ihrer niedrigeren taxonomischen Kategorie kann das Wurm-Bild eine pejorative Bedeutung haben, aber wegen der Assoziation mit dem Tod können Würmer als aasfressende Tiere die menschliche Vergänglichkeit zum Ausdruck bringen. Der wurmartige Charakter des Volkes Israel in Jes 41:14 deutet darauf hin, dass das exilische Diaspora in einem Todes-nahen Zustand ist, und wegen seiner Kleinheit keine Kraft hat, sich selbst zu erlösen. Die Tiermetapher in den Worten des Propheten ist keine Kritik, sondern ein tröstlicher Hinweis auf den wesentlichen Unterschied zwischen Gott und seinem Volk.

4) Göttliche Strafe

Im Danielbuch begegnen wir der Animalisierung als göttliche Strafe. Das 4. Kapitel des Danielbuches berichtet über die Verbannung Nebukadnezzars, und seine zeitweilige Verwandlung zu einem Tier. Die Animalisierung ist in diesem Fall keine verbale Atrozität oder diskursive Dehumanisierung, sondern eine tatsächliche Strafe Gottes. Der Hochmut des babylonischen

---

[34] Jeremias, *Die Propheten Joel, Obadja, Jona, Micha*, 161.

[35] *Herodotos történeti könyvei. Görögül és magyarul*, 2. kötet: *IV–VI. könyv* (transl.: Geréb József), Budapest, 1893, 157.

[36] Vgl. Corzilius, *Michas Rätsel*, 305.

[37] Georg Fischer, *Jeremia 1–25*, Freiburg 2005, 168.242.

Königs wird von Gott mit einer "Exkommunikation" bestraft, dass ein temporäres Tier-Werden mitbringt. Es geht nicht einfach um eine Ausweisung des Königs, sondern es wird das Menschsein – damit auch die Gottebenbildlichkeit – des Königs in der Strafzeit aberkannt.[38] "Sein Verstand (לְבַב) wird verwandelt, dass er nicht mehr der eines Menschen ist, und der Verstand (לְבַב) eines Tieres wird ihm gegeben [...]" (Dan 4,13). Die Isolation bedeutet nicht wie übrigens das "soziale Tod," sondern eine Gleichsetzung mit Tieren, eine untermenschliche, tierische Lebensform.

Diese Animalisierung des Königs wirkt als Kontrastbild zu der Beschreibung Nebukadnezzars in Dan 2,31-32.37-38. In der Erklärung des Traumbildes kommt die Vorstellung der *dominium terrae* vor, die mit der priesterlichen Schöpfungserzählung verwandt ist.[39] Wie der Ur-Mensch als *imago Dei* eine Herrschaft über die Tierwelt ausübt, so hat Nebukadnezzar auch die königliche Macht über "die Tiere auf dem Felde und die Vögel unter dem Himmel (LXX: und die Fische des Meers)" (Dan 2:38). Auch Jer 27,5-6 versteht Nebukadnezzar als Verkörperung Adams, und Ebenbild Gottes.[40]

Die bestrafende Animalisierung betrifft nicht nur das Verständnis, sondern auch das körperliche Aussehen ("sein Haar lang war wie Adlerfedern und seine Nägel lang waren wie Vogelkrallen") und das Essverhalten ("wie das Vieh aß er Kräuter"). Diese göttliche Strafe hat keine richtige Parallele im Alten Testament. Es muss aber darauf unbedingt hinweisen, dass dieser Zustand zeitweilig und reversibel ist (Dan 4:31), und Gott selbst ist, der den König bestraft.

Ein anderer Text, wo die Animalisierung sich durch göttliche Strafe vollziehen scheint, steht im Buch Jeremia. Jeremia prophezeit den unwürdigen Tod des judäischen Königs Jehojakim/Jojakim. "Nicht werden sie um ihn klagen [...] [Mit] einem Begräbnis eines Esels wird er begraben werden, fortschleppen und werfen über die Tore Jerusalems hinaus. (Jer 22:18–19* [übers. G. Fischer]). Eine Eselsbestattung wirkt weitgehend

---

[38] Áron Németh, "The Ideal and the Bestial Human: Anthropological Aspects of Dan 1–6*," *Academia Letters* (2021), https://doi.org/10.20935/AL836 (09.11. 2023).

[39] Choon Leong Seow, *Daniel*, Louisville 2003, 44; Klaus Koch, *Daniel 1–4*, Neukirchen-Vluyn 2005, 189; Uta Schmidt, "Anthropologie, Körper und Macht in Daniel 2," in Jürgen van Oorschot, Andreas Wagner (Hg.), *Anthropologie(n) des Alten Testaments*, Leipzig 2018², 231.

[40] Jürgen-Christian Lebram, *Das Buch Daniel*, Zürich 1984, 56; André LaCocque, *The Book of Daniel. Second Edition*, Eugene 2018², 70.108.

dehumanisierend, besonders wenn es um einen König geht. Es gibt keine verwandtschaftliche und mitmenschliche Sympathie, darum wird keine rituelle Totenklage angestimmt, und der Leichnam des Königs wird eines Tieres behandelt werden. Es findet durch dieses Begräbnis eine postmortale Exkommunikation statt. Der gewalttätige und ungerechte König endet wie ein Tier, weit außerhalb der menschlichen Gemeinschaft.[41]

Saul M. Olyan in einer Studie macht darauf aufmerksam, dass sich die Dehumanisierung des toten Königs durch ein reklassifizierendes Strafritual vollzog. Die Ablehnung der Totenklage, das Fortschleppen und Herausschmeißen der Leiche sind Elemente eines demütigenden Anti-Rituals, nämlich das des "Eselsbegräbnis." Eine Reihe von Keilschrifttexten beschreibt die Demütigung gefangener feindlicher Könige durch ihre rituelle Reklassifizierung als Haustiere. Ein wichtiger Unterschied zu den altorientalischen Parallelen ist einerseits, dass in Jer 22:18–19 nicht ein siegreicher König, sondern Gott (JHWH) den animalisierenden Strafakt ausübt, andererseits, dass der Opfer dieser Dehumanisierung kein lebendiger Mensch ist.[42]

5) Das alttestamentliche Recht

Der fünfte Kontext, in dem man einer animalisierenden Dehumanisierung begegnet, ist das alttestamentliche Recht und der Bereich der Ethik. Bestialität und tierisches Verhalten werden im Alten Testament teilweise verboten und gesetzlich sanktioniert (Ex 22:18; Lev 18:23; 20:15–16).[43] Unter den Sexualdelikten in Ex 22:18 und Lev 20:10-21 wird Sodomie/Zoophilie mit Todessanktion versehen. Geschlechtsverkehr zwischen Mensch und Tier ist ein Gräuel, denn sie nicht nur eine freiwillige Selbst-Animalisierung darstellt, sondern auch die Humanisierung des Tieres mit einschließt. Dieser Gräuel bringt Todesstrafe mit, in Lev 20 wird sie auch über das Tier verhängt.

Das Hauptproblem liegt darin, dass aus solchen Praktiken, "keine Nachkommenschaft für JHWH entsteht",[44] und die soziale Dimension der

41 Fischer, *Jeremia 1–25*, 664.
42 Saul M. Olyan, "Jehoiakim's Dehumanizing Interment as a Ritual Act of Reclassification," *JBL* 133 (2014), 271–279.
43 Riede, Tier, https://www.bibelwissenschaft.de/de/stichwort/35794/ (09.11. 2023).
44 Thomas Hieke, *Levitikus 16–27*, Freiburg 2014, 687.

Sexualität außer Acht bleibt.[45] Das bedeutet, dass die Bestialität des Menschen in solcher Perversitäten auch negative gesellschaftliche Folgen hat, gegen die Gesellschaft wirkt. Sodomie gefährdet die menschliche Gesellschaft von Grund auf. Das Gebot vertritt die scharfe Trennung Mensch und Tier, deren Begründung in Gen 2 in dem Motiv erhalten ist, dass der Mann die ihm entsprechende Hilfe nur in einer Artgenossin erkennt.[46] Wenn der Mensch im Tier einen ihm adäquates Gegenüber finden versucht, lässt die Beziehung zum Mitmenschen und gleich damit die eigene Gottebenbildlichkeit verloren gehen.[47]

6) Extreme Notsituation

Extreme Notsituationen, wie Naturkatastrophen oder Kriegsnot, haben eine dehumanisierende, bzw. animalisierende Auswirkung.

In den Kriegsnotschilderungen des Alten Testaments kommt das Phänomen des Notkannibalismus vor. Lange Belagerung verursacht Hungersnot innerhalb der Stadtmauer, wo im Extremfall die Bewohner Anthropophagie/Teknophagie begangen. Solche Schilderungen von Belagerungsnot finden wir in der Beschreibung der Belagerung Samarias (2Kön 6:28–29), im Buch der Klagelieder (Klgl 2:20b; 4:10), und die gleiche Grausamkeit kommen in einigen prophetischen Strafankündigungen (Jer 19:9; Ez 5:10) und in Fluchworten des Deuteronomiums vor (Deut 28:52–57, vgl. Lev 26:27–29).[48]

Keiner dieser Texte spricht dezidiert aus, dass der Mensch in diesen Situationen zum Tier wird, aber das Wort "essen" beschreibt einen Akt, dessen Subjekt und Objekt normalerweise nicht gleichzeitig beide menschlich sein dürften. Ein Menschenfresser könnte nur ein großes Raubtier sein. Der Alte Testament kennt den literarischen Topos, in dem die Tiere (Aasfresser) die Leichen am Schlachtfeld auffressen (z. B. Jer 7:33; 12:9; 15:3; 16:4; 19:7).[49] Auch das Objekt des Essens dürfte nur ein tierisches

---

45 Janowski, *Anthropologie*, 114.
46 Silvia Schroer, "Grundlinien hebräischer Anthropologie," in Walter Dietrich (Hg.), *Die Welt der Hebräischen Bibel. Umfeld – Inhalte – Grundthemen*, Stuttgart 2021², 308.
47 Christoph Dohmen, *Exodus 19–40*, Freiburg 2012², 170–171.
48 Oeming, Kannibalismus, 158–163.
49 Van der Zwan sieht auch einen positiven Aspekt der Teknophagie in Klgl 2:20 und 4:10: Die Mütter essen ihre Kinder aus Mitleid, um weiteres Leiden der Kinder

oder pflanzliches Lebensmittel sein. Wenn der Mensch von einem anderen Menschen gegessen wird, geht es um eine radikale Dehumanisierung, bzw. Animalisierung des Menschen. Der Opfer der Antropophagie wird zum Schlachtvieh, und das Subjekt dieser tierischen Verhaltensweise wird zum Raubtier.[50] Die Teknophagie zeigt plastisch, wie in der Hungersnot der Überlebensinstinkt den Fortpflanzungstrieb unterdrückt.

Menschen können in einer Krisensituation nicht nur gegessen, sondern auch kultisch geopfert werden. Das Opfertier wird in diesem Fall mit einem Menschen ersetzt, denn ein Mensch genug wertvoll ist, die Gottheit in einer extremen Not zu besänftigen (2Kön 3:26-27).

7) Der heutige Kontext

Die Entmenschlichung durch Animalisierung ist in der Geschichte Europas nicht unbekannt. Die Sklaverei im Römischen Reich, die Menschheitsverbrechen der totalitären Diktaturen im 20. Jahrhundert, und der islamische Fundamentalismus/Fanatismus heutzutage setzen die institutionalisierte Aberkennung der Menschenwürde voraus. Dem "Feind" wird die Menschlichkeit abgesprochen. Die Unterdrückung von Randgruppen, die Gewalt gegen Frauen und Kinder, die Unterdrückung der Armen und der ethnischen/religiösen Minderheiten, Krieg, Rassismus, Völkermord und Terrorismus sind alles Phänomene, die mit der Vorstellung verbunden sind, dass der andere kein gleichwertiger Mensch oder überhaupt kein Mensch ist.

Ein grausamer Höhepunkt der pejorativen Animalisierung des Menschen in neueren Zeiten zeigt sich in der Nazi-Propaganda. Die Entmenschlichung der Juden durch Tierdarstellungen war zu dieser Zeit ganz gewöhnlich. Sie spielten häufig auf jüdische Familiennamen an wie etwa Hirsch, Löwy oder Bär. Diese antisemitischen Karikaturen hatten das Ziel, die Juden einerseitz lächerlich zu machen, andererseits sie zu entfremden. Jüdische Menschen wurden häufig auf Plakaten, Postkarten und in Zeitungen in Form von Geiern, Raben, Pferden, Ungeziefern, Läusen, Ratten oder Schlangen abgebildet, um sich über ihr Aussehen lustig zu machen

---

zu verhindern. In dieser Weise kehren die Kinder in den Mutterleib zurück, Pieter van der Zwan, "The Punished and the Lamenting Body," *HTS Teologiese Studies / Theological Studies* 75 (2019), 7.

[50] Zur Antropophagie in der Bildsprache siehe z. B. Num 23:14; Ps 27:2; Spr 30:14; Mich 3:3; Zef 3:3; Zak 11:9.

oder um klischeehafte Eigenschaften hervorzuheben. Zudem Juden wurden oft mit Schweinen in Zusammenhang gebracht, vermutlich um das jüdische Verbot, Schweinefleisch zu essen, zu verspotten.

Der Anti-Schwarze-Rassismus verwendet auch häufig das Instrument der Animalisierung, um Hass und Entfremdung zu erzeugen. Das Grundnarrativ des animalisch-primitiven Schwarzafrikaners wurde durch den transatlantischen Sklavenhandel begründet und global verbreitet.[51] Im 20. Jahrhundert wurden schwarze Männer sogar in den Akten der ordentlichen Justiz mit wilden, verständnislosen Tieren verglichen.[52] Als Muhammad Ali in 1967 die Teilnahme am Vietnamkrieg mit starken Worten ablehnte, wies auch auf die Ungerechtigkeit hin, dass die sogenannten "Negro people" in Louisiana wie Hunde behandelt seien und ihnen die Menschenrechte aberkannt werden.[53]

Wie die Nazis benutzte die rassistische Propaganda der Hutu-Mehrheit in Ruanda (1994) auch Tiermetapher für ihren Völkermord und stellte die Tutsi-Minderheit als bösartig und entmenschlicht dar, indem sie sie immer wieder als "Kakerlaken" bezeichnete.[54]

Der Abu-Ghuraib-Folterskandal zeigt, dass es nicht nur eine systemische oder kulturelle Animalisierung gibt, sondern auch individuelle Perversionen, die selten ans Licht der Öffentlichkeit kommen. Die irakischen Gefangenen im Abu-Ghuraib-Gefängnis wurden vom Wachpersonal misshandelt und gefoltert. Bilder dieser Affäre wurden in 2004 und 2006 veröffentlicht. Ein Foto beispielsweise zeigt eine US-Soldatin mit einer Hundeleine in der Hand. Am anderen Ende der Leine ist ein nackter, auf dem Boden liegender Mann zu sehen. Manchmal wurden die Gefangene wie Tiere geritten und gezwungen, auf Händen und Füßen zu gehen.

In Bezug auf den Terroranschlag auf Israel (2023) berichten die meisten Medien über "grenzenlose Bestialität." Bestialität bedeutet in diesem Zusammenhang die unmenschliche Grausamkeit gegen die israleitischee Zivilbevölkerung.

---

[51] Tarek Naguib, Kurt Pärli et al., *Anti-Schwarze-Rassismus. Juristische Untersuchung zu Problem und Handlungsbedarf im Auftrag der Eidgenössischen Kommission gegen Rassismus* EKR, Basel 2017, 32.

[52] Jürgen Martschukat, "'Little Short of Judicial Murder'. Todesstrafe und Afro-Amerikaner, 1930–1972," *Geschichte und Gesellschaft* 30 (2004), 501–502.

[53] Tracy M. Lemos, *Violence and Personhood in Ancient Israel and Comparative*, Oxford, 2017, 171–198.

[54] Lemos, Neither Mice nor Men, 253.

8) Schlussfolgerungen

"Wie sollen wir mit der langen und beschämenden Geschichte von Tiervergleichen umgehen, die ein wesentliches Element der Rhetorik der sozialen Marginalisierung, des Missbrauchs und der Tötung von Menschen darstellt, die als Mitglieder nicht-dominanter ethnischer Gruppen identifiziert werden?"[55] – Diese Frage von Alice Crary ist nicht nur aktuell, sondern führt zu der eigentlichen Fragestellung unserer Untersuchung weiter: Wie sollen wir mit alttestamentlichen Texten umgehen, die eine pejorative Animalisierung des Menschen unterlegen?

Meine Schlussfolgerung ist, dass wir aus alttestamentlicher Sicht nicht vom Verlust der Gottebenbildlichkeit sprechen können, aber die implizite Aberkennung oder Infragestellung der Gottebenbildlichkeit durch die Animalisierung der (Mit-)Menschen ist im Alten Testament eindeutig belegt. Gottesbildlichkeit ging nach dem Sündenfall nicht verloren, sondern in vieler Hinsicht falsch verstanden, indem der sündige Mensch entweder nicht herrschen mag, oder als Tyrann über Tierwelt herrscht, oder über anderen Menschen mit Gewalt herrschen will. Das letztere führt zu einer Dehumanisierung, bzw. einer pejorativen Animalisierung des Menschen.

Aus alttestamentlicher Sicht gibt es m. E. zwei legitime Formen einer Animalisierung des Menschen.

Die eine legitime Form einer dehumanisierenden Animalisierung ist die Entmenschlichung durch Gott selbst. Der Schöpfer des Menschen hat das souveräne Recht, die Gottebenbildlichkeit aufzuheben. Im Buch Daniel Gott nimmt diese Gelegenheit wahr, nimmt aber die Gottebenbildlichkeit nur zeitweilig zurück. Im Buch Jeremia findet eine göttliche Animalisierung nur postmortal statt. Diese Strafen betreffen individuelle Personen, von einer allgemeinen Abschaffung der Gottebenbildlichkeit durch Gott erwähnt das Alte Testament kein Wort. Im prophetischen Gerichtswort haben die pejorativ verwendeten Tierbilder eine rhetorische Funktion, die abwertende Aussagen sind aber Wort Gottes durch seinen Propheten.

Zweitens, das Klagegebet. Nach dem Gebot Jesu sollte man eigentlich auch für die Feinde beten, es sind aber Situationen, wenn der traumatisierte Mensch darauf unfähig ist. In der individuellen Klage steht man vor

---

[55]   Alice Crary, Animalität und Ethnizität, in Martin Hähnel, Jörg Noller (Hg.), *Die Natur der Lebensform. Perspektiven in Biologie, Ontologie und praktischer Philosophie*, Paderborn 2020, 177.

Gott, wo keine politische Korrektheit erwartet wird. Das Gebet ist der sprachliche Raum, wo Hass, Zorn und Rache unter Kontrolle halten werden kann. Die Feindklage der individuellen Gebete schadet nicht und tut keinem leid, kann aber therapeutische Kräfte freisetzen.[56]

---

[56] Grohmann, Feindpsalmen, 47.

DEUTEROCANONICAL LITERATURE

Sin and Virtue
Consequences of the Fundamental Choice between Death and Wisdom in the Book of Wisdom

Marcin Zieliński

Introduction

The Book of Wisdom, which was written in times close to the New Testament (after 30 CE), presents a very rich theological reality. It is a sapiential reflection, inspired primarily by the Old Testament, and also by Hellenistic philosophy. Its inspired author predominantly draws boldly on Stoic philosophy, emphasizing the importance of wisdom, virtues, the search for happiness, and self-discipline. Importantly, he adjusts the biblical teaching to a new philosophical and theological context, trying to interestingly present the Jewish religion to young people, who, being tempted by prospects of social careers in Alexandria in Egypt or by attractive mystery cults, depart from the faith. The Book of Wisdom depicts the rich intellectual life of the Jewish community in Alexandria, where the Hebrew Bible was translated into Greek, and where the Jewish thinker Philo of Alexandria was born and worked.

The topic under analysis concerns anthropological issues, i. e. the human condition according to the Book of Wisdom. This study juxtaposes two opposing realities: on the one hand, sin and perfection, and on the other, ungodliness and virtue. This seems to be one of the characteristic features of the inspired author's style, a kind of endless *syncrisis*, i. e. a comparison of contraries and opposites. In the first part of the book, the ungodly and the righteous are set against each other, while in the third part – the Egyptians and the Israelites. Similarly, the author describes and compares life and death, wisdom and folly, joy and sorrow, true worship and idolatry, and many other realities. Only in part two, does he create the encomium of Wisdom as the highest good, which seems to have no opposites. However, it should be assumed that such an opposite may exist, and a possible discovery of this opposite would help us better understand the nature of Wisdom itself.

This paper deals with the fundamental relation, which, in consequence, gives rise to antagonistic realities, i. e. sin and virtue. Both categories not only refer to earthly life, but also affect the specificity of life after death, because according to the Book of Wisdom, man was created in a state of immortality, and the consequences of his choices are everlasting as well. It seems that in the Book of Wisdom, the essence and source of a person's morality and, more broadly, of his every activity, is the lifelong bond he forms with a specific being or idea. A cursory reading of the Book of Wisdom makes us see that man, in his freedom, makes a choice between death or Wisdom. What is specific to this relationship is that its nature is love, although it concerns different entities and has dramatically different consequences. We intend to discuss the nature of man's relationship with Wisdom or death, and its consequences (virtue or sin, the latter understood as evil and unreasonable activity). Our purpose is to show that human choices are consequences of the specific bond that people form with death or Wisdom, respectively. In both cases, this relationship means a fundamental, existential choice, and actually is a loving, or even spousal, relationship. Furthermore, both relationships, with Wisdom and death, lead to diametrically different attitudes to life.

1. Earthly and Eternal Consequences of Human Choices

The importance of virtue and sin, along with the fundamental choices associated with them, is emphasized by the truth that the consequences of human choices concern both earthly life and eternity. The Book of Wisdom unambiguously introduces the idea of life after death, which is not just a colourless existence in Sheol, but has the character of a reward or punishment. This is possible thanks to the belief in the immortality of the human "I." The concept of immortality appears several times in the Book of Wisdom. Immortality is what people expect and hope for (Wis 3:4), and it results from virtue (4:1). The key text is Wisdom 8, where immortality is presented as a gift of personified Wisdom and a fruit of man's relationship with her (8:13.17). The terms do not refer to the soul understood as a spiritual element of man (if we can really talk about the soul in the Book of Wisdom), but to the entire person, understood as a unity in the Old Testament sense. This is emphasized in Wis 3:1, speaking about the righteous (this is how the word ψυχή in this verse should be translated; it is not a reference to man's spiritual element), and that no suffering will ever touch them. In the Greek text, the pronoun αὐτῶν is masculine and refers to the righteous. Similarly, in Wis 3:3, the article οἱ (masculine nominative plural) concerns concrete persons and not souls. The subject of interest and activity of Wisdom is man as a human person, and not a spiritual element or a material body, treated.[1]

When speaking about life after death, the author introduces new terms, previously missing in the Old Testament. In Wis 2:23, there is ἀφθαρσία – "incorruptibility," which is not a stylistic alternative for ἀθανασία ("immortality"). The word appears twice in the Fourth Book of Maccabees and seven times in the New Testament.[2] It was deeply rooted in Epicurean philosophy, as attested in the writings of Philodemus of Gadara, found at Herculaneum, Italy. The Epicureans assumed that the gods, although they had bodies made of matter, could live forever and knew no diseases or weaknesses.[3] This incorruptibility was caused by a physical force that bound the atoms of the body so tightly that it did not allow them to disintegrate, which is usually caused by time or the influence of the world. The author of the Book of Wisdom might have been inspired by this reasoning. Looking for some force that would guarantee human incorruptibility, he found it in God and Wisdom.[4]

Describing incorruptibility, the inspired author shows the nature of this gift. The key seems to be the interpretation of the expression ἐπ' ἀφθαρσίᾳ. It is suggested to give this preposition a final value and treat every human being as created "for the purpose of being immortal." In this understanding, immortality would be a reward for living a life according to the commandments, and achieving immortality would be reserved for those who successfully pass the test of life, guided by Wisdom and the commandments.[5] It is worth noticing that blissful immortality appears in various philosophical and biblical traditions. However, in the Book of Wis-

---

[1] Luca Mazzinghi, *Libro della Sapienza. Introduzione, traduzione, commento,* Roma 2020, 159.

[2] An analysis of these terms, including their biblical backgrounds, can be found in Tomasz Zaklukiewicz, *Nieśmiertelność sprawiedliwych. Idea nieśmiertelności sprawiedliwych w Księdze Mądrości,* Wrocław 2017, 210–253.

[3] Marco V. Fabbri, "Incorruttibilità e salvezza corporale. Il significato del termine ἀφθαρσία in Sap. 2,23," *Annales Theologici* 24 (2010), 318–320.

[4] Bogdan Poniży, *Księga Mądrości. Wstęp – Przekład z oryginału – Komentarz,* Łódź 2012, 121–122.

[5] This understanding of virtue appears in Agric. 100.

dom there is an important *novum*: it seems that man was not created for the purpose of achieving immortality (finality), but received this gift immediately, at the moment of creation.[6] Exegetes have long debated the meaning of the preposition ἐπὶ in the Book of Wisdom. Reese's opinion seems important, as he was a pioneer of research into the influence of Hellenism on this book. He wrote an important, and still inspiring, study concerning this issue. Reese brought up an essential argument in the discussion, emphasizing that out of twenty-two uses of ἐπὶ with a dative, none means finality, but informs about a specific state.[7] For instance, Wis 1:13, just like Wis 18:13, speaks of destruction as a concretely existing situation. In the light of this statement, man appears to have been created from the beginning in the state of immortality, understood as a vocation to eternal existence. The parallel stich suggests that God made man as an image of his nature. There is a textual problem here, as there are two possible readings (ἰδιότητο and ἀϊδιότητος). The first one, proposed by Ziegler's critical edition, seems more likely.[8] The other variant, meaning "eternity," may be an attempt to clearly show the essence of man's likeness to God – man has been endowed with the privilege of immortality, i.e. the ability to exist even after his physical death. The Book of Wisdom emphasizes that the entire human being (not only the soul or not only the body) as personal "I" is immortal. Thus, the real problem is not a physical death, which is a natural element of life and does not stop the human existence, but the man's fate after death. The immortal human being may be rewarded after death in the form of a blissful existence or "spiritual death," understood as punishment, i.e. a miserable existence. In this context, the issue of life choices is extremely important, because it concerns both earthly life and life after death. Hence, every choice is of fundamental significance, and its consequences are long-lasting.

[6] Chrysostome Larcher, *Études sur le livre de la sagesse*, Paris 1969, 280–284.
[7] James M. Reese, *Hellenistic Influence on the Book of Wisdom and its Consequences*, Rome 1970, 66–67.
[8] For instance, this variant is opted for by Mazzinghi, *Libro della Sapienza*, 132; see also Giuseppe Scarpat, *Libro della Sapienza. Vol. 1*, Brescia 1989, 189.

2. Man's Relationship with Death and Wisdom

The Book of Wisdom strongly underlines the role of free choice. It can be argued that lifestyle is determined by the relationship a person enters into. Choosing death or Wisdom seems to be so fundamental that it affects the entire ethical life. Being associated with a specific reality also translates into the person's fate after death. It should be noted that in both cases, this relationship is, paradoxically, a loving one.

2.1. Nature of the Relationship with Death

This section addresses the surprising topic of love of death, which is present in biblical literature. In its Greek version, Prov 8:36 speaks of people who hate wisdom but love death. Similarly, Isa 28:15 speaks of the covenant that the scoffers have made with death. In an attempt to escape from death, people try to somehow tame this inexorable reality, but in effect, they invoke death with all the consequences of their choice.[9]

The topic of death is introduced in Wis 1:12, where death is, by way of parallelism, juxtaposed with destruction (ὄλεθρος). Both words refer to a spiritual reality, a specific failure in life. In this way, the author gives a clear assessment of death, which brings only destruction and misfortune.[10] The topic of death is developed in vv. 13–15. The author shows lying as killing the ψυχή, i.e. life (v. 11). For those living in Greek culture, lying against another person was treated as one of the greatest crimes, and its consequence could be death, even understood as killing, taking someone's life. It mainly affected the liar.[11] The author of the Book of Wisdom might have wanted to show morally reprehensible behaviour as absolutely fatal (the verb is used in the future tense). The problem is how to interpret the word "death," which always remains ambiguous: it can refer to both earthly life and life in the future world.[12] It seems that in this particular case, it is about spiritual death, associated with the loss of friendship with God, which anticipates the later punishment, i.e. a dramatic and miserable existence after physical death.[13]

---

[9]   Mazzinghi, *Libro della Sapienza*, 105.
[10] José Vílchez Líndez, *Sapienza*, Roma 1990, 163–164.
[11] Scarpat, *Libro della Sapienza. Vol. 1*, 96.
[12] Mazzinghi, *Libro della Sapienza*, 89.
[13] Scarpat, *Libro della Sapienza. Vol. 1*, 163.

Although death itself is initially presented as a decidedly negative phenomenon, it attracts people's attention and seems to have a specific power to arouse interest. What is important for our analysis is the fact that v. 12 shows death as an object of seeking. The word ζηλόω emphasizes not only the aspect of seeking, but also the effort made and the involvement in seeking death. This word refers to love, along with the passionate search for the object of love. In this context, there occurs πλάνη, an important word conveying the idea of being deceived, seduced. According to the inspired author, seeking death relates to ignorance, error, which puts the seeker in a bad light. It is important to know the true goals of life, and this happens only with the help of Wisdom and the light of the Law, to which the author refers in several places.[14] Seeking death is presented as a passionate quest that is fraught with the cognitive error from the very beginning. The ungodly do not call death by its own name (θάνατος), but use other expressions (e. g. τελευτή). This may indicate the fear of death, which manifests itself as an inexorable and invincible reality.[15]

The aspect of a loving relationship with death can clearly be seen in Wis 1:16, where the ungodly are moved with love at the sight of death. Here three expressions require analysis: the nouns φίλος and συνθήκη, and the verb τήκω. The word φίλος occurs twice in the Book of Wisdom: in 7:27, referring to Wisdom, whose presence in the world makes holy souls friends of God. Noticeably, this noun is used in two completely different contexts, with opposite meanings. The author does not present Wisdom in her cosmic dimension, but as forming friends and prophets of God. The term "friend" may bring to mind the closest people who function in the king's court as trusted and proven advisors.[16] On the other hand, in Wis 1:16, the ungodly are shown as those who want to regard death as their friend. No reason for this behaviour is given. It may result from fear or ignorance related to rejecting God's wisdom, which leads to erroneous and irrational behaviour. In Wis 1:16, death is described as a reality that

---

[14] Luca Mazzinghi, "Law of Nature and Light of the Law in the Book of Wisdom (Wis 18:4c)," in József Zsengellér, Géza G. Xeravits (eds.), *Studies in the Book of Wisdom*, Leiden 2010, 39–42. This topic has been updated in Marcin Zieliński, "Światło jako symbol mądrości i Prawa w Księdze Mądrości," *Verbum Vitae* 29 (2016), 104–112, focusing on the importance of the Law as an essential guideline on the path to immortality.

[15] Mazzinghi, *Libro della Sapienza*, 108.

[16] Scarpat refers to Greek texts showing the king's friends in the Egyptian court; cf. Giuseppe Scarpat, *Libro della Sapienza. Vol. 2*, Brescia 1996, 80.

affects only and exclusively the ungodly. For this reason, it cannot be only physical death, because this death affects the righteous as well; they sometimes die prematurely. In this context, the death in v. 16 would refer to spiritual death or punishment after death.

The other noun is "covenant" (συνθήκη), which can have legal dimension or a dimension related to love.[17] This seems to be the understanding of the text by the Latin translator, who makes a clear allusion to the marital relationship (the Latin translation reads: sponsionem posuerunt). A similar image appears in Isa 28:15, where the opponents of the prophet speak about their covenant with death (in parallel lines there are death and Sheol, understood as a place of death). It seems that seeing no other alternative, the ungodly want to completely entrust their lives to death.[18] It is emphasized that they have not discovered God's plans and the promise of eternal happiness, so they try to appease the reality they fear. This surrender to death is not associated with any expectation, but only expresses the desire to belong to it. This sense is strengthened by the word μερίς, which in the Old Testament describes the portion, share God allotted to every Israelite as his special possession (cf. Deut 32:9) or underlines that it is God who is Israel's share and possession (cf. Num 18:20; Ps 119:57). The use of this expression may be ironic, because those who should be God's possessions become the possession of death.[19]

The image of the loving relation is completed with the word τήκω, used five times in the Book of Wisdom. In Wis 16:22.27 and 29, it describes the physical phenomenon of melting by the sun, which is the basic meaning of the word. Yet, τήκω has a lyrical meaning, related to love, as used in Alexandrian poetry. In his commentary, Scarpat quotes verses of several classical authors, including Theocritus, who uses the word in the sense of "being absorbed in love" (cf. Ps 21:15; 67:3).[20] A similar sense of τήκω can be found in Longus the Sophist (1,18,1). He describes the psychophysical state of a person who, under the influence of falling in love, literally "melts" in front of the object of his love, referring to the basic

---

[17] In Winston's commentary, there are numerous examples of covenants with various entities. Cf. David S. Winston, *The Wisdom of Solomon. A New Translation with Introduction and Commentary*, Garden City 1979, 113.

[18] Vílchez Líndez, *Sapienza*, 168. Commenting on this text, Vílchez Líndez refers to a similar covenant with death in Isa 28:15.

[19] Adalberto Sisti, *Il libro della Sapienza. Introduzione – Versione – Commento*, Assisi 1992, 108.

[20] Scarpat, *Libro della Sapienza. Vol. 1*, 132.

meaning of the word. This is a reaction affecting the physical and emotional sphere, which appears when one feels a strong love stimulus. This interpretation allows us to suggest that the ungodly become lovers of death, desiring to enter into a relationship with it. The choice of death is not just a simple error resulting from ignorance or cold calculation, but a kind of love fascination. Such a bond is comparable to the relationship that the righteous person builds with Wisdom. These bonds share a similar nature, although the consequences of the choices will be dramatically different.[21]

2.2. Nature of the Relationship with Wisdom

Analysing the love relation with Wisdom, it is worth focusing on the image of the figure of Wisdom, as it has a considerable influence on the nature of the future relationship. Following the rules of encomium, the author writes about the nature of Wisdom, its origin and deeds in the history of mankind. In Wis 7:22–8:1, he mentions 21 attributes of Wisdom. The first ten attributes occur in pairs, the eleventh φιλάγαθος seems to be in the centre and opens the second series, which is naturally connected with φιλανθρώπως. This repetition of the lexeme φιλ- seems to emphasize, on the one hand, an inclination towards goodness and perfection, and on the other hand, it shows Wisdom's love and care for people. At the same time, already in this section, the inspired author clearly defines Solomon's goal, which is the community of life with Wisdom and the experience of God's love.[22]

It has to be pointed out that the presence of Wisdom and its mode of operation are not hidden or visible only to a small group of people. Wisdom manifests herself to all who seek her help. Emphasizing this presence, the author uses the word "secret" (μυστήριον), which may be an allusion to mystery cults, because Wisdom is not reserved only for those initiated.[23] Importantly, this word also refers to the eschatological dimension, since Wisdom reveals the truth about reward after death and shows how to obtain it. Writing positively about this presence, the author defines it as passing into holy souls (7:27), dwelling in them even like the Pauline image of God's Spirit dwelling in believers (cf. 1:4). It is Wisdom that allows

---

[21] Marcin Zieliński, "La morte nel libro della Sapienza. Il rapporto tra la figura della Sapienza e la realtà della morte," *Biblical Annals* 7 (2017), 313–321.

[22] In his commentary, Engel even emphasizes that this image is "erotic." Cf. Helmut Engel, *Das Buch der Weisheit*, Stuttgart 1998, 137.

[23] Mazzinghi, *Libro della Sapienza*, 122.

people to know God and his plans (8:4), and then the structure of the world (7:17–21). Wisdom is the mother of all good things: power, wealth, beauty and health; she helps manage these gifts (7:11–12). Finally, she is the one that gives virtue (4:1) and in consequence, she leads mortals to blissful immortality (8:17).[24]

After presenting Wisdom as a reality that is close to God and offering priceless gifts, the inspired author seems to suggest that the next natural step will be to enter into a relationship with her. Inspired by spousal metaphors, used by the prophets, and the images from the Book of Proverbs, he depicts the downright marital nature of this relationship referring to Solomon (Wisdom 7–8). A series of expressions emphasize the aspect of closeness; hence it seems right and possible to talk about a spousal metaphor. We can notice significant progress in building this relationship based on Wisdom 6–8, and especially on 8:9–16. After describing the beauty and noble origin of Wisdom, she becomes the object of loving desire (Wis 9:2), and then this unity is realized in everyday life. The author expresses this in the programmatic beginning of the pericope, where he decides to make Wisdom his companion (bride, 8:2).

This process culminates in the image of marital nature in Wis 8:16. The word προσαναπαύω stresses the familial and spousal nature of rest. Scarpat cites passages that use this word in the context of marriage.[25] The word συναναστροφή shows that this relationship is associated with constantly being together, like συμβίωσις. It also emphasizes the aspect of friendship, which is characteristic of the Song of Songs.[26] Finally, in 8:18, highlighting all the attributes of Wisdom, the author speaks of seeking how to get her for himself.[27] Attention should be paid to the word λαμβάνω, which may be a cliché of the Hebrew expression meaning "taking as wife" (לקח). It is worth noting that also in Greek, λαμβάνω, used to render the Hebrew expression, may refer to taking to wife. Scarpat observes that Codex S uses ἀγάγω in 8:18, which is a technical term referring to getting married. This correction might have aimed at making the text less ambiguous for the reader, and at the same time, it could clearly have indicated the marital sense of this expression. Moreover, the use of the lo-

---

[24] Sisti, *Il libro della Sapienza*.

[25] Scarpat, *Libro della Sapienza. Vol. 2*, 197–198.

[26] A detailed analysis of the terms and a presentation of the dynamics of this process in Wis 8:10–16 can be found in Zieli ski, "La morte nel libro della Sapienza,« 313–317.

[27] Scarpat, *Libro della Sapienza. Vol. 2*, 202.

cution εἰς ἐμαυτόν, instead of the simpler ἐμαυτῷ (dative), may emphasize the loving dimension of this relationship. Scarpat refers to Gen 6:2 and, above all, to Tob 8:7, the description of the wedding of Tobias and Sarah, understood as "taking" Sarah as his wife. The next problem is how to interpret the expression εἰς ἐμαυτόν, which, according to some exegetes, should be replaced with εἰς ἐμαυτοῦ (sc. οἰκία). In this case, the correction would refer to taking Wisdom to one's "home." It seems that it is more correct to keep the original version (Ziegler's critical version also supports this solution) and translate it as "to take into oneself, into one's soul." Such a translation is made possible both by the numerous examples that Scarpat cites and by the logic of the text itself.[28] The inspired author must have intended to emphasize the profound loving and personal relationship, which unites Pseudo-Solomon with Wisdom. Being inspired with the spousal metaphor, occurring in the Bible, the author shows that the essence of this bond is to create a spousal relationship, in which Wisdom is treated as the ideal spouse. The nature of this bond and the nature of love itself mean that Solomon's behaviour, his choices and way of thinking are consequences of the deep relationship that determines his personal and public life. To sum up, it should be emphasized that these images point to the dynamic development of these relationships and show that for the inspired author, the ideal is a spousal and intimate relationship with Wisdom, encompassing all dimensions of human life (public, family, religious).

3. Effects of the Relationships with Death and Wisdom

The relationships with death and Wisdom have the character of a deep affectionate fascination and, as a result, influence the whole life. Since the realities of death and wisdom are opposing, the consequences of these choices seem to be the same. Analysing the selected verses, we can note that the author juxtaposes these effects and further highlights their opposing nature.

---

[28]   Scarpat, *Libro della Sapienza. Vol.2*, 203.

3.1. Effects of the Relationship with Death

After establishing their relationships with death, the ungodly state that this reality evokes fear so much that they avoid applying the word θάνατος to it. In Wis 2:1–5, they underline that life is a sad and short-term experience. Despite these sad perspectives, they attempt to enjoy their lives. Verses 2:6–9 show their uninhibited use of goods, combined with sexual promiscuity. In the Stoic context, the word εὐφροσύνη (2:9) meant joy related to the reasonable use of goods. It was the joy that accompanied works of the sage.[29] This word is used in a similar meaning by Philo of Alexandria, who writes about the relationship between joy (εὐφροσύνη) and passion (ἡδονή) in his work entitled *De Sacrificiis*. He emphasizes that the goods he treasures do not come from partaking in a feast where the body is seized by the pleasures of the stomach. The real pleasure is from the mind nourished and dancing with virtues, which allows one to experience authentic and lasting joy (Sac. 33). Since in the Book of Wisdom, true joy is always related to the relationship with Wisdom and good life, the use of the term εὐφροσύνη is ironic in this context. It is worth noting that this false joy becomes the lot (μερίς) of the ungodly only. The author uses this word three times (1:16; 2:9.24) to describe what the ungodly receive as a result of their efforts: these are, respectively, adherence to death, false joys, and again belonging to the company of death.

The author of the Book of Wisdom emphasizes that the lives of the ungodly were fruitless. Chapter five describes the situation of a righteous person and the unrighteous at the moment of eschatological judgment. The unrighteous discover that the very righteous person they despised turns out to be the child of God (the words of the righteous person from Wis 2:16 are confirmed) and stands before the court with great confidence. The ungodly emphasize that their lives were fleeting and very short experiences. They lack happy perspectives, which they notice already in 2:1. However, the problem is not life expectancy itself. Although life is short, one should be guided by virtue, because it leaves a lasting trace in people's memories and, at the same time, being the fruit of co-operation with Wisdom, it ensures blissful immortality. The ungodly left traces of their carefree fun (σύμβολα τῆς εὐφροσύνης – 2:9) and no sign of virtue (ἀρετῆς μὲν σημεῖον οὐδὲν – 5:13). The particles μέν and δέ (v. 13) additionally empha-

---

[29]   SVF III,105,32.

size the contrast between virtue and godless life, showing the eschatological value of bad choices. Their evil earthly lives do not allow them to enjoy blissful immortality.[30]

The consequence of the first choice of the ungodly is their tragic lives, combined with moral evil, which ultimately manifest themselves as existential failures in Wisdom 5. The assessment of the moral behaviour of the unrighteous is scattered throughout the first part of the Book of Wisdom, and considering the variety of images and terms used, it is impossible to discuss it in this paper. However, it is worth emphasizing the consequences of choosing death, which manifest themselves practically at the moment of choice. These disastrous consequences may suggest a different meaning of the verb τήκω, which refers to the process of body decomposition and the process of digestion. Examples of this meaning can be found in Plato (*Timaeus*, 82e), Sophocles (*Antigone*, 905) or Galenus (6.192.784). The author might have wanted to show contrast with the images of love through the ambiguity of the word he had chosen. Death, by its nature, does not guarantee any long-term relationship or blissful immortality (cf. Wis 8:17), but only announces decay and suffering during earthly life and the afterlife.

3.2. Nature of the Relationship with Wisdom

The key effect of the relationship with Wisdom is virtue, which seems to be a value in itself, sufficient to give a person joy and fullness in every dimension of his human life.[31] The concept of virtue in a philosophical sense is rarely found in the Greek Bible. It appears only in 2–4 Maccabees and the Book of Wisdom, and its use is related to the influence of Stoic philosophy, where it was one of the central themes. In the Book of Wisdom, it is closely associated with two concepts: righteousness and immortality. Virtue is understood as the developed habit of acting fairly. It is related to human nature and being created in the image and likeness of God (cf. Wis 2:23). It is also the result of constant being in kinship with Wisdom (cf. Wis 8:7.18).

Virtue itself seems to have two dimensions. On the one hand, it is the result of being inspired by a beautiful lifestyle that is described as desirable,

---

[30] Mazzinghi, *Libro della Sapienza*, 232–233.
[31] Chrysostome Larcher, *Le livre de la sagesse, ou, La sagesse de Salomon. Vol. 1*, Paris 1983, 314.

to be imitated and triumphant (cf. Wis 4:2).[32] At the same time, possessing virtue is related not only to the presence of Wisdom, but also to the work and spiritual exercise that the righteous person undertakes. As it is emphasized in Wis 8:18, the right way of thinking and acting requires the constant practicing of good deeds. The word συγγυμνασία, appearing only here in the entire Greek Bible, points to the need for creative cooperation with Wisdom in developing virtues.[33] This understanding of virtue is consistent with the Stoic vision, for which the author seems to have respect. The Stoics, inspired by Aristotle, emphasize that virtue is the ability to live morally and in accordance with the vocation given to every person. At the same time, it is emphasized that virtue requires constant practice so that it can be rooted in a person's life, especially in the sphere of his moral choices.[34]

The consequence of possessing virtue is immortality. In Wis 4:1, virtue appears in the context of eternal memory, which results from the influence of Greek culture, in which the memory of the deceased was a substitute for immortality. In the Book of Wisdom, the concept of immortality is associated with happiness in the present and future life, which God guarantees. He is the one who remembers the righteous, and this has real consequences after physical death. On the other hand, any memory of the unrighteous will disappear, both in the memory of people and God. The lot of the ungodly, outlined in Wisdom 6, manifests itself as the sad remembrance of wrong decisions and the suffering resulting from the fact that this fate can no longer be changed in any way.[35]

Writing about virtue, the author also presents it as a reality that attracts and encourages people to follow, perhaps transferring to virtue certain images associated with the figure of Wisdom. Wis 4:2 emphasizes that virtue becomes the object of seeking. Scarpat suggests that the author depicts virtue as a beautiful woman who becomes an object of attention and even adoration. In his commentary, he quotes Xenophon of Athens, who describes Wisdom as a reality communing with the gods and men, a reality

---

[32] It is worth noting that Wisdom is also shown as attracting her devotees with the promise of a fulfilled life.

[33] This aspect is rightly emphasized by Leproux, observing that in Wis 8:18, φιλία is connected with παιδεία, i. e. friendship with Wisdom leads to developing virtues and makes mortals friends of God (Wis 7:27) and not of death. Cf. Alexis Leproux, *Un discours de sagesse. Étude exégétique de Sg 7–8*, Roma 2007, 269.

[34] SVF III,49,214; SVF III,48,197–198.

[35] Mazzinghi, *Libro della Sapienza*, 188.

that is most valued of all things. Scarpat also notes that in Wis 4:1, the inspired author uses the word γινώσκω, rendered as "to come to know, recognize." In his opinion, the author's preference for this word over τιμάω may be due to the connotations this word has in the Bible. Γινώσκω emphasizes love, including its sexual value. In this context, virtue manifests itself not only as the result of a simple choice, but also as a reality with which the righteous create an emotional, loving bond, characterized by admiration and affect.[36]

Conclusion

To sum up the above analyses, it should be emphasized that the problem of sinfulness and perfection is not only a matter of moral choices or specific deeds. Deeds are consequences of the first choice – the choice of a relationship, which then translates into the quality of life. Man is faced with the choice of two realities: devil and death as well as Wisdom and God. It seems that the key role in making this choice is knowledge of salvation history and the role of Wisdom in the salvation process, which the author has, and this knowledge is generally available to all seekers.

In the Book of Wisdom, people's key choices are described as creating bonds of a loving nature. As for the relationship with Wisdom, the author practically sees it in terms of the New Testament concept of grace, where the relationship of faith with Christ becomes the key to justification.[37] In this context, it seems strange that people try to build a bond with death, a bond that is characterized by fascination. It seems that the relationship with death, even if described using words and images of a loving nature, cannot be put on an equal footing with love of Wisdom. Sinners do not create lasting relationships that will later have positive effects. They are portrayed as those who do not understand God's secrets, but are rather subject to passion and delusion. They see no alternative to their choices and, therefore, lead sad lives without any prospect of blissful immortality.

From the point of view of biblical anthropology, it is important to emphasize that in the Book of Wisdom, man is portrayed as a relational being. He does not make choices autonomously, but relates himself to a specific reality and, being inspired by it, he takes decisions. It seems that a natural

---

[36] Scarpat, *Libro della Sapienza. Vol. 1*, 260.
[37] Maurice Gilbert, *La sapienza di Salomone. Vol. 1*, Roma 1995, 120.

element in human life is the creation of bonds of love that involve the whole person. The inspired author, juxtaposing the motifs of death and Wisdom, as well as virtue and sin, emphasizes that man's wrong choice of the subject of interest leads to his fall that begins in this world and is completed after death. On the contrary, man's good choice of the object of love brings positive effects in the intellectual and spiritual aspect and makes his life happy both on earth and after death.

"Male and Female" as Limits
Genesis, the Book of Tobit, and God's Creative Intentions

Francis M. Macatangay

Introduction

The creation stories in Genesis 1–2 provide the paradigm of order necessary for life to prosper. God creates harmony by placing boundaries and
assigning limits. When categories and functions are mixed, chaos that is
detrimental to the flourishing of life ensues. This essay looks at the theme
of limits that is reflected in Genesis 1–2 and explores the ways this creation
theme is embedded in the Book of Tobit. In particular, the study considers
how the narration of the journey of Tobias, the story's young hero, weaves
the fundamental theological claims of these creation stories in order to address the life-draining afflictions of two families in exile.

With this end in view, the study first delineates the theme of limits or
boundaries in Genesis 1–2 as a principle of order. It then examines the
central section of the Book of Tobit, which is the journey of Tobias that
concludes with his marriage to Sarah. Interestingly, the Book of Tobit
makes a rather bold claim in specifying the partner and helper of Genesis
2 as a kinswoman named Sarah. Tobit's claim thus projects the practice of
endogamy all the way back to God's intentions in creation. This hermeneu-
tical move opens up to some considerations of same-sex partnerships. In
the end, it is argued that though Tobit may have opened up a space for
such a possibility, the narrative of Tobit nonetheless witnesses to the validity of the claims of Genesis understood canonically.

1. God's Creative Actions in Genesis 1

In the Priestly account of creation in Genesis 1, God sets up limits to create order out of the whirling mass of chaos. The divine action of placing limits is an act of differentiation. In imposing boundaries, God separates and so distinguishes the elemental realities of creation one from the other. For example, God places a disc to contain the waters from above and the waters from below. The waters from below are further separated, limiting them to a particular place in order to make dry land for plants and fruit trees to thrive. In a similar manner, the lights in the dome of the sky are made to distinguish day from night and light from darkness. God's creative word activates the process of ordering all the elements in place by assigning them their own respective functions (cf. also Ps 104:9-18; Job 38; Prov 8:22-29; Sir 33:7-13; Isa 45:12). As Bernard Och has observed, the mutual co-existence in creation is a result of differentiation, separation, and the proper allocation of limits upon the elements of the universe.[1] This harmonious relationship in creation is at risk when the divinely imposed limits are disrespected. The confusion of boundaries and categories results in disorder and dysfunction.

After the elements of creation have been assigned a proper place, God gives a blessing to "every living creature that moves" (Gen 1:21), saying "be fruitful and multiply and fill the waters in the seas and let the birds multiply on the earth" (Gen 1:22). Genesis 1 also reports that God gives a similar blessing after making humankind. First, God distinguishes humankind as male and female. God then blesses and commands them, saying "be fruitful and multiply, and fill the earth and subdue it" (Gen 1:28). Finally, God delegates them as the divine representative to all of creation. The Priestly vision then shows a creative pattern in which God separates and differentiates humankind for life to flourish. As God places limits on his creation in its first stage to pave the way for living creatures to grow, so God has also set up the limits of male and female in humankind for human life to develop in its quantitative and qualitative dimensions.

Since the distinction of humankind as male and female follows the patterns of God's boundary-setting activity that gives birth to life in the created universe, it is reasonable to view male and female as *a priori* limits God has imposed upon humankind. Humankind is indeed made in God's

---

[1] Bernard Och, "Creation and Redemption. Towards a Theology of Creation," *Judaism* 44 (1995), 226–243, see especially pp. 227–228.

image and likeness.[2] And yet, humankind is differentiated as male and female. Humankind may be the more immediately linked to God than any other living creature but the distinction stresses the fact that they are not God.[3] Lest they be mistaken for God, they are created with limits as male and female as an ordering principle.

God created humankind with limits, thus opening up to God's creative word of blessing. His command "to be fertile and multiply" is the divine blessing that respects the limits that inhere in humankind. It is only as male and female that humankind is able to perform their function as God's agent to other created beings. Humankind's limits allow the creation and the proliferation of life, which is consistent with the way God has acted upon the rest of his creation. After placing the limits on his final creation, God makes humankind the agents of the ongoing process of creation. To respect the limits God has imposed on humanity is to receive the blessing of life in all its dimensions. In Genesis 1, limiting humankind as male and female has in view the creative process that proliferates and makes human life fruitful. Consequently, humanity in their limitedness as male and female represents, images, and points to the living God as they participate in the process of creation.[4]

2. God's Creation of Humanity in Genesis 2

Genesis 2 offers a different account of the creation of humanity. God forms the first man by breathing into a hunk of clay formed from the dust of the earth (Gen 2:7). Here, it is the divine breath, not God's image and likeness, that closely connects the first living man to God (Gen 2:7). God places him in the garden of Eden that teems with life to work and guard it (Gen 2:15). And yet, after ensuring that the garden has all the elements necessary for life for the first man, God remarkably finds something in the set-up that is not good. God identifies the problem as the aloneness and helplessness of Adam: "it is not good for man to be alone" (Gen 2:18).

[2] For a brief survey of interpretive possibilities for the claim that humankind was created in the image and likeness of God, see Moshe Reiss, "Adam. Created in the Image and Likeness of God," *Jewish Bible Quarterly*, 39 (2011), 181–186.

[3] See the comments of Phyllis Trible, *God and the Rhetoric of Sexuality,* Philadelphia 1978, 20–21.

[4] See the comments of Mark Smith, *The Priestly Vision of Genesis 1*, Minneapolis 2010, 101, 135.

To address the problem, God forms out of the ground all the wild animals and all the birds of the air so that the man can identify and name them (Gen 2:19-20). To name the animals is to know their nature. To name them also implies not only that the animals are subject to Adam but also that they enjoy a harmonious relationship with humans.[5] These animals are paraded before Adam in order to find him a helper or companion. Adam realizes that no one of these, not all of them together, like to him though they are, are like enough to him. In none of them does he find a partner fit for him for none corresponds to him; none can play the helper that God has in mind. The animals are meant to be "'assistants and encouragement" for humans in various ways "but not yet worthy assistants in the ultimate sense which God seeks."[6] Since none of the animals are found to be a suitable support and partner to Adam, God performs a second and surgical procedure while Adam sleeps, taking a rib from him and building it into a woman (Gen 2:22). It is only after the creation of the woman that Adam finds a proper counterpart, a fitting partner, and a corresponding companion.

For Genesis 2, the main problem God addresses in creating humanity is the solitariness of Adam, or his lack of an equivalent partner. To this end, God provides him a helper in Eve who is astonishingly like him yet extraordinarily different. Since God has cast the man into deep sleep to create the woman, the man does not know her origins. In fact, he is not meant to know how she came to be. And yet, when God brings him the woman, the first man does not name her the way he did with the animals. Instead, he identifies what they share in common and ignores their differences: "this one at last is bone of my bones and flesh of my flesh" (Gen 2:23). Somehow, the first man who was fast asleep when it happened understands the woman to be like him on their first encounter.

The first man is limited in two ways. First, he lacks true knowledge of his partner and he ignores the fact that he does not possess any knowledge of what happened and how the woman came to be. Second, he is now in-

---

[5] Claus Westermann, *Genesis 1–11. A Continental Commentary*, Minneapolis 1994, 229: "Names are given first to living beings because they are closest to humans ..." Gerhard von Rad also notes that naming is "an act of copying and an act of appropriative ordering" (*Genesis. A Commentary*, Philadelphia 1972, 83). In the words of Karl Löning and Erich Zenger, *To Begin With, God Created ... Biblical Theologies of Creation*, Collegeville 2000, 113: human beings are "ordering representatives of the creator God."

[6] Von Rad, *Genesis*, 82.

complete because a rib from his side has been taken away from him. In the creative act of giving the first man a companion and helper, the first man has become limited and weaker. He is able to make up for what he lacks only by leaving his father and mother and by clinging to his wife. The creation of the woman surfaces not only the aloneness but also the limitedness and dependence of the first man. The aloneness of the first *ish* has been decided with the creation of the *ishshah* but at a cost: the first man has become lesser. That God has made a support and helper for the first man only underlines the man's limitedness.

The woman certainly corresponds to the man but she is not like him. Her origin is different as she is not made from the dirt in the ground that God moulds and breathes into life. She is instead constructed or derived from the side of the first man. She has no knowledge of her origin either. She too is limited and has a certain lack. Furthermore, she does not go to the man out of her own will. Rather, God brings her to the man. This divine action of drawing them to each other overcomes the limitedness that inheres in both of them. In doing so, God forms a relationship of partnership between the first man and woman so that life may be enriched. God connects them to each other and the relationship of mutual assistance and companionship that is formed makes up for what they lack as individuals for the purpose of enhancing life.[7]

3. Ways of Reading the Journey of Tobias

The journey of Tobias in the Book of Tobit forms the heart of the story. Six out of fourteen chapters narrate the young man's travel with his angelic companion Raphael disguised as a kinsman named Azariah. The central section of the book, from the sixth to the eleventh chapter, shows the ordinary and extraordinary adventures that transform the young boy into a man. The journey of Tobias then can be viewed as a *bildungsroman* that describes the young hero's rite of passage into adulthood.[8] Tobias' journey is not only physical but also educational.

---

[7]   For a rehearsal of the various readings of Gen 2:24, see, for instance, Angelo Tosato, "On Gen 2:24," *Catholic Biblical Quarterly* 52 (1990), 398–404. The concern of this piece, however, is on the witness of Tobit. It is tempting to describe this as "completing" the other in order to address their respective lacks. However, completion is never really possible, since the point of God's creation of the woman is to be a helper and partner to the man.

The story offers the recovery of a sizable sum of money as reason for Tobias' journey. Tobit, the young man's father, has entrusted the money to a cousin in the distant Persian city of Ecbatana, which today is the Iranian city of Hamadan (see Tob 4:1-2.20; 5:1-3). Believing that his death looms on the horizon after asking God for it in prayer, Tobit decides to send his son Tobias on a dangerous journey with this mission in mind. The story implies that Tobit intends to have the money as a sinecure for his family after his death.

As the young man's obstacle-ridden journey unfurls, the hidden but real reason for the journey emerges. It becomes the vehicle in fact for the unfolding of the divine plan previously announced (Tob 3:16-17). While traveling together, the angel informs the young boy that he will marry Sarah, a kinswoman who has been married seven times unsuccessfully. Each of her seven husbands turned up dead on their honeymoon because the demon Asmodeus is jealously in love with Sarah. This tragic turn of events has not only moved Sarah's maidservants to accuse her of killing her husbands but has also pushed Sarah to despair. In prayer, Sarah asks God to take her life away but changes her mind after considering the possible impact of her death on her father. Instead, Sarah asks God to pay attention to her condition of disgrace. In response, God sends the angel Raphael with the twofold mission to heal Tobit's blindness and to unbind Sarah from the demon Asmodeus so that she can be given to Tobias in marriage. In short, marriage is the real force behind the young man's quest.

As Tobias' journey takes him away from his father's home in Nineveh and leads him to the home of Sarah's father Raguel, Raphael initiates the marriage arrangements while Tobias asks Raguel for Sarah's hand in marriage. In marrying Sarah, Tobias shows that he has matured and acquired some wisdom, ready to take on the responsibility of an adult kinsman who saves Sarah from shame and reproach (see Tob 3:13). While the marriage clearly benefits Sarah, it also makes Tobias the inheritor of the estate of Sarah's family and head of the household (see Tob 3:17; 6:12; 14:13). The marriage serves as a safety net for Tobit's family, the need for which is the impetus behind Tobit's decision to send his only son to Media (see Tob 4:21; 5:17-19). When Tobias returns home with Tobit's deposited money

---

[8] See, for instance, Cristián Barría Iroumé, "El matrimonio de Tobías y la sexualidad. un estudio psicológico," *Teología y Vida* 46 (2005), 675–697; Pierre Charland, *Le jeune Tobias et son ange. Filiation, autonomie et identité*, Montreal 2006.

and half of Raguel's estate after his marriage to Sarah, Tobit's household is doubly enriched. Marriage, which is the stated divine solution, not only points to Tobias' maturity but also addresses Tobit's financial concerns.

The journey will also lead Tobias to find the cure for his father's blindness, thanks to the angel who shares with him some special medical knowledge after a dangerous encounter with a giant fish (see Tob 6:6-8). Following the instruction of the angel, Tobias smears the gall of the fish he had caught on his father's eyes and it restores his father's eyesight. The journey of the young hero bestows boon upon the afflicted characters as the misfortunes of Tobit and Sarah are resolved. From the point of view of the narrative, Tobias' journey enables the fulfilment of the divine intentions to remove the white films from Tobit's eyes and to give Sarah to Tobias in marriage (Tob 3:16-17).

Another way to describe the journey of Tobias is in theological terms. The journey is not simply a rite of passage from boyhood to adulthood with marriage as the marker of transition. The resolution of the misfortunes of Tobit and Sarah, thanks to the journey of Tobias, is also about the restoration of order and the reinstatement of limits in the chaotic world of the suffering characters. To this end, it is not surprising that creation motifs and themes are echoed in the narration of Tobias' journey.[9] Just as in creation the joining of man and woman in marriage concludes God's creative actions, so does the wedding of Tobias and Sarah conclude the journey of restoration. The prayer of the couple on their wedding night, which alludes to the creation of man and woman in Genesis 1–2, hints at this discernment. Their marriage forms part of a creation theology.[10] It also fulfils a major instruction of Tobit on the kind of spouse his son Tobias ought to marry (Tob 4:12). Tobias' journey therefore is a significant piece of the story not only because it functions as the means for resolving the story's dramatic conflicts but also because it serves as the motor for running the story's theological convictions.

---

[9]   The journey of Tobias also resonates with Exodus; see Francis M. Macatangay, "Election by Allusion. Exodus Themes in the Book of Tobit," *Catholic Biblical Quarterly* 76 (2014), 450–463. Since Exodus can also be understood as a type of creation, it is not surprising to find echoes of these creation accounts in Gen 1–2 in the journey narrative of the book of Tobit.

[10] See Joseph A. Fitzmyer, *Tobit*, Berlin 2003, 464; Benedikt Otzen, *Tobit and Judith*, London 2002, 40.

4. The Theme of Limits from Genesis 1–2 in the Journey of Tobias

Tobit, the young man's father, becomes blind and poor while Sarah suffers the disgrace that comes from having seven husbands killed on the evening of the honeymoon. Their misfortunes reflect the chaos of their world. The journey of Tobias shows the conquest of chaos and the repair of transgressed boundaries in the world of the suffering characters. His journey speaks to the disorder when limits are trespassed and to order when they are re-established. As the accounts of creation show, life is possible and thrives when boundaries are respected. This is precisely what happens to Tobit and Sarah after the transgressed boundaries are normalized. There are at least two elements in the journey narrative that contribute to this discernment: the encounter with the fish and the exorcism of Asmodeus.

On the first night of the journey, Tobias confronts a giant fish, ιχθυς μεγάς, that leaps out unexpectedly of its natural environment in order to devour him whole on the riverbank (6:2).[11] The big fish may recall the great fish that swallowed Jonah, the prophet who resisted God's command to warn Nineveh (Jonah 1:17). It also evokes the traditional symbolism of water monsters that are often linked to death and known to swallow all living creatures. The sudden appearance of the giant fish is likely less of a folktale motif and more of an echo of the combat myth whereby God defeats the dragon and the sea.[12] Crushing the chaos monsters, God reinstates order in creation by keeping them at bay by restricting them with boundaries.

Amy-Jill Levine has noted that the fish crossing into improper realms contravenes the normal relationship between humans and animals in

---

[11]   In G^I, the fish jumps out of the water to devour the boy. In G^{II}, the fish jumps out to devour the *feet* of the boy.

[12]   See Francis M. Macatangay, "God's Conflict with the Chaos Monster in the Book of Tobit," in Michael Duggan et al. (eds.), *Cosmos and Creation. Second Temple Perspectives*, Berlin 2020, 321–329. See also Anathea Portier-Young, "'Eyes to the Blind'. A Dialogue Between Tobit and Job," in Jeremy Corley, Vincent Skemp (eds.), *Intertextual Studies in Ben Sira and Tobit. Essays in Honor of Alexander A. Di Lella, O.F.M.*, Washington DC 2005, 23; Irene Nowell, *The Book of Tobit. Narrative Technique and Theology*, CUA PhD Dissertation 1983, 219; Géza G. Xeravits, "Stranger in a Strange Land. Tobiah's Journey," in Géza G. Xeravits, Jan Dusek (eds.), *The Stranger in Ancient and Medieval Jewish Tradition*, Berlin 2010, 87–89; Naomi S. S. Jacobs, *Delicious Prose. Reading the Tale of Tobit with Food and Drink*, Leiden 2018, 108–125.

which the fish is "a consumer rather than the consumed."[13] The fish vaulting out of its usual bounds is a breach of boundaries that God established in creation. Moreover, God's command to humankind to "have dominion over the fish of the sea" (Gen 1:29) is subverted. Humans are supposed to subdue animals, not the other way around. If not for the guidance of Raphael, God's divine representative, Tobias would not have known how to manage the unforeseen encounter with the transgressive fish. By following the angel's instructions, however, Tobias controls and subdues the monstrous fish. The water creature, now returned to its suitable function, becomes "the means of creation."[14] Tobias roasts and eats the fish (Tob 6:5). Later, its parts are used to exorcise the demon Asmodeus from Sarah and to clean up Tobit's scales-covered eyes. Both events will restore the life and well-being of Tobit and Sarah.

Tobias confronts a riskier threat. Asmodeus, a demon that exemplifies transgression of the essential boundaries between two realms, is in love with a daughter of a mortal. The jealous demon has killed all the seven husbands of Sarah on their wedding night as they approached her to consummate the union (Tob 3:8; 6:14-15). Asmodeus "violates marriage boundaries by killing Sarah's husbands, and the union of a demon with a woman offers no fully human offspring, only anomalies."[15] More importantly, Asmodeus and his unexplained longing for Sarah naturally recalls the desire of the fallen angels or the Nephilim for the daughters of men as told in Gen 6:1-4.[16] This mixing of categories is a contravention of the limits God established in creation.

---

[13] Amy-Jill Levine, "Diaspora as Metaphor. Bodies and Boundaries in the Book of Tobit," in J. Andrew Overman, Robert S. MacLennan (eds.), *Diaspora Jews and Judaism. Essays in Honor of, and in Dialogue with A. Thomas Kraabel*, Atlanta 1992, 113. See also J. Robert C. Cousland, "Tobit. A Comedy in Error," *Catholic Biblical Quarterly* 65 (2003), 550. See also Francis M. Macatangay, "Divine Providence and the Dog in the Book of Tobit," *Journal of Theological Interpretation* 13 (2019), 128–143.

[14] Nowell, *Narrative Technique and Theology*, 219. See also Fitzmyer, *Tobit*, 203, who notes that Tobias' struggle with the fish is in keeping with the typical motif found in romantic quests in which the hero battles a dragon or sea monster (Tobias versus the big fish) which when conquered becomes a source of healing (205).

[15] J. Edward Owens, "Asmodeus. A Less than Minor Character in the Book of Tobit," in Friedrich Reiterer et al. (eds.), *Angels. The Concept of Celestial Beings – Origins, Developments and Reception*, Berlin 2007, 287.

[16] On the seduction of mortal women by fallen angels, see the *Test. of Naphtali* 3.4–5; *Test. of Reuben* 5.4–7; Jub 4:15, 22; 5:1–11; 1 Enoch 6:1–6; 7:1–6; 9:6–9.

In an important respect, Asmodeus also represents the total Other.[17] For this reason, the demon does not correspond to Sarah as a suitable partner that God has envisioned at creation. The demon's desire for Sarah is a dysfunction and a deviation from the order of nature. In this way, Asmodeus signals "a return to primordial chaos."[18] The situation therefore calls for a remedy in which boundaries are re-set in place. The reinstatement of the natural boundaries occurs in the evening of the honeymoon. Remembering the instruction of Raphael, Tobias takes the liver and heart of the fish out of his bag and places them on live coals, giving off a repulsive odour that sends the demon out of the bridal chamber into the remotest parts of Egypt (Tob 8:1-3). There, the angel Raphael has him bound; Asmodeus is kept within proper limits. Now that the demon is bound, he is permanently away and unable to return to Sarah. The life-giving marriage between Tobias and Sarah is made possible now that the transgressed boundaries have been healed.

In this light, the journey of Tobias with the angel Raphael is not simply a journey to ensure the security of the family in a time of instability. It is not merely an educational journey that bestows Tobias knowledge, wisdom and maturity. It is also a passage in which the violated limits and trespassed boundaries to the detriment of the characters are re-established. The journey is the vehicle through which God reconstitutes the chaotic world according to his original design.[19] The restoration of these boundaries paves the way for the realization of another creational intention, namely, the marriage of Tobias and Sarah along with its purposes. Since marriage is so much a part of God's creative activities, it is hardly surprising that Tobias and Sarah would rehearse the creation of man and woman in their wedding prayer.

---

[17] On this point, see Beate Ego, "'Denn er liebt sie' (Tob 6:15 MS 319). Zur Rolle des Dämons Asmodeus in der Tobit-Erzählung," in Armin Lange et al. (eds.), *Die Dämonen. Die Dämonologie der israelitisch-jüdischen und frühchristlichen Literatur im Kontext ihrer Umwelt = Demons. The Demonology of Israelite-Jewish and Early Christan Literature in Context of their Environment*, Tübingen 2003, 309–317.

[18] Owens, "Asmodeus," 281.

[19] See Ida Fröhlich, "Creation in the Book of Tobit," in Tobias Nicklas, Korinna Zamfir (eds.), *Theologies of Creation in Early Judaism and Ancient Christianity in Honor of Hans Klein*, Berlin 2010, 35–50.

4.1 Genesis 1 in the Wedding Prayer of Tobias and Sarah

Genesis 1 offers the pattern in which God creates the man and woman as male and female in his image before resting on the seventh day from all his work. While the seventh day is described as holy (Gen 2:3), God pronounces as good the creation of man and the woman, God's last creative act (Gen 1:31). The establishment of limits necessary for life to grow in its qualitative and quantitative dimensions concludes in the creation of man and woman. This pattern in Genesis is reflected in the journey of Tobias which ends in marriage. After the re-establishment of boundaries, Tobias and Sarah are married, the high point of the narrative.

In fact, the marriage prayer of Tobias and Sarah alludes to the creation story in Genesis 1.[20] Starting with a call to the heavens and all of creation to bless God, who is referred to as the "God of our ancestors" (8:5), the couple's prayer moves to the creation of man and woman. It is likely that the prayer echoes the creation of man and woman as found in Genesis 1. First, the use of the Greek verb *poiein* (to do, to make) in "You made Adam" suggests the first account in Gen 1:27 because the LXX version restricts this verb for translating the Hebrew *barah* or *asah* in describing the divine action and the creation of humanity in Genesis 1.[21] The second creation account in Gen 2:7 states that God formed (*eplasen*) the first human from the dust, a description that is absent in the prayer.

---

[20]   Patrick Griffin, *Theology and Function of Prayer in the Book of Tobit*, CUA PhD Dissertation 1984, 172–173, notes that it is not a prayer by or for Tobias alone but the prayer of the married couple. Carey A. Moore, *Tobit. A New Translation with Introduction and Commentary*, New York 1996, 241, notes that the prayer is a vehicle for the narrator to state "his understanding of the nature and purpose of marriage."

[21]   See Griffin, *Theology and Function of Prayer*, 177 n.22. In G^{II} (Sinaiticus), the verb *poiein* of Gen 1 is also utilized for Eve, reading literally: "And you made Eve his wife as a helper and support to him" (Tob 8:6). The other Greek versions and the Vetus Latina (VL) use the verb "to give." The Vulgate adds "de limo terrae" to make the reference to the creation of Adam more conformed to Gen 2:7, but this is not in the Greek versions (see Vincent Skemp, *The Vulgate of Tobit Compared with Other Ancient* Witnesses, Atlanta 2000, 270–271). Although the statement "let us make him a helper like him" echoes Gen 2:18 where God decides to make a "fitting helper for him," the use of the Greek ποιήσωμεν nevertheless echoes Gen 1:26, where God says, "let us make ... ." It is also followed by the Vulgate. But see Geoffrey Miller, *Marriage in the Book of Tobit*, Berlin 2011, 141 n.461, preferring the reading of G^{I} and the VL, "to give."

Tobias also notes the fulfilment of God's blessing to multiply in citing Adam and Eve as the primogenitors of humankind. His claim in the prayer that "from the two of them has come the whole human race" (rendered by the Old Latin as "and from them you multiplied human offspring") resonates with the divine blessing of fruitfulness given in Genesis 1. That the Old Latin adds "give us children as a blessing" to the petition to grant them to grow old together is thus understandable and not out of place.

This theme of proliferation and fecundity of life, which is not an explicit concern of Genesis 2, is also found in Raphael's response to Tobias who felt fear upon learning that he will marry Sarah. Raphael assures Tobias that Sarah has been destined for him from the beginning and that Tobias will have children by her (6:18; 4Q197 4 ii 18).[22] The blessings of Sarah's parents Raguel and Edna before the couple returns home to Tobit also include petitions to see children (10:11).[23] The conclusion of the story reports that Tobias and Sarah indeed have seven sons (14:3; 4Q196 18:15-16), which proves the fulfilment of God's command at the creation of humankind as male and female.[24]

4.2 Genesis 2 in the Wedding Prayer of Tobias and Sarah

The prayer is also reminiscent of God's plan for Adam and Eve as told in Gen 2:18-24.[25] Tobias notes the role of Eve as helper (*boethos*) and support (*sterigma*).[26] Tobias also cites the divine judgment in Gen 2:18 that "it is

---

[22]   The Qumran fragment reads: "I am sure that there will be [children from her] for you, [and] they [w]ill be ..." See Fitzmyer, *Tobit*, 218.

[23]   This is in the long text-type (G^{II}), in G^{III} and in the Old Latin (VL); the mention of children from the marriage of Tobias and Sarah is lacking in G^{I}.

[24]   See Fitzmyer, *Tobit*, 324–325. Miller, *Marriage in the Book of Tobit*, 151, notes that the number seven connotes perfection and says that "Tobiah and Sarah have been perfectly fruitful."

[25]   For instance, see Miller, *Marriage in the Book of Tobit*, 141: "The parallels with Gen 2:18–24 are unmistakable." See also Fitzmyer, *Tobit*, 241, 245; Tobias Nicklas, "Marriage in the Book of Tobit. A Synoptic Approach," in Géza G. Xeravits, József Zsengellér (eds.), *The Book of Tobit. Text, Tradition, Theology*, Leiden 2005, 149. Angelo Tosato claims that the reference in Tob 8:6–8 to Gen 2:18–24 implies that it acts as "a normative matrimonial model" ("On Genesis 2:24," 408 n. 53). See also John Collins, "Judaism in the Book of Tobit," in Géza G. Xeravits, József Zsengellér (eds.), *The Book of Tobit. Text, Tradition, Theology*, Leiden 2005, 33; William Loader, *The Pseudepigrapha on Sexuality. Attitudes towards Sexuality in Apocalypses, Testaments, Legends, Wisdom, and Related Literature*, Grand Rapids 2011, 172, 174.

[26]   For an analysis of these terms, see Griffin, *Theology and Function of Prayer*,

not good for the man to be alone" as reason for the creation of Eve. The allusion to Gen 2:18-24 implies that Tobias sees the role of his wife Sarah to be the same as that of Eve. God brought and gave Sarah to Tobias like Eve to Adam (cf. Tob 3:17).[27] Sarah is the helper and partner God has intended for Tobias. They have been brought together by God into a relationship just as Adam and Eve were brought together by God to overcome their limits. That the heart of Tobias clings or is drawn to Sarah upon learning that she is a kinswoman whom he has the right to marry (Tob 6:18) likely echoes Gen 2:24, which states that the husband clings to his wife.[28] In alluding to Genesis 2, the marriage of Tobias and Sarah harmonizes with God's creational intentions.[29] The mutual partnership and assistance that obtains from this marriage is meant for the flourishing of their lives in its qualitative dimensions.

The marriage prayer's reference to the creation of Adam and Eve is a way to make sense of Raphael's claim that God has destined the marriage of Tobias and Sarah from the beginning (Tob 6:17). Indeed, God has decreed the marriage between the two as a response to the prayer of Sarah (Tob 3:16-17). The prayer's twice-repeated reference to "helper" (cf. Tob 8:6) gives the impression that their marriage participates in God's intentions expressed at creation. In the same way that God brings Eve to Adam in creation to resolve the problem of the first man's existential aloneness, so too it is part of God's plan to bring Sarah to Tobias in marriage as his helper and support so that they can enjoy a marriage of mutual partnership that fosters life in all its aspects. God is at work in this marriage because their marriage follows the pattern God has set forth for the life-giving relationship between man and woman in Genesis 2.[30] The marriage of Tobias

---

178–179; Napoleón Fernández Zaragoza, "La Oracion de Tb 8,5–9 en el contexto del libro y a la luz de Gn 2,18," *Estudios Biblicos* 74 (2016), 150–154.

[27] The Greek verb in Tob 3:17 is "to take," which is a typical verb in the Hebrew Bible for indicating something like marriage. On this, see Ken Stone, "Marriage and Sexual Relations in the World of the Hebrew Bible," in Adrian Thatcher (ed.), *The Oxford Handbook of Theology, Sexuality, and Gender*, Oxford 2015, 175.

[28] The Greek verb in Tob 6:18 echoes the LXX of Gen 2:24 (see Loader, *Pseudepigrapha on Sexuality*, 172).

[29] Ryan Schellenberg, "Suspense, Simultaneity, and Divine Providence in the Book of Tobit," *Journal of Biblical Literature* 130 (2011), 326 n. 60, says "that the account of Eve's creation in Genesis 2 evokes precisely the notion of correspondence that informs Tobit's narrative structure. God makes for Adam 'a helper as his partner,' the NRSV translates the construction," or the more literal translation "corresponding to him."

and Sarah, viewed in terms of mutual assistance and suitable partnership, realizes God's creative intentions from the start of time.[31]

From a socio-historical perspective, "the circumstances of Hellenistic times made such mutual support desirable; faithful spouses could help one another in the practice and knowledge of their faith."[32] Furthermore, the concluding petition of the prayer for God to have mercy on them and to allow them to grow old together is consistent with emphasizing and commending the value of partnership and support in the relationship between husband and wife. Indeed, it is in the ripeness of age that one has greater need of a companion and helper.

5. Tobit's Idea of a Suitable Partner and Companion

The Book of Tobit proposes that the helper and partner God has intended for Tobias is in fact a kinswoman, one who shares the lineage of their ancestors. At the beginning of the story, Tobit claims that when he became a man, he married a woman who is a member of his own family (1:9). In his instruction to Tobias, Tobit warns his son against marrying a foreign woman, or one who is not of his father's tribe (4:12). When Raphael informs Tobias that he will be married during their journey, the angel says that Tobias is Sarah's next of kin and so, he has "hereditary claim" on her (6:12). To assuage Tobias' fear that his marriage to Sarah may result in his own death, Raphael reminds him of Tobit's command to take a wife from his father's house (6:16). Before handing Sarah to Tobias in marriage, Raguel tells Tobias to take his kinswoman (7:11-12).[33]

---

30   See the remarks of Griffin, *Theology and Function of Prayer*, 178: "There is a notable parallel between God's activity on behalf of Adam and Eve, and what he does for Tobiah and Sarah."

31   The argument is along the lines of Schökel's observation: "Cada matrimonio repite el misterio de la primera pareja, creada por Dios para la mutua ayuda y la fecundidad. En ese sentido, Sara había sido creada para Tobias, que aún estaba solo, como Adán" (Luis Alonso Schökel, *Rut, Tobías, Judit, Ester*, Madrid 1973, 76–77). But see also the comment of Miller, *Marriage in the Book of Tobit*, 139: "This divine intervention does not reveal that all marriages are 'made in heaven' but constitutes a manifestation of God's providential care for his people, enabling two afflicted Diaspora families to survive and prosper in the exile and to insure the survival of Judaism in a hostile environment."

32   Griffin, *Theology and Function of Prayer*, 179.

33   On endogamy in Tobit, see Thomas Hieke, "Endogamy in the Book of Tobit, Gen-

In light of this information from the story, the wedding prayer's reference to the woman as helper and support is understood specifically as a woman from Tobit's tribe. The story insists that this practice is in keeping with the Law of Moses.[34] In recalling the role of the woman as described in Gen 2:18, Tobit's narrative discourse claims that endogamous marriage has its roots in creation. Sarah, a kinswoman of Tobias, is the suitable wife God has intended for Tobias as his helper and support from the beginning. For Tobias to take his kinswoman Sarah out of truth instead of lust means that Tobias follows not only the Mosaic Law but also the truth and the proper purpose willed and established by God at the creation of man and woman.[35] In sum, the story seems to project such preference for a kinswoman as the proper marriage partner all the way to God's intentions in creation.[36] Such an interpretation may have been motivated by a desire to protect Israel's economic, ethnic and religious identity from dissolution in the dispersion that it has become part of the "Torah for exile."[37]

The Book of Tobit has folded the theological claims of the two creation accounts in Genesis into its story. With its likely allusion to Genesis 1, it acknowledges that the limits God has imposed on humankind as male and

---

esis, and Ezra-Nehemiah," in Géza G. Xeravits, József Zsengellér (eds.), *The Book of Tobit. Text, Tradition, Theology*, Leiden 2005, 103–120; Nicklas, "Marriage in the Book of Tobit," 139–154; Jean-Jacques Lavoie, "L'interdit des mariages mixtes comme stratégie identitaire en Tobit 4,12–13," in André Gagné et al. (eds.), *Constructing Religious Identities During the Second Temple Period. Festschrift for Jean Duhaime on the Occasion of his 68th Birthday*, Leuven 2016, 75–90.

[34] On this point, see Francis M. Macatangay, "The Wisdom Discourse of Tobit as Torah," *Biblische Notizen* 167 (2015), 99–111.

[35] The word *porneia* used in the prayer, which is translated as lust, is in antithetical parallel with *aletheia*. The word has been interpreted to mean any relations between a man and a woman that is not willed by God. For Lavoie, "L'interdit des mariages mixtes," 82, *porneia* "désigne un comportement sexuel non sincère." See also Griffin, *Theology and Function of Prayer*, 182, and Lucca Mazzinghi, "'Non per passione, ma con verità'. un aspetto del matrimonio secondo Tb 8,7," in José E. Aguilar Chiu et al. (eds.), *Bible et Terre Sainte. Mélanges Marcel Beaudry*, New York 2008, 94–96.

[36] It has to be noted, however, that the seven previous husbands are also close kin. Nicklas notes that the two Greek versions of Tobit (GI and GII) have different approaches to endogamy, with GII having a stricter approach ("Marriage in the Book of Tobit," 139–154). Lavoie, "L'interdit des mariages mixtes," 84, also notes that Tobit's notion of endogamy is stricter than that of Ezra and Nehemiah because he limits Tobias's future spouse to one tribe, Naphtali, the tribe of Tobit.

[37] Devorah Dimant, "Tobit and the 'Torah for Exile' in Light of the Qumran Texts," *Zeitschrift für Theologie und Kirche* 119 (2022), 29.

female open up to God's word of blessing, making fecundity and the proliferation of human life possible. This can be called the pro-creative aspect
of marriage. Moreover, it recognizes the claim of Genesis 2 that God has
healed the inherent lack and limitedness of the human person by bringing
man and woman into a relationship of partnership and mutual assistance
for the enhancement of life. This can be referred to as the unitive aspect
of marriage. And so, Tobit agrees that marriage as part of God's creative
plan has these pro-creative and unitive purposes in mind. Tobit, however,
specifies the kind of suitable partner and helper intended for the man. As
the marriage of Tobias and Sarah shows, a kinswoman is the corresponding
companion for the man. A marriage outside of close kinship bonds constitutes an improper marriage.[38]

Concluding Remarks

The Book of Tobit participates in the conversation about appropriate and
inappropriate marriages, offering the kinswoman as the companion and
partner God intended to heal the aloneness of the first man. This interpretation of mutual partnership and assistance for the flourishing of life, which
is one of the purposes of marriage, invites questions related to same-sex
unions. If Tobit can employ Gen 2:18-24 and identify the corresponding
partner and companion God intended for his son Tobias as a kinswoman,
why would it not be possible to expand the implied meaning of Gen 2:18-
24 to include same-sex partners? After all, if the primary concern of the
second creation account in Genesis 2 is the powerful draw of relationship
in terms of partnership and mutual help as a way of resolving the aloneness
of the human person, or as a way to enhance life for the better, then the
companion and mutual support can be another man or another woman.[39]
If Tobit can include kinswoman as part of its understanding of the partner
and helper that Genesis 2 has in view, then surely, a man can play the
partner to another man or a woman can be the mutual support to another
woman. To live in intimate relationship and mutual partnership, no matter

---

[38] See Hieke, "Endogamy," 103–120.
[39] For von Rad (*Genesis*, 82) and Westermann (*Genesis 1–11*, 233), Gen 2:24 does
not establish a normative standard for marriage. Instead, it is a descriptive explanation of the extraordinarily strong pull that moves human beings to marry or
enter into relationships even with the normative standards that parents and society
normally try to enforce.

the companion, is to live still in accordance with God's original intentions.

In fact, it has been argued that Gen 2:18-24 is not a normative regulation or restriction of marriage but a descriptive definition of "the strong draw and attraction that calls men and women into relationship with one another" or an acknowledgement of "the propensity of men to pursue 'inappropriate' marriages that defy the wishes and schemes of their parents and, by implication, society and religious institutions."[40]

While this interpretation is possible, it has to overcome nonetheless the fact that the two accounts of the creation of man and woman in Genesis 1–2 cannot be taken in isolation of each other. The Book of Tobit certainly entwines them together in the story and prayer of the couple Tobias and Sarah on their wedding night, albeit coloured by the story's unique claim that Genesis 2's mutual support and partner is restricted to a kinswoman. Later tradition repeats and reinforces this canonical pattern. In Matthew's gospel, for instance, Jesus responds to the question of divorce by citing both Gen 1:27 ("God made them male and female") and Gen 2:24 ("a man leaves his father and mother and be joined to his wife), concluding that "what God has joined together let no one put asunder" (Matt 19:4-6; cf. Mark 10:5-9). In other words, what has been scripturally and canonically joined cannot be set apart from each other. Needless to say, Catholic theology has always maintained that marriage has both pro-creative and unitive ends. And so, the return to the beginnings as told in Genesis 1–2 and as witnessed in the Book of Tobit shows that God's creative plan of marriage always includes the flourishing of life in both its quantitative and qualitative dimensions.

---

[40] See the arguments of Megan Warner, "'Therefore a Man Leaves his Father and Mother and Clings to his Wife'. Marriage and Intermarriage in Genesis 2:24," *Journal of Biblical Literature* 136 (2017), 269–288, 288.

NEW TESTAMENT

Logos as Imago Dei in John's Prologue
The Meaning of Logos in John's Prologue
(A Narrative Critical Study)

Mirjam Piplica

Introduction

John's Gospel is renowned for a somewhat different presentation of Jesus than the one present in the Synoptic Gospels. For his readers to understand the human and divine natures of Christ, the author had to employ well-known terms and some which shed new light on his presentation of Jesus. *Logos* has been introduced so that John's Christology could be recognized in categories of cosmology, eschatology and soteriology (Creator, Revealer, and Saviour).

This narrative-critical study aims to observe the function of *Logos* in John's Gospel from the perspectives of its *implied* and *real* readers. I shall extract the meaning of the Logos in the *Prologue* (John 1:1–18) and trace its usage in the Fourth Gospel, prioritizing those passages which most poignantly shed light on how *Logos* functions within the Gospel of John. My focus will be on the meaning of Logos that provokes the readers' response, taking into account that Logos is a dynamic substance. In the course of the Fourth Gospel this dynamic is attested. Logos revealed as Jesus Christ has been leading dialogues and discourses for the most part in the narrative. The word (Logos) as in incarnation (i.e. Jesus Christ) becomes endowed with explicit manifestation and deprived of divine "otherness." –

Logos' traits which are presented in the Prologue through his dialectical performances, inducing the reader's response, become known in the narrative part of the Gospel as the divine qualities of Christ.

The divine qualities of Christ which develop into the tenets of Christianity are easily apprehensible for new Christians, Gentiles, Jews and for contemporary readers. These divine properties as presented in John's Gospel may be historically and semantically (religiously and philosophically) rooted. However, they may also be easily understood from a given narrative, without previous knowledge or religious practice that may facilitate understanding and espousing those principles.

Narrative Criticism: Method

According to James L. Resseguie "Narrative criticism focuses on how biblical literature works as literature. The what of a text (its content) and the how of a text (its rhetoric and structure) as an organic whole."[1] It examines the complexities and nuances of a text and emphasizes the effect of a narrative on the reader. Narrative analysis studies how a text tells a story in such a way as to engage the reader in its "narrative world" and the system of values contained therein (How does the narrative undermine or subvert the reader's accepted norms, values and beliefs? What are the standards of judgment-ideological point of view?).[2]

The Pontifical Biblical Commission's Document, "*The Interpretation of the Bible in the Church*" defines the roles of "the real reader" and "the implied reader" in the following way:

The text functions as a "mirror" in the sense that it projects a certain image – a "narrative world" – which exercises an influence upon readers' perceptions in such a way as to bring them to adopt certain values rather than others. The *real reader* is any person who has access to the text – from those who first read it or heard it read, to those who read or hear it today. By *implied reader* one means the reader which the text presupposes and in effect creates, the one who is capable of performing the mental and affective operations necessary for entering into the narrative world of the text and responding to it in the way envisaged by the real author through the instrumentality of the implied author. What is asked of narrative exegesis is that it rehabilitate in new historical contexts the modes of communicating and conveying meaning proper to the biblical account in order to open up more effectively its saving power.[3]

---

[1] James L. Resseguie, *Narrative Criticism of the New Testament. An Introduction*, Grand Rapids 2005, 18–19.

[2] Resseguie, *Narrative Criticism,* 38–40.

[3] *The Interpretation of the Bible in the Church,* The Pontifical Biblical Commission Pope John Paul II (23 April 1993), *Origins* 6 (1994), http://www. catholic-resources.org/ChurchDocs/PBC_Interp-FullText.htm.

Derek Tovey in his article, "Narrative Strategies in the Prologue and the Metaphor of ὁ λόγος in John's Gospel" portrays this process. According to Tovey, the Logos in the Prologue (John 1:1–18) functions as sequence signal, and character-substitute, to pique the reader's curiosity as to the identity of the Logos, as a preparation for the introduction of the name "Jesus Christ" in v. 17. These narrative dynamics create a strong link in the implied reader's mind between the Logos and Jesus. The implied author uses the implicative force of this connection to add metaphorical freight to the term when used later in the Gospel.[4] This metaphorical freight will unfold in the course of the Gospel, in forms which would indicate the presence of Logos, talk plenty about the Logos' nature, without explicitly stating his presence. His presence, throughout this metaphorical grid, is to be discerned in the person of Jesus Christ.

Introductory Remarks on the Prologue

The Prologue exhibits a few themes which enunciate key dimensions of the Gospel's Christology. We are informed concerning the origin and the destiny of Jesus the Logos and his relationship to other figures, notably the Father. Jesus is introduced as a Revealer, a function which then invites a response. Our focus will stay with the way and means of revelation and the human response to it.

The Prologue begins with the Logos, who is with God, moreover himself God. "He exists with God before the creation of all that exists" (vv. 1–2). He gave life to all that is created and sustained it with the light that He emits (metaphysical light, v. 4). That revelatory light continues to shine in humankind despite a darkness which is present from its origins (vv. 4, 9). The quality of this light is "true" which, therefore, designates its uniqueness and points to its divine nature (v. 9). As Logos, he was always in the world and yet was not known by his creation, a reference to the Jews, but probably to humankind in general, who in their ignorance (blindness) did not receive him.[5] He renounces his safe distance, and embraces proximity to humans, to offer "sonship" (the children of God status) to all who be-

---

4   Derek Tovey, "Narrative Strategies in the Prologue and the Metaphor of ὁ λόγος in John's Gospel," *Pacifica* 15 (2002), 138–153.
5   Elisabeth Harry, *Prologue and Gospel. The Theology of the Fourth Evangelist*, New York 2004, 159.

lieved in his name (v. 12). In his humanity, he was given the revelation agency of divine glory. The glory is defined in terms of sonship as that which belongs to the one who is unique – the only begotten.[6]

John the Baptist (vv. 6–8), witnessing the light, now introduces the historical figure of Jesus Christ, who is the source of the fullness of grace and truth (vv. 15–18). The function of this figure has been to communicate to human beings the heavenly things.[7] In vv. 1–5, the Word in God becomes the Light of the World. The Word is embodied, coming into the world – the Word is the light of the world (vv. 6–15). After v. 14, the concentration is on our appropriation of the gift of the Word. As the darkness has not overcome the light (v. 5), one can accept or refuse to accept the Word (vv. 15–18). If one accepts the revealed Word (the right response to the gift of Logos, the Revealer), he then is in position to experience Logos, the Saviour.

Francis Maloney competently summarizes the Prologue in one sentence: "The author informs the reader of the Word, his coming as the light of humankind, and the response to the gift who is Jesus Christ, the Son of God."[8] To introduce his Gospel, John takes a different approach than the Synoptics. In John, the presentation of Christ is theological rather than biographical or historical. John uses a cosmogony as the background for his message of salvation. The Prologue is "the key to the understanding of this Gospel," for the same topics of the Gospel are all embodied in the Prologue. However, the most characteristic term in the Prologue is not used elsewhere in the Gospel in the titular sense. Nonetheless, it frequently appears exhibiting and reproducing all the meanings attached to it in the Prologue. The "Word" in the Prologue is not only the instrument of revelation, it is revelation. The Prologue thus emphasizes the universal and cosmic importance of the Logos before the particularistic incarnational work of the Logos is presented.[9] In what it says about the Logos, the Pro-

---

[6]   Harry, *Prologue and Gospel*, 160.
[7]   Phanuel O. Osweto, *Analysis of the Gospel of John in Light of Christology* (MA Dissertation), Prague 2008, 36–37.
[8]   Francis J. Moloney, *Belief in the Word*, Minneapolis 1993, 26–27.
[9]   *Logos Christology and the Johannine Prologue. Confessional Identification and Function*, 19–20, http://kingstonnychurchofchrist.org/yahoo_site_admin/assets/docs/Logos_Christology.113145548.pdf; Gheorghe Dobrin, "The Introduction of the Concept of Logos in the Prologue of the Fourth Gospel," *Perichoresis* 3 (2005), 209–218, 209.

logue shows us the perspective from which the Gospel as a whole is to be understood.[10]

The Prologue is to be viewed, according to Warren Carter, as part of the Gospel's "cluster of sacred symbols" which legitimates and interprets the experiences and self-understanding of John's community (there is common understanding among scholars that the Prologue was written the latest out of all Johannine corpus).[11] The Gospel of John expounds on the deity of Jesus probably more than any New Testament document. John's Logos Christology is revealed in his Prologue, but merely hinted at in his narrative.[12] The Prologue serves to deepen the theological understanding of the reader. John's objective was to establish the identity of Jesus (Jesus is the Christ, the Son of God – Jesus is God) resulting in the gift of life for those who confess that identity.[13]

It is evident, given the Prologue and a subsequent narrative section of the Gospel, that we face two different forms and modes of expression: one poetic and the other a prosaic kind of narrative.[14] The Prologue is also logically distinct from the main body of the Gospel, thus most also believe it to be or to contain a Christological hymn, the "Logos Hymn."[15] For Brown the Prologue was: "An early Christian hymn, probably stemming from Johannine circles, which has been adapted to serve as an overture to the Gospel narrative of the career of the incarnate Word."[16] Down that line, Bultmann sought to trace the hymn's origin to Gnostic circles, via a sect of John the Baptist's adherents.[17] The origin of this poetic material is explained in various ways, mainly by locating it within the broader Hellenistic world.[18]

It could be stated that John used the tradition as an instrument of communication.[19] With regard to lyric (attributed to the Hymn's origin)

---

[10] Dobrin, "The Introduction of the Concept of Logos," 215.
[11] Warren Carter, "The Prologue and John's Gospel. Function, Symbol and the Definitive Word," *Journal for the Study of the New Testament* 39 (1990), 35–58, 37.
[12] *Logos Christology and the Johannine Prologue*, 24.
[13] *Logos Christology and the Johannine Prologue*, 19–20.
[14] Carter, "The Prologue," 48.
[15] Ed. L. Miller, "The Johannine Origins of the Johannine Logos," *Journal of Biblical Literature* 112 (1993), 445–457, 446.
[16] Dobrin, "The Introduction of the Concept of Logos," 211.
[17] Richard Van Egmond, "An Exegetical Study of the Prologue of John (John 1:1–18)," *McMaster Journal of Theology and Ministry* 4 (2001), http://www.mcmaster.ca/mjtm/4-7.htm.
[18] Van Egmond, "An Exegetical Study of the Prologue."
[19] Walther Bindemann, "Der Johannesprolog. Ein Versuch, ihn zu verstehen," *Novum Testamentum* 37 (1995), 330–354.

and prose sections of the Prologue, this material can be identified as stylistic prose.[20] However, its poetic elements bear narrative devices used to create a certain effect on the reader, anticipating a reaction. As the larger part of the Prologue is poetry, it indicates a strong likelihood of a metaphorical interpretation of personification and parallels.[21] As James Resseguie conceives: "Everyday language is made difficult in poetry so that we attend to the words and their sounds."[22] Viewed from a novel perspective, commonplace points of view must be made odd to awaken the reader from the lethargy of the habitual.[23] Those devices warrant the reader's involvement. Repeated words or phrases that alert the reader and ambiguities of the words that complicate the nuances of the narrative, create the view that the narrator wants the reader to adopt.[24] The narrative strategy is to induce "the reemployment of the reader."[25]

Meaning of Logos – Word

In Bible translations and commentaries, Logos in John is most frequently rendered as "Word." A survey of commentaries suggests that the term is deeply rooted in Old Testament thought (e. g. Genesis 1, Proverbs 8). The role of the Johannine Logos also parallels that of personified Wisdom in a number of traditions within Judaism.[26] In association with Hellenistic thought, the term "Logos" played a key role both in Stoic thought (the Greek or pre-Christian speculation on the subject is marked by Heraclitus, Plato and the Stoics) and in the work of Hellenistic Jewish thinkers such as Philo.[27] Thus, "it is likely that John's audience would have had some pre-understanding of the Logos as an active-creative force of God, bringing God's revelation into the world."[28] Nonetheless, the Fourth Gospel's em-

---

20 Van Egmond, "An Exegetical Study of the Prologue."
21 Raymond C. Faircloth, "The 'Logos' in John's Prologue," 15, http://www.christian monotheism.com/media/text/1-17.%20THE%20LOGOS%20IN%20JOHN%60S %20PROLOGUE.pdf.
22 Resseguie, *Narrative Criticism,* 34.
23 Resseguie , *Narrative Criticism*, 34.
24 Resseguie , *Narrative Criticism*, 20.
25 Resseguie , *Narrative Criticism*, 32–33.
26 Van Egmond, "An Exegetical Study of the Prologue."
27 Van Egmond, "An Exegetical Study of the Prologue."
28 Dale Loepp, Analyses of Important Johannine Vocabulary, http://catholic-resources.org/John/Vocab-Logos.html.

ployment of the term turns out to be quite contrary to a Hellenistic world-view, as well as distinct from previous Jewish uses.[29]

Logos bears multiple meanings which all point to mental faculty: word, thinking, reasoning, regard, reason, cause, ground. Does that point to a person, or a – more abstract – thought?[30] Danijel Časni provides a plausible answer: "The most common meaning was 'word,' particularly the word which remains in a person, but also the word which is uttered. In other words, it is a non-verbalized thought which remains in the mind, but it is also the expression of the thought through the uttered word."[31] Here, the word is personalized, but also uttered expressing or revealing the thought, the "Word."

In the Prologue, Logos is used also in a third sense, as a plan or a concept. The Logos is a person with a special relationship to God.[32] The Logos in the Prologue could be seen as pointing towards three directions (the Logos functions in threefold way): as Creator, Revealer and Saviour (Redeemer). We mainly focus on the Logos as Revealer, which then prepares the ground for Logos the Saviour to step on the stage. This shall be illustrated by referring to how the Prologue employs the metaphor of the Logos as the incarnated light. The Light which the Logos embodies refers to the light of revelation, since it is in Christ that all wisdom and knowledge are hidden (Col 2:3). Furthermore, as Ronald H. Nash remarks: "All human knowledge is possible because of the unique human participation in the eternal Logos of God, Jesus Christ."[33] That takes us from the realm of the Logos as Revealer to the Logos-Saviour realm.

It should be clear at this point that in the Prologue the term "word" is as such inadequate to express the meaning of Logos.[34] The naming of the Logos as Jesus Christ is a climactic moment for the reader of the Prologue.[35] The deity of the Logos could only be apprehended with the final surren-

---

[29] Van Egmond, "An Exegetical Study of the Prologue."

[30] Kirby Hopper, "The Logos of John 1:1 – First a Plan, Then a Person," http://kirby-hopper.com/logos-of-john-1-what-is-it/.

[31] Danijel Časni, "Christ. The Logos Incarnate," *KAIROS – Evangelical Journal of Theology* 9 (2015), 187–199, 192.

[32] Darryl Wood, "The Logos Concept in the Prologue to the Gospel of John," *The Theological Educator* 38 (1988), 85–93, 85.

[33] Ronald H. Nash, *The Word of God and the Mind of Man. The Crisis of Revealed Truth in Contemporary Theology*, Grand Rapids 1982, 9.

[34] Faircloth, "The Logos in John's Prologue," 15.

[35] Moloney, *Belief in the Word*, 47.

dering contention "I do," as a token of embracing Christ fully in one's life, and the recognition that "He truly is God."

Logos' presentation at an earlier stage is easily grasped without possessing the background knowledge which associated the Logos with the familiar Hellenistic and Jewish traditions. The implied reader whom the author had in mind has either a Greek or a Jewish background. The real reader, which is our targeted audience, might have none of that. However, the real reader is still invited to take part in Christ's glory and is presumed to require no background knowledge pertaining to the usages of "Logos" in other traditions.

Alan Culpepper indicates how Logos and Christ in the readers' mind are to be joined and perceived as one and the same reality: "The Gospel presents Jesus as the incarnation of the Logos continuing the work of revelation, healing (soteriology), and creation. Jesus is introduced elaborately, but somewhat indirectly."[36] The Prologue presents the Logos as light and life, while Jesus's name is first mentioned under the title "Christ" in v. 17. Hence only from this context is it then possible to link the Logos and the Christ (Messiah) as being One.[37]

The Prologue in Relation to the Rest of the Fourth Gospel

Interestingly, the ideas previewed in the Prologue do not attest, as we might expect, corresponding instances in the Gospel itself.[38] Logos, later being identified as Jesus, nominally was discarded and not used anymore in the rest of the Gospel.[39] Thus, "word" dominates the Fourth Gospel with a certain Christological transparency. If we were to accept the identification of "word" and other ideas such as "truth" and "light," then we should also consider the many discourses of Jesus in which a certain metaphor is used (Bread, Water, Resurrection and Life, Good Shepherd, Door, Vine, etc.), each of which accounts for a kind of extended appearance of the Word which characterizes the Johannine Christ and his activity.[40]

---

[36] R. Alan Culpepper, *Anatomy of the Fourth Gospel. A Study in Literary Design*, Philadelphia 1983, 106–107.
[37] Culpepper, *Anatomy of the Fourth Gospel*, 106–107.
[38] Miller, "The Johannine origins," 447.
[39] Wood, "The Logos Concept in the Prologue," 91.
[40] Miller, "The Johannine origins," 452.

In respect of Jesus's human nature as depicted in John's Gospel, Alan Culpepper detects how Jesus's identity bears the burden of his Logos-nature as presented in the Prologue. In John, Jesus is less emotional than in the Synoptics, an observation that Culpepper relates to His incarnation of the pre-existent Logos who is not of this world. Jesus's "Logos-nature" is responsible for the failure to give a portrayal of Jesus's "human nature." John insists on the recognition of Jesus's divinity and his origin from above. Jesus's function is not to give insight into his nature but only to enable others to share in his relationship to the Father.[41]

John goes beyond the familiar concept of Logos held by Jewish and Gentile readers and presents Jesus Christ not as a mere mediating principle, but as a personal being, fully divine, fully human, God's perfect revelation in the flesh.[42] "There is no longer need for 'Logos language.' The incarnate word will hereafter be known as Jesus Christ." Logos has hitherto just "been," whereas now has become light, to engender belief in humans, by disclosing the glory of God.[43]

Logos as Revealer and Saviour

As shown above, key themes in John's Prologue and narrative could be encapsulated in three main fields: creation, revelation and salvation. Paul Anderson propounds this sustainable model: "John 1:1–5 – the creative word of life; John 1:9–13 – the redemptive light of the world; John 1:14–18 – the flesh-becoming word."[44] We are now to engage with "the redemptive light," (the Logos as Saviour and Redeemer) and "the flesh-becoming word" (the Logos as Revealer) presented within the Prologue in terms of "light," "truth," "glory" and "grace."

---

[41]   Culpepper, *Anatomy of the Fourth Gospel*, 115.
[42]   What Do John 1:1,14 Mean When They Declare that Jesus is the Word of God? https://www.gotquestions.org/Jesus-Word-God.html.
[43]   Christopher W. Skinner, *Characters and Characterization in the Gospel of John*, London 2013, 116–117.
[44]   Paul N. Anderson, "The Johannine Logos-Hymn. A Cross-Cultural Celebration of God's Creative-Redemptive Work," in R. Alan Culpepper, Jan G. Van der Watt (eds.), *Creation Stories in Dialogue. The Bible, Science, and Folk Traditions*, Leiden 2015, 219–242, 224–225.

John 1:9–13

> [9] The true light that gives light to everyone was coming into the world. [10] He was in the world, and though the world was made through him, the world did not recognize him. [11] He came to that which was his own, but his own did not receive him. [12] Yet to all who did receive him, to those who believed in his name, he gave the right to become children of God –[13] children born not of natural descent, nor of human decision or a husband's will, but born of God.

Logos draws attention to himself as the Revealer and Redeemer who descends as the light.[45] As Revealer, he discloses God to humans, and He proposes partaking in "the sonship." As Redeemer, to those who accept His proposal, He gives life, to ultimately become children of God. The life granted to those who believed in his name is both a present possession (have life in his name) and a future reality (becoming sons of God).[46] As Saviour, he gives life to those who accept light over darkness. Also as Redeemer (Saviour), he concedes "the sonship" to all who believe in his name, while at the same time retaining the status of the only begotten Son himself.

Light is the first Logos principle. Logos is regarded through the symbol of light as a cosmic illuminator of human beings.[47] The Gospel of John was written for the Greek Christians towards the close of the first century. Light was a familiar theme in the Johannine environment. The dualism of the era drew heavily upon the light-dark (good vs. evil) theme.[48] This can be felt in the remark "But his own did not receive him" (v. 11), which tells about the darkness in which they stand, as opposed to the light which came to them as enlightenment and a proposal of eternal light. The darkness, on the contrary, is defined in the Prologue as the life "of natural descent, of human decision or a husband's will," and the light signifies being "born of God" (v. 13).

---

45   Clyde Muropa, "The Johannine Writings. Symbolism and the Symbol of 'Light' in the Gospel of John," *The Asbury Journal* 67 (2012), 106–113, 112–113.
46   Wood, "The Logos Concept in the Prologue," 90.
47   Osweto, *John in Light of Christology*, 60.
48   James Still, The Gospel of John and the Hellenization of Jesus, https://infidels.org/library/modern/james_still/gospel_john.html.

The Prologue sums up the characteristics of Light: Light is true, shining in the world, and ethical. As the adjective "true" (ἀληθινός) means "dependable, real," this implies that the Logos is, then, the genuine-real revelation of God. By consequence, all other lights are false.[49] Logos is more than anything truthful. In the Prologue, the truth is attributed to Light, whereas later in the Gospel, after the incarnation, the Logos as Christ is itself the Truth (e.g. John 14:6). On multiple occasions, when leading dialogues and interacting, Jesus uses the locution "truly, truly" (amen, amen) as in John 5:21: "truly, truly I tell you." Jesus uses this to highlight his validity as the only truth, opposed to all who might pretend to know the truth, though in reality they stand in the darkness. Logos became light coming into the world, "light that gives light to everyone was coming into the world. He was in the world, and though the world was made through him" (vv. 9–10). Logos as the light is this-worldly. He came to the world to illuminate "his own" (v. 11), so that they might see that they stand in the darkness. Those who beheld the Light as the source of illumination are the ones who believe in his name. Light represents that which is morally good, hence opposes the dark, which represents the morally wrong (1:5). We are given the understanding of God, as the Logos is the one who explained God (1:18). That calls for a decision, to be the children of the light or the darkness. That decision will be of chief importance when the last judgment comes.[50] The reader is reminded that the light is the means of salvation. Light is true – which speaks of the revelation of Logos, as the unique revelation, like no other. Light is truthful in his dynamic agency towards humanity. Truthful stands for trustworthy, dependable, credible. All this entails belief in him, to believe in his name.

Logos as Revealer

John 1:14–18

> [14] The Word became flesh and made his dwelling among us. We have seen his glory, the glory of the one and only Son, who came from the Father, full of grace and truth.
> [16] Out of his fullness we have all received grace in place of grace already given. [17] For the law was given through Moses; grace and truth came through

---

49   Wood, "The Logos Concept in the Prologue," 89.
50   Wood, "The Logos Concept in the Prologue," 89–90.

Jesus Christ. [18] No one has ever seen God, but the one and only Son, who is himself God and is in closest relationship with the Father, has made him known.

According to this passage, Logos' revelatory agency begins with the Word's incarnation. Logos as Son reveals the Father, but we are to comprehend that appearance through glory and grace. From the Old Testament, we know that glory belongs exclusively to the Father's realm, however, glory now becomes a visible proposal to those who are to accept this proposal and as a result will become the sons of light. Grace is God's property which is now in fullness revealed through the Son and enables humans to take part in the sonship. Logos reveals this grace which is a call to share in the sonship. The glory is the absolute fullness of grace and truth. The grace of the old covenant, mediated by the Law, is replaced by the fullness of the grace of the new covenant in the flesh of Jesus Christ (1:17).[51] Logos is "full of grace and truth" (1:14). Logos is revealed as Jesus Christ, true God. His objective is to reveal God, whom we might not see but we might come to know Him through his Son. His Son, as God himself, shares in the same properties belonging to the Father – grace and truth. Truth, as he is the only true God, all others are false. And grace, as the readiness to offer salvation to those who believed that He truly is God. Glory is Father's property which is made visible in Logos' incarnation as Son. Glory unfolds then in communication of the heavenly things to humans as grace and truth. Grace and truth are heavenly categories, which are not alike, however not in opposition to the earthly categories as, for example, the law given through Moses. In the following narrative section of the Gospel, grace is concretized in Jesus's dialogues and actions. We learn what the salvation consists of and how we are to take part in the redemptive history.

Conclusion

Logos is the word, the personalised word containing certain properties which speak about its nature. Logos is also the uttered word, an active-creative force, which communicates God to humans in a revelatory modal-

---

[51] William J. U. Philip, "The Light of Glory. An Exposition of the Prologue of John s Gospel," 113–126, 123, https://biblicalstudies.org.uk/pdf/churchman/116-02_113.pdf.

ity. There are three theological themes that expound "the plan or the concept" of Logos and the process in which the Logos' active force is displayed: Cosmology, Eschatology and Soteriology.[52] *Cosmology* refers to Logos as Creator and Revealer. Here, Logos is presented as the true Light. Light is the creative word which brings life, but it is also the means of revelation, introducing the Son, as the True God. *Eschatology* pertains to Grace, which is the Logos' competence to offer salvation to all who are enlightened, and have chosen light over darkness in which they stood so far. *Soteriology* introduces the Logos viewed as Redeemer. We are to see the glory of the Father. By way of that glory the "sonship" is available to humans. The Son is revealed in the property which exclusively belonged to the Father. We are invited to take part in this Son-Father relation. We are redeemed through the incarnate Logos which is now known as Son, the only begotten Son, Jesus Christ. The Logos is the Son who reveals the Father and enables humans to share in his relationship to the Father.

[52] Osweto, *John in Light of Christology*, 35.

Paul's Disabled Body
To be "kata sarka" or not to be?

György Kustár

Regrettably, Brian Brock and John Swinton did not involve the biblical fundaments in their reader, titled *Disability in the Christian tradition*. This proposal would be a supplement to this volume from a New Testament perspective.

The key concept in my proposal is imitation: who imitates whom and in what way? The text in 2 Cor 5:16-18 has nothing to do with emulation. On a theological level, this verse was hotly debated and, by Bultmann, associated with the division between the historical Jesus and the heavenly Christ. "Kata sarka" meant knowing Christ as a historical figure that has no relevance for the faith, just as "knowing Christ in Spirit" means receiving God's grace through faith alone. This division is not only historical but also ontological and epistemological: to have Christ is to obtain a different perspective, a radically new understanding, which is indescribable since it hides behind the language. This understanding has much truth in it, but fails in many respects. My purpose is to argue for a different perspective that is reflected in these verses. From the point of view of disability studies, I will examine Paul's argumentation in 1 and 2 Corinthians and ask the question: what relevance does his argumentation have for people living with hindrances.

1. Paul's Appearance

In the Acts of Paul, we find an interesting description of the apostle:

> And he saw Paul coming, a man little of stature, thin-haired upon the head, crooked in the legs, of good state of body, with eyebrows joining, and nose

somewhat hooked, full of grace: for sometimes he appeared like a man, and sometimes he had the face of an angel.[1]

It is obviously dangerous to build an assumption on another assumption, but it is worth playing with the idea of what we can learn about Paul if we take this description under serious consideration.[2] In any case, it is worth suggesting the authenticity of this characterization, as it draws a distinctly "ugly" man, and ancient physiognomy suggests that these traits reveal an unappealing personality.[3] Who would have intended to undermine the apostle's prestige with such a portrait? On the contrary, I personally do not think that the description has a devaluating purpose.

But first, it may be important to give a second thought to the description because there might have been some people in Paul's Corinthian congregation who practiced physiognomy, although not at the scientific level, but at the level of ordinary correlations. Furthermore, his opponents, who most likely had serious rhetorical training,[4] could consciously use physiognomy to destroy their opponents' reputations.[5] Jennifer Larson notes that

[1] Acta Pauli 3. From Montague R. James (Translation and Notes), *The Apocryphal New Testament*, Oxford 1924.

[2] According to Malherbe, this look expresses nobility in ancient times; for example, Suetonius describes August as a short man with an unibrow and hooked nose, but Hermes also appears small, hooked-nosed figure with thick eyebrows in a description of Clement of Alexandria. See Abraham J. Malherbe, "A Physical Description of Paul," *Harvard Theological Review* 79 (2011), 173–174. However, I prefer to follow the idea of Jennifer Larson, "Paul's Masculinity," *Journal of Biblical Literature* 123 (2004), 85–97; Albert Harril, "Invective Against Paul (2 Cor 10:10). The Physiognomics of the Ancient Slave Body, and the Greco-Roman Rhetoric of Manhood," in Adela Yarbro Collins and Margaret M. Mitchell (eds.), *Antiquity and Humanity. Essays on Ancient Religion and Philosophy Presented to Hans Dieter Betz on His 70th Birthday*, Tübingen 2001, 189–213; or Peter Marshall, *Enmity in Corinth. Social Conventions in Paul's Relations with the Corinthians*, Tübingen 1987.

[3] Malherbe, for example, based on the portrayal of early catacombs and autobiographical notes in Paul's letters, believes that this image may go back to "historical memory" (Malherbe, *Physical Description*, 171). In contrast, Robert M. Grant argues that the image seeks to describe Paul as a warlord, which is why the author forms that image of him. So, the description has nothing to do with reality, see Robert M. Grant: "The Description of Paul in the Acts of Paul and Thecla," *Vigiliae Christianae* 36 (1982), 1–4.

[4] This is pretty much the majority opinion. The exact nature of the teaching divides the commentators, see Craig S. Keener, *1–2 Corinthians*, Cambridge UK 2005, 145.

[5] Marshall, *Enmity in Corinth*, 398–399.

the meticulous descriptions of rhetorical textbooks on the head and neck postures, permissible movements, and rules for using speech sounds show that the speaker's appearance was examined continuously by the ancient audience and highly experienced crowd or by the opponents looking for errors. They often did it to discredit the professional speaker, not by attacking the oration's content but the speaker. Not even Cicero could avoid such attacks:

> Calvus, one of the Atticists who prided themselves on their masculine severity and strength, described Cicero as 'limp and enervated' (solutum et enervem), while Brutus derided him as 'subdued and feeble in the loins' (fractum et elumbem).[6]

Peter Marshall mentions that an orator might have been discredited in several ways: "Common themes of mockery are [...] social background, immorality, physical appearance, religious or political views, speech, greed, personal pursuits."[7] Moreover, 2 Corinthians 10–13 speak of the apostle being attacked, among other things, because of his appearance. 2 Cor 10:10, in particular, deserves attention. It is about the weakness of Paul's "physical appearance." What could it be? If we take a closer look at Paul's portrait and what these body features suggest, we find the following in Pseudo-Aristotle's *Physiognomics*: those with touching eyebrows are annoyed, irritable (δυσάνιος); the hooked or too long nose refers to shamelessness (ἀναίδεια). While there is no reference to hoop legs or baldness, according to 812a5, the high forehead reflects insensitivity (ἀναίδεια). If we play with the possibility that Gal 6:11 refers to Paul's weak eyes, it becomes evident in what a difficult situation the apostle may have been: according to 807b5 the weak eye is a characteristic of the cowards. Also, the same work describes the narrow-minded man as follows:

> These are the marks of the low-spirited man. His face is wrinkled, his eyes are dry and weak, but at the same time, weakness of the eye signifies two things, softness and effeminacy on the one hand, depression and lack of spirit on the other. He is stooping in figure and feeble in his movements. (808a913)

---

6   Larson, *Paul's Masculinity*, 88. She emphasizes the same in her analysis of Quintilian's rhetoric, see also Eric Gunderson, *Staging Masculinity. the Rhetoric of Performance in the Roman World*, Ann Arbor 2000, 59–86; especially 71–72.
7   Marshall, *Enmity in Corinth*, 54.

Quintilian (1st century AD) claims that any imperfection in appearance, or a thin tone, is a disadvantage that cannot be eliminated and makes high-level oratory deliverance impossible (*Institutio Oratoria* 11.3.12-13). If Paul's voice might be weak, the opinion of him is negative when he speaks. This assumption should also be considered, although we do not know what 2 Cor 10:10 means by ἐξουθενημένος λόγος. According to Aristotle, "The great-souled man is slow of step, possesses a deep voice, and a deliberate form of speech. For a rapid gait and a shrill voice bespeak an intense and nervous person, who ponders nothing fundamentally great."[8] The less-noticed connection between voice and character, which can also be traced back to Aristotle, is medical: the deep voice helps the pneuma evenly circulate in the body, while the high-pitched voice constrains it. The latter is thus a sign of some disease or character defect.[9] Of course, even if we assume that there are some deficiencies related to the way of Paul's performance (among other things), it remains uncertain whether the contempt refers to some kind of a capability (speech error, high voice) or some speech technique deficiency (over-gesticulation, wrong pitch choice, or accent).[10] It is clear that a negative perception of physical weakness and rhetorical abilities are interrelated. More generally, physical endowment, opinion about rhetorical education, and character are inseparable. Is it possible that the devaluation of Paul's action and speech is due to his failure in performance and not to his actual rhetorical knowledge?[11]

---

[8]   Elizabeth C. Evans, "Physiognomics in the Ancient World," *Transactions of the American Philosophical Society, New Series* 59 (1969), 1–101, 22.

[9]   Larson, *Paul's Masculinity*, 90.

[10] Keener enumerates these speech-technical instruments expected on the occasion of rhetorical performance (*1–2 Corinthians*, 218–219).

[11] On the one hand, this is likely only because when Paul speaks of his rhetorical shortcomings, more specifically, (according to Dale B. Martin, *The Corinthian Body*, New Haven 1995, 49) that he is "laymen with regard of speech," "he is saying that he is not a professional orator or a teacher of rhetoric; but he is not denying that he has had a rhetorical education." Interestingly, Paul himself uses various rhetorical tools to criticize himself, either the speaking ability of "debaters" in general or his own belief in the persuasive power of professional oratory. When evaluating this self-critical remark, we should also bear in mind that when an orator speaks of his lack of qualification with disrespectful words, it is also part of his rhetorical toolkit and aims to win over the potentially sceptical listeners of the audience by showing himself closer to them; see Christopher Forbes, "Comparison, Self-Praise and Irony. Paul's Boasting and the Conventions of Hellenistic Rhetoric," *New Testament Studies* 32 (1986), 1–30, 10.

Ben Witherington points out that criticism of the speakers is not just about what they look like (*schema*) but about their appearance in general (*hypocrisis*), which includes the oratory performance.[12] So the problem may not be the deficiency in the speech composition, as his opponents must recognize his letters' persuasive power. Instead, it may be that his speech and appearance (and/or the elocution) are not in harmony with each other.[13] Based on the thinking of that time, which combines power, rhetorical knowledge, and beauty and links them with social respect, in Paul's case, it results in deprivation of that honour. This is because the "weakness" discredits the speaker, and this "weakness" does not necessarily mean any visible diseases or physical defects, only the feebleness of the body and appearance, or discomfort due to the strange proportions of the body, or some distracting factors in the performance, be it an error in the implementation of the speech. For example, Quintilian advises the aging orator to retire when he feels the signs of weakness in himself because his appearance will be unworthy of his speech, and his feebleness may cause disdain (*Ars Oratoria* 12.11.23).

2. Paul and Disease

The following is written in 2 Cor 10:10: "For some say, 'His letters are weighty and forceful, but in person he is unimpressive and his speaking amounts to nothing'" (ὅτι αἱ ἐπιστολαὶ μέν, φησίν, βαρεῖαι καὶ ἰσχυραί, ἡ δὲ παρουσία τοῦ σώματος ἀσθενὴς καὶ ὁ λόγος ἐξουθενημένος). Paul's appearance is ἀσθενής. According to the Liddell-Scott-Jones dictionary, this term can express many things: physical weakness, sickness, poverty, insignificance, and weakness in a moral sense. This is interesting because the mysterious "thorn" given into Paul's body is interpreted accordingly by some commentaries. To name just a few examples: István Tőkés agrees with Wenland, Bousset, and Bultmann, who say that it is a kind of

---

[12] Ben Witherington, *Conflict and Community in Corinth. A Socio-Rhetorical Commentary on 1 and 2 Corinthians*, Grand Rapids 1995, 437. Against Hans D. Betz, according to whom the main target of the critic against Paul is the tension between his appearance and the content of his speech; see Hans D. Betz, *Der Apostel Paulus und die sokratische Tradition. Eine exegetische Untersuchung zu seiner Apologie 2 Korinther 10–13*, Tübingen 1972.

[13] Larson, *Paul's Masculinity*, 89.

illness.[14] Cserháti also thinks that we need to take the thorn literally: "The commentators agree that it can be something of a disease that sometimes causes severe pain, possibly a headache or perhaps epilepsy."[15] Although he does not name his sources, in the case of epilepsy, he probably refers to Windisch's thesis.[16] The theory of migraine appears in Ulrich Heckel's work,[17] although this interpretation can be traced back to Tertullian himself.[18] Hartmut Göbel, Hansruedi Isler, and Hans-Peter Hasenfratz's brief analysis likewise concludes that it is a migraine based on the symptoms in Acts.[19] Alan Hisey and James S. P. Beck think that the haemorrhage caused by the fall may have partially damaged part of the brain that controls the hearing and the vision and resulted in permanent and disturbing visual disorder and hearing problems. They say that Paul does not recognize the high priest in the Council not because of his ignorance but because of his poor sight.[20] Those who read this passage in comparison with the epistle to the Galatians, especially in the light of his handwritten signature of 6:11 (Ἴδετε πηλίκοις ὑμῖν γράμμασιν ἔγραψα τῇ ἐμῇ χειρί) also conclude that the apostle had myopia.[21] Moreover, according to Timothy J. Leary, Paul asks Timothy to bring scrolls (membrana) (2 Tim 4:13) that made reading easier for the short-sighted.[22] Many say that there are references to Paul's weak eyes elsewhere in the letter (Gal 4:12-15):

[14] István Tőkés, *A Korinthusbeliekhez írt második levél magyarázata*, Kolozsvár 1996, 391.
[15] Sándor Cserháti, *Pál apostolnak a korinthusiakhoz írt második levele*, Budapest 2009, 403.
[16] Hans Windisch, *Der Zweite Korintherbrief*, KEK 6, Göttingen 1924, 386–387.
[17] Ulrich Heckel, "Der Dorn im Fleisch. Die Krankheit des Paulus in 2 Kor 12,7 und Gal 4,13f.," *Zeitschrift für die Neutestamentliche Wissenschaft* 84 (1993), 65–92.
[18] Some of the viewpoints are presented here: Candida R. Moss, "Christly Possession and Weakened Bodies.
Reconsideration of the Function of Paul's Thorn in the Flesh (2 Cor 12:7–10)," *Journal of Religion, Disability & Health* 16 (2012), 319–333, 321.
[19] Hartmut Göbel, Hansruedi Isler and Hans-Peter Hasenfratz, "Headache Classification and the Bible. Was St Paul's Thorn in the Flesh Migraine?," *Cephalalgia* 15 (1995), 180–181.
[20] Alan Hisey and James S. P. Beck, "Paul's 'Thorn in the Flesh'. A Paragnosis," *Journal of Bible and Religion* 29 (1961), 125–129, 128.
[21] James D. G. Dunn, *The Epistle to the Galatians*, Peabody MA 1993, 234, 236; Ben Witherington, *Grace in Galatia. A Commentary on Paul's Letter to the Galatians*, Grand Rapids 1998, 309–310.
[22] Timothy J. Leary, "A Thorn in the Flesh – 2 Corinthians 12,7," *Journal of Theological Studies* 43 (1992), 520–522.

I plead with you, brothers and sisters, become like me, for I became like you. You did me no wrong. As you know, it was because of an illness that I first preached the gospel to you, and even though my illness was a trial to you, you did not treat me with contempt or scorn. Instead, you welcomed me as if I were an angel of God, as if I were Christ Jesus himself. Where, then, is your blessing of me now? I can testify that, if you could have done so, you would have torn out your eyes and given them to me.

Keener, on the other hand, believes the last sentence refers not to physical illness: "Treating another as dearer than one's eyes" was part of the ancient figurative discourse.[23] So the theory of eye disease is not infallible either. In any case, it is a thought-provoking possibility. Of course, there are other opinions as well: according to Moss, it may be that Paul's physical weakness makes him liable to be possessed by the demons, i. e., the "thorn" means vulnerability to all sorts of demonic harm.[24] And after Mullins and others, the issue should not be approached here from the point of view of medicine, as it is one (or more) enemy that torments Paul.[25] Those who support this viewpoint refer to Numbers 33, where we read that the Canaanites will become "thorns in your eyes" and also to the powerful image of the verse: the thorn is like a punch to the face which the angel constantly torments the apostle with.[26] This could even be a plausible statement if the theme of "weakness" and infirmity did not run through both Corinthian letters. It is not the super-apostles who are the thorns, but the attack from them, which in turn targets Paul's physical weakness. The fact that it is indeed a disease of some kind or even a predisposition to diseases (this can also be deduced from the apparent physical weakness) is precisely possible in the broader context.

Nevertheless, if Paul had some other visible illnesses (e. g., lameness, physique problem, thin voice), it also set back his honour as a rhetor. In this context, it may be interesting to note that the apostle calls himself ἔκτρωμα in 1 Cor 15:8. The term is somewhat confusing and leaves many unresolved questions. According to Munk, Hollander, and Van der Hout's theory, there are two possible interpretations: one is that Paul referred to

23 Keener, *1–2 Corinthians*, 240.
24 Moss, "Christly Possession and Weakened Bodies," 325.
25 Terence Y. Mullins, "Paul's Thorn in the Flesh," *Journal of Biblical Literature* 76 (1957), 299–303, 302.
26 Michael L. Barré, "Qumran and the 'Weakness' of Paul," *Catholic Biblical Quarterly* 42 (1980), 216–227.

his past when he had persecuted Christians, which is why he is the most vicious. According to Munk, the other option is "referring to someone who is to be formed."[27] The correlation does not support the second explanation; the term is too harsh, and the connotations of being worthless and useless are stronger in their meaning.[28] However, the first explanation alone is also unsatisfactory. Why does the apostle call himself "an abortive person"? Maybe an accusation echoes here? Recently, Ben Witherington raises the possibility, with which I agree, that this may also have been a mocking remark about Paul's physical appearance – maybe because of a visible ailment.[29] In this case, the term "abortive" does not make sense in the particular context, but in the broader one of the two Corinthian letters, in light of the accusations against Paul.[30]

If we give thought to this context, the term becomes understandable. The apostle is "ugly and unviable," not worthy of the revelation: this is partly due to his appearance, weak look, illness, and, of course, burdened past.[31] Thus, as an unpleasant person, he cannot be associated with excellence or real and reliable knowledge.

---

[27] Johannes Munck, "Paulus Tanquam Abortivus," in Angus J. B. Higgins (ed.), *New Testament Essays. Studies in Memory of Thomas Walter Manson 1893–1958*, Manchester 1959, 180–193, 190.

[28] Harm W. Hollander and Gijsbert E. Van der Hout, "Paul Calling himself an Abortion. 1 Cor 15:8 Within the Context of 1 Cor 15:8–10," *Novum Testamentum* 38 (1996), 224–236, 231.

[29] "Perhaps this was a term of scorn some used behind his back. It might suggest that he was disfigured or odd in appearance." See Witherington, *Conflict and Community*, 300; Barrett holds the same opinion. Cf. also Charles K. Barrett, *A Commentary on the First Epistle to the Corinthians*, London 1968, 344. One more datum: in the Twelve Tablets, a fragment appears: "Quickly killed as, according to the Twelve Tablets, the dreadfully deformed child." (Cito necatus, tamquam ex XII tabulis insignis ad deformitatem puer.) (*A Tizenkéttáblás törvény töredékei*, Ford. Zlinszky János, Budapest 1995, IV.1. – I significantly modified the available English translations as they differ from the original Latin text.) This means that the deformed/miscarried child is both repugnant and sentenced to death (declared unworthy of living).

[30] This interpretation fits into the context and is also connected to Num 12:12, which the commentators often cite as a parallel: "Let her not be as it were like death, as an abortion coming out of his mother's womb, when *the disease* devours the half of the flesh" (LXX: μὴ γένηται ὡσεὶ ἴσον θανάτῳ ὡσεὶ ἔκτρωμα ἐκπορευόμενον ἐκ μήτρας μητρὸς καὶ κατεσθίει τὸ ἥμισυ τῶν σαρκῶν αὐτῆς). According to this passage, Miriam's leprosy is disgustful, similar to a premature baby's deformity.

[31] Of course, the interpretation of the term ἔκτρωμα should not be limited to a single

3. The Theology of "kata sarka"

Let us return to κατὰ σάρκα, which arises, first, in connection to the knowledge of Christ and others (2 Cor 5:16), and then concerning the accusation that Paul lives "by the standards of this world/by the flesh" (2 Cor 10:1-3). It is interesting to read through both Corinthian letters keeping in mind some of the possible shameful flaws of Paul's physique. It turns out that humiliation, the weakness of the body, inferiority, and the idea of grace, in contrast, are constant and recurring themes of both letters. Paul speaks of his weakness right away in 1 Corinthians 2: κἀγὼ ἐν ἀσθενείᾳ καὶ ἐν φόβῳ καὶ ἐν τρόμῳ πολλῷ ἐγενόμην πρὸς ὑμᾶς. He is weak when he appears. This self-critical sentence is, of course, also a rhetorical device, part of a strategy to shame the self-esteemed teachers. Nevertheless, he articulates the truth, the compelling truth: Paul has a weakness and something to worry about, which he cannot deny. In his argument, therefore, he must do something with this endowment. 1 Cor 4:6-13, which responses to the selection among teachers, is essentially the same as the arguments against the "super-apostles" (2 Cor 6:1-10; 12:1-10). This common topic places the message of the two passages next to each other.[32]

aspect. All the accusations concerning Paul are related, which includes the explanation that the scornful characterization that distinguishes Paul from the apostles also plays a role in the use of the term. See Matthew W. Mitchell, "Reexamining the 'Aborted Apostle'. An Exploration of Paul's Self-Description in 1 Corinthians 15.8," *Journal for the Study of the New Testament* 25 (2003), 469–485.

[32] Moreover, the criticism levelled at Paul also targets his way of life. For this reason, the apostle must emphasize that apostleship is not the path to exercise power and strength but to experiencing humiliation, moreover, suffering that a "common person" bears. Paul's esteem is also undermined because he does not accept money for his teachings but works for his living with his own hands (1 Cor 9:1-18); Witherington, *Conflict and Community*, 208–209. This may also be part of his "fleshly existence" for he does not live from the fruit of his spiritual work but from despised physical work (1 Cor 9:11–12). I believe that in this context, weakness arises as social contempt in cases Paul speaks of the composition of the church ("Not many of you were wise by human standards – κατὰ σάρκα [!] – are wise, influential, or noble," 1 Cor 1:26); when he mentions that he will be weak for others (9:22; 10:33), or when he says that God will treat the "weaker" and less honourable parts of the body with special honour (12:23–24). Perhaps it is not an exaggeration to find an autobiographical reference to the latter, primarily since divisions within the church and rivalry among teachers also affect him (cf. 1 Cor 4:18–21). For example, the Pauline principle of "becoming all things to all people" may have been disliked because it seemed "flattering." The male ideal is the au-

The situation in 2 Corinthians is much more acute, and there is a direct attack in the background. As we have mentioned, the passage on the clay jar is an apparent reference to the vulnerable earthly existence. In 2 Corinthians 4, Paul speaks about the jars of clay, the fragility of bodily existence, in chapter 5, the desire to undress the body, and then the fact that we do not know anyone according to the flesh. It might not be an overinterpretation if we suggest that Paul here probably talks about himself, his own body. Cserháti mentions a sentence from Seneca: "What is man? He is a claypot that can be smashed by any wobbling or bumps."[33] However, in the image of pottery, we find much more than a general idea of human fragility. Ralph P. Martin cites the b. Ta'an 7a, describes Joshua ben Hanina, who was far from being an attractive man, as "glorious wisdom in a disgusting earthly vessel."[34] However, Paul does not even accept the compliment inherent in this possible parallel, namely, that only the one who is humble enough and acknowledges one's own fragility can carry the "treasure." Here the apostle speaks of a simple fact: the treasure is in clay jars. The *soma*, the earthly existence, is defined by this condition, and here again, it is important to emphasize: it determines not only humans in general, but the apostles in particular, and more specifically, Paul's way of existence.[35] What Cserháti mentions is related to this: "The apostle acknowledges that there is a contradiction between apostleship and apostolic destiny."[36] He must provide a theological reflection on this; otherwise, he will lose his persuasive power and audience. Analysing 10:1, which is closely related to the section on the clay pot, Margaret Thrall lists several possibilities for the nature of the accusation against Paul (that the apostle "lives by the flesh").

tonomous being who is free, and those who submit themselves to the others' will (and the flatterers are such) are weak, like women, the deviants, or servants. Marshall, *Enmity in Corinth*, 281–325.

[33] Cserháti, *Pál apostolnak a korinthusiakhoz írt második levele*, 150.

[34] Ralph B. Martin, *2 Corinthians* (Word Biblical Commentary 40), Nashville 1986, 85.

[35] Although Hughes also talks about Paul's sufferings, he basically simplifies the message of the passage and talks about fragility in general. He is right about this, but in doing so, the emphasis is shifted: Paul's apologetic tone and his deeply personal message are left out of consideration. Philip E. Hughes, *The Second Epistle to the Corinthians* (The New International Commentary on the New Testament), Grand Rapids 1992, 141–144.

[36] Cserháti, *Pál apostolnak a korinthusiakhoz írt második levele*, 149. See also Tőkés, *Korinthusbeliekhez írt második levél*, 127–128.

a) The Holy Spirit does not control Paul's deeds. b) The previous criticism can be outlined even more precisely in the fact that because of his many weaknesses (cf. v.10; 2 Cor 12:6c) Paul cannot be considered truly a "divine man" or a "man of God" (θεῖος ἀνήρ), namely an extraordinary person who has outstanding abilities and overcomes all obstacles. c) Paul is inclined to such fallible fears and feelings, as shown in the chapter's first verse or 2 Cor 1:12-17. d) But the accusation may be even more contemptuous if, according to the faultfinders, Paul juggles with words in such a way that he turns his weaknesses into arguments for his apostleship (2 Cor 1:12; 2:17; 4:2; 11:24). e) The opponents may refer to in what Paul intends to discover the work of Satan (2 Cor 12:7), they see an incurable disease and hence incompetence for apostolic ministry.[37]

Several possible accusations relate to this very contrast: on the one hand, Paul is unsuccessful, weak, physically powerless, maybe ugly, or perhaps physically ill, but on the other, he preaches something firmly that his poor appearance does not legitimate. That is why the apostle vehemently states that to know someone κατὰ σάρκα is the wisdom that judges the body; more precisely, it focuses on the body (1 Cor 1:26) – and forms an opinion on the soul accordingly.[38] Conzelmann refers to the connection between "according to the flesh" and σοφία σαρκική in 2 Cor 1:12.[39] Corinthians who rival teachers – and thus, in effect, claim their own authority and prestige – or glorify the super-apostles coming from outside enforce their environment's values and peer their teachers' appearance and words the same way as anyone from the upper class trained in rhetorics. This is the wisdom that "looks at the body." However, Bultmann is right when he speaks of σάρξ, saying that "σῶμα is the man himself, while σάρξ is a power that lays claim to him and determines him."[40] Perhaps we should

---

37 Cserháti, *Pál apostolnak a korinthusiakhoz írt második levele*, 344. We should note that the theory of *theios aner* cannot be proved, which is why it is no longer used as a comparative religious science category today.

38 Bultmann calls the term κατὰ σάρκα περιπαεῖν a description of the ungodly life, where *soma* stands for "the self under the rule of *sarx*"; see Rudolf Bultmann, *Theology of the New Testament* (transl. Kendrick Grobel), New York 1951, 200. This is justifiable, but it is also worth considering translating this concept in the light of physiognomy. Those living by human standards judge in judgment by human standards.

39 Hans Conzelmann, *1 Corinthians*, Philadelphia 1975 (1969), 50.

40 Bultmann, *Theology of the New Testament*, 201.

not be talking here so much about cosmic powers but points of view and value judgment, because an ancient person's existence is determined by the others' judgment, the extent to which he meets or differs from the social elite's standards. As we have seen, this affects all areas of life: the proportionality that defines the ideal of physiognomy, clothing, the ideal that specifies masculinity, the definition of the range of virtues, the degree of work and education. This is also the case when Paul presents this as a cosmic power as the "law of the world," and he is undoubtedly right in this: he must compete with this ideal-enforcing power that measures everything and everyone. Paul can only override this if he presents a deeper, more universal standard that questions the value system that labels him weak. From this, the apostle reproaches his opponents: they do not judge by what is in the heart, but by the outward (ἐν προσώπῳ) (2 Cor 5:12); this "by appearance" is synonymous with κατὰ σάρκα, in the sense in which the story of Zopyrus speaks of the value of physiognomy.[41]

Cicero, who tells the story, is facing a contradiction similar to that of concerning Paul. Although Socrates is ugly, his teaching and soul are "beautiful." If physiognomy were right, the philosopher would have to be considered a seducer and foolish, which is obviously ridiculous. In *Tusculan Disputations*, we read another version of the story, which is significant from our point of view: –

> ... for when Zopyrus, who professed to know the character of everyone from his person, had heaped a great many vices on him in a public assembly, he was laughed at by others, who could perceive no such vices in Socrates; but Socrates kept him in countenance by declaring that such vices were natural to him, but that he had got the better of them by his reason. (Cicero, Tusc. 4.80-81.)[42]

---

[41] Malherbe and Harril approach the issue differently but come to a similar conclusion. They see the debate over Paul's contemporary philosopher self-representation as the background to Paul's argument about Odysseus's story. During the Trojan War, he puts on the schema (form) of a slave to deceive his opponents. The question is if it was not cowardice to appear like this instead of standing up as a brave warlord; Abraham J. Malherbe, *Paul and the Popular Philosophers*, Philadelphia 2006, 91–119; Harril, "Invective against Paul," 211–212.

[42] Marcus Tullius Cicero, *Cicero's Tusculan Disputation. Also, Treatises on the Nature of the Gods, and on the Commonwealth* (transl. Charles D. Yonge), New York 1877, 161.

Böhme sees this story as a critique of physiognomy, a display of its contradiction.[43] For Socrates acknowledges his weakness and does not attack physiognomy. At the same time, he claims that he has transformed himself through knowledge or at least tries to keep these character flaws under control. We find a similar line of argumentation in the reasoning of the Corinthian letters. Paul acknowledges his weakness as an evident and visible irritation, a "thorn." However, he points out that he who is "in Christ, is a new creation" (2 Cor 5:17). It does not only mean that the inner nature of a believer in Christ changes but also that different values will take effect: being for others (5:15), reconciliation (5:19) and openness (6:11). At the same time, the veil that obscures the gospel from the unbelievers is also there when these people look at the apostles. They look, but they do not see because the knowledge that would offer a new perspective is a mystery (1 Cor 2:6-16) revealed by the Spirit of the Lord (2 Cor 3:17-18). But he who looks without a veil sees the treasure in the earthenware, namely that Paul's ugly appearance carries a beautiful personality, for "we all, who with unveiled faces contemplate the Lord's glory, are being transformed into his image with ever-increasing glory, which comes from the Lord, who is the Spirit" (2 Cor 3:18). However, this formation is Socratic: the *inner* changes. Eikon is the image of the invisible God, that is, the invisible soul, the inner being becomes like it.[44]

If we read between the lines, some features of this "beautiful soul" also appear. Paul does not judge by what is visible (2 Cor 5:12). He does not preach himself (2 Cor 4:5). He is faithful (1 Cor 4:2), has inner steadfastness and strength (1 Cor 4:20), his celibacy strengthens his impeccability (1 Cor 7:32-34), does not work for profit (2 Cor 2:17; 7:2), he is not deceptive (4:2), has peace (7:4), he is masculine (see pictures of military service 10:4-6; and picture of sport cf. 1 Cor 9:24-27),[45] does not boast

---

[43] Gernot Böhme, "Über die Physiognomie des Sokrates und Physiognomik überhaupt," in ibid., *Atmosphäre. Essays zur neuen Ästhetik*, Berlin 2014, 171–196, 171. Éva Vígh describes that in the Middle Ages, the therapeutic value of physiognomy was formulated on the basis of this story: "Physiognomy is also useful because we can not only infer the morals of others but equipped with will and reason, it also helps us to become better." ("Fiziognómikus gondolkodás az ókori görög kultúrában," *Corollarium, AAA Szeged Suppl.* XIII (2010), 352, n. 14).

[44] The body is not capable of this. For a thorough analysis of the "spiritual body" and for ideas of Paul's contemporaries about the relationship between body and soul, see Dale B. Martin, *The Corinthian Body*, New Haven 1999, 108–128.

[45] Larson, *Paul's Masculinity*, 96.

about others' work (10:16), has knowledge (2 Cor 11:5-6), and has special revelations (12:1-6), which are also accompanied by miraculous powers (12:12).

4. To Overcome the Visible – The Mystery of the Imitation of Christ

πᾶς δὲ προφήτης διδάσκων τὴν ἀλήθειαν, εἰ ἃ διδάσκει οὐ ποιεῖ, ψευδοπρφήτης ἐστί.

And every prophet teaching the truth, if he doeth not what he teacheth, is a false prophet.
(Didache 11:10)[46]

As Ben Witherington points out, Paul does not deny the relation between beauty, knowledge, and aptitude but begins to speak of the gospel as contempt.[47] At the same time, he does not make an abstract theological explanation of it but fights to defend the coherence of his way of life and the message. Furthermore, this is a key aspect of the letter (see 1 Cor 4:16-17):

Therefore I urge you to imitate me. For this reason, I have sent to you Timothy, my son whom I love, who is faithful in the Lord. He will remind you of my way of life (τὰς ὁδούς μου) in Christ Jesus, which agrees with what I teach everywhere in every church.

Paul's whole argument depends on the following question: Can he demonstrate that his way of life matches up with that of Christ's? If so, then he has won and can rightly reason with the theology of humiliation and contempt against the super-apostles who preach some "gospel of glory."

Paul connects the suffering of Christ to his own body in a somewhat mystical way in 2 Cor 4:10. But it is not only the parallel of the image of the dying and resurrected Jesus that appears (cf. 2 Cor 13:3-4), but also his imitable mentality on earth. Although Hughes points out that for Paul, the earthly Jesus and the glorified Christ are one, he still focuses on the risen Lord, through whom the human existence is reconnected with his

---

[46]   Online source: http://www.romans45.org/didache.htm (accessed: 05.05.2022.).
[47]   Witherington, *Conflict and Community*, 143.

body, without which it could not be complete.[48] All of this is right, but in the catalogue of suffering, we find a concrete reference to the mentality of Jesus' earthly life and a concrete mode of imitation. Furthermore, this attitude appears in 1 Cor 4:12: "When we are cursed, we bless; when we are persecuted, we endure it." The same idea appears in 1 Pet 2:21-23, just after the letter's author points out that bearing blasphemy is a paradigmatic act (1 Pet 2:21)! The refusal to return curses is rooted in one of the crucial thoughts of the Sermon on the Mount (the later tradition of Luke 6:28 emphasizes this: "bless those who curse you") and is a stable element of the Jesus tradition.

Therefore, during the persecutions, Paul's behaviour is Christ-like: the apostle's self-devotion is the opposite of the rivalry, social discrimination, and arrogance in Corinth. Meekness and humbleness that appear in 10:1 are also Jesus' features (Matth 5:5). Ταπεινός and πραΰς are practically synonyms,[49] and πραΰς in 10:1 echoes the expression of Matth 5:5: "blessed are the meek." One of Jesus' Logia states that this behaviour is to be followed "ἄρατε τὸν ζυγόν μου ἐφ ὑμᾶς καὶ μάθετε ἀπ ἐμοῦ, ὅτι πραΰς εἰμι καὶ ταπεινὸς τῇ καρδίᾳ, καὶ εὑρήσετε ἀνάπαυσιν ταῖς ψυχαῖς ὑμῶν ·/ "Take my yoke upon you and learn from me, for I am gentle and humble in heart, and you will find rest for your souls" (Matth 11:29 cf. Matth 21:5). The two concepts stand side by side in this sentence, as in Paul's apology. This kind of gentleness, which has clearly negative connotations in the Greco-Hellenic world, is considered the characteristic of those from lower social classes or women, namely those deprived of exercising power,[50] here receives positive content. The persecution, contempt and humbleness of the apostles in the church will reflect the life of Christ.[51] The brilliance of Paul's argument lies in not denying the relationship between external and internal traits but in claiming that the point of reference is wrong; thereby, Paul overturns a whole system of values, for he can justify the close connection of his own life with the Christian way of life and the deviation from it in the case of his opponents.

---

[48] Philip E. Hughes, *The Second Epistle to the Corinthians*, Grand Rapids 1992, 144.

[49] For the connection between the two notions, the relationship between the Hebrew עָנָו, and the translations appearing in LXX, see Olexandr Levko, "The Word tapeinos in the New Testament and its Rendition in Ukrainian Translations," *Studia Slavica Hungarica* 63 (2018), 283–295, 285–286.

[50] Larson, *Paul's Masculinity*, 93.

[51] The line can still be continued: the reason for Paul's contempt is that he does not practice his "righteousness in front of others to be seen by them." This fits in with the message of Matth 6:1 par.

Furthermore, with that, he does one more thing. When 2 Cor 4:10 speaks of carrying the death of Jesus in our bodies, he binds the imitation even closer. The despised death of Jesus, the distorted body hanging on the cross, and Paul's body, weakness, and contempt become the basis of imitation, one of the criteria of the election. "According to the flesh," Jesus and Paul share in the rejection of misunderstanding and incomprehensibility.

And now, let us turn back to the description of Paul in the *Acta Pauli*. Why is he portrayed with such traits? Maybe exactly to demonstrate this duality: the flaws of the outer appearance and the nobility of his person. This contrast is a demonstration of the new wisdom: in Christ, we do not look at anybody "kata sarka," but through the eyes opened to the "treasures in earthenware." Paul, the ugly, the distorted, the weak, and thus despised, is transformed by God – that is why he looks like, according to the description in the *Acta Pauli*, an "angel."

5. Disability and Paul

But what does this all mean when we talk about disabilities? First of all, we have to admit that we generally share the values of physiognomy. Princeton University scholars Alexander Todorov, Sean G. Baron, Nikolaas N. Oosterhof carried out an experiment in 2007 by computer modelling, looking for facial traits that make the impression of being competent and sympathetic. By the judgment of the attendants, the most competent persons had wider faces, and the most sympathetic persons had U-shaped mouths and eyes that formed almost a surprised look. On the contrary, the most unsympathetic persons have mouths curled down, low inner eyebrows, thin and accentuated chins and wide faces with shallow cheekbones. Another article signed among others by Jonathan B. Freeman comes to similar conclusions:

> Interestingly, the notion that individual differences in conceptual associations between traits shapes perceptions comports well with seminal person perception research that posited a role of 'implicit personality theory' in nonface trait impressions (16, 17). The results, therefore, suggest that these classic insights with respect to general impression-formation patterns (outside of face perception) may apply to face-based trait impressions as well.[52]

[52] Ryan M. Stolier, Eric Hehman, Matthias D. Keller, Mirella Walker, Jonathan B. Free-

What this means is that perception of others is connected to our pre-understanding and our lay conceptual beliefs of others, and this is connected to the facial impressions we gain from superficial observations. More interesting is another article written by Eva Louvet, Odile Rohmer, and Nicole Dubois.[53] They explore the connection between biased presuppositions of disabled persons with visible disadvantages and expectations of their competence in a work environment. What they find is a confirmation of earlier experimental results that to disabled persons (who have motoric harms) more social warmth and caring are attached but lower competency levels.

John Swinton calls attention to a similar bias against mentally disabled persons. In an article, he criticizes Peter Birchenall, who states that persons with severe mental ailments cannot develop faith as they are devoid of the cognitive representation of God.[54] Swinton agrees here with Ben Witherington, who, while commenting 2 Cor 5:9, says that judging "not according to human standards" means to experience Christ and each other differently. Swinton debunks Birchenall's argument as an over-intellectualization of faith. I should add that this initiative of Birchenall is in line with the general prejudice against disabled persons. Swinton rightly tries to balance this inadequacy by stating that faith has other aspects besides the purely cognitive. Experiencing is more than knowing; to be the image of God is to be in a relationship. With Paul, we would say: we are earthen vessels – fragile and carriers of treasures. This means that disability, fragility and ailment are not denied but held in tension with the transforming "treasure," Christ, with whom we are in a relationship. This relation has a transforming power, and so Paul can be a different man, judged not from the outward appearance but from Christ's point of view, who gave the example of living for others. This mentality can be common to all – whether somebody is considered "normal" or "disabled." Paul strives for the same we should strive for: to gain a new perspective. This is not the worthiness of the human soul, as the Stoics would say, but Christ, who can transform everybody, regardless of one's appearance, ailment or disability. If we imi-

man, *The Conceptual Structure of Face Impressions, Psychological and Cognitive Sciences, Proceedings of the National Academy of Sciences*, 2018, offprint, 4.

[53] Eva Louvet, Odile Rohmer, Nicole Dubois, "Social Judgment of People with a Disability in the Workplace. How to Make a Good Impression on Employers," *Swiss Journal of Psychology* 68 (2009), 153–159.

[54] John Swinton, "Restoring the Image. Spirituality, Faith, and Cognitive Disability," *Journal of Religion and Health* 36 (1997), 21–27, 23.

tate Paul as he imitated Christ, then we arrive to what Ben Witherington states:

> Paul knows Christ better and wants to be evaluated better by his converts. The implication is that when one is converted, one ought to give up such superficial criteria for judging people. Here again, is evidence that the Corinthians were inadequately socialized converts. They still evaluated things by the criteria they had imbibed from the rhetoric-infatuated culture in Roman Corinth.[55]

Seeing through the eyes of Paul, we might treat persons with disability not "kata sarka," but as persons who can receive divine wisdom. But most importantly we ourselves can gain a new perspective: to look at them as if they were already accepted and transformed by the divine grace, since we do not anymore think like the world, according to human standards. We look and now we can see, as we discovered the glorious Christ in the distorted figure of the one hanging on the cross, and the graceful man in the weak stature of Paul, who might have had severe ailments.

---

[55] Witherington, *Conflict and Community*, 395.

The Beast as an *Imago Diaboli*
Εἰκών and θηρίον in the Book of Revelation

József Nagy

Anthropology has gained significant attention within theology in recent years. The growing interest is visible in each area of theology. Concerning the exegetical writings, numerous aspects are explored and many exegetical works delve into the examination of human nature within the context of the divine-human-animal boundaries.[1]

As will be demonstrated, Scripture offers several key passages that aid in defining these boundaries. In this study, special focus will be dedicated to see the relationship between the words "θηρίον" and "εἰκών" in Genesis, Daniel, and Revelation, and exploring the implications of these words for our understanding of human nature.

This study seeks not only to align with the theme of this volume (*imago Dei*) but also to enhance our understanding of the Book of Revelation. In this context, our study provides several noteworthy contributions. First, we introduce the concept of *imago Diaboli*, which assists in our comprehension of the nature of the beast in Revelation. Second, this study proposes a fresh interpretation of the oft-debated phrase "image of the beast" ("εἰκὼν τοῦ θηρίου") in Revelation 13:14–15.

God-Human-Animal Boundary in the Old Testament

Before delving into this interpretation, we consider how εἰκών and θηρίον are interconnected in various passages within the Septuagint (LXX).

The term "θηρίον" in both classical Greek and biblical texts is primarily associated with the concept of wild or predatory animals,[2] or land animals.

---

[1]   Cf. P. J. Atkins, *The Animalising Affliction of Nebuchadnezzar in Daniel 4: Reading Across the Human-Animal Boundary* (LHBOTS 733), London 2023.

In the LXX, θηρίον is encountered on numerous occasions, mostly as a translation of חַיָּה and בְּהֵמָה. The word "θηρίον" first appears in Genesis 1:24. This passage along with the broader context of Genesis 1:24–31, deserves special attention because θηρίον is used within a framework that aids in our understanding of the divine-human-animal boundaries. Genesis 1:24 discusses God as the creator and distinguishes land animals as his creatures. Specifically, the verse categorizes land animals into three groups: cattle, creeping things, and wild animals (θηρίον). According to Wenham, these categories can be interpreted as domestic animals, small creatures, and wild animals.[3]

Several intriguing similarities can be seen between the creation of humans and land animals. 1. Both humans and land animals were crafted by God. 2. God brought both into existence on the sixth day of creation. 3. Both humans and land animals were formed from the dust of the earth (Gen 2:7, 19). 4. God bestowed the breath of life upon both humans and animals (Gen 1:20–24; 2:7, 19). 5. Initially, both humans and animals were nourished by vegetation alone (Gen 1:29–30). 6. Although God's blessing in Genesis 1:22 specifically mentions sea creatures and birds, it is noteworthy that in Genesis 1:28, God also blesses humans and commands them to be fruitful and multiply. Additionally, some scholars argue that this blessing includes land animals.[4] The intimate relationship between humans and animals continues to be evident throughout the rest of the Bible: 1. Genesis 3:1–5 illustrates the possibility of communication between the woman and the serpent.[5] 2. Noah's ark accommodated a variety of animals (Gen 6:20). 3. After the flood, God's covenant encompassed both humans and animals (Gen 9:9–10, 16).

While there are evident similarities between beasts and humans, it is equally important to acknowledge their distinctions. Here are a few key points that highlight these differences: 1. Only humans are created in the image (εἰκών) and likeness of God (Gen 1:26[LXX]). 2. God called man to exercise dominion over beasts (Gen 1:28). 3. Humans were granted the authority to name animals (Gen 2:19–20). 4. Among all the animals, humans did not find a suitable companion (Gen 2:20). These distinctions in the

---

[2]   W. Foerster, "θηρίον," *Theologisches Wörterbuch zum Neuen Testament* (Hrsg. Gerhard Kittel), Stuttgart 1939, I 133–136, 134.
[3]   G. J. Wenham, *Genesis 1–15* (WBC 1), Waco, TX 1987, 25.
[4]   E. g. C. Westermann, *Genesis 1–11* (CCS), Minneapolis, MN 1985, 141–142.
[5]   Atkins, *Daniel 4*, 159.

text also serve to underscore how Genesis 1–2 envisions the boundaries between God, humans, and animals. In this narrative, God, as the Creator, holds supreme power and elevates humanity to a position of authority over the animals.

However, as a consequence of the fall, this order has been disrupted. There are numerous instances in which the animal is depicted as an adversary of humanity (e. g. Gen 9:2.5; 37:20). The presence of these creatures often serves as a symbol of the desolation of cities (e.g. Isa 13:21; Ezek 31:13; 32:4). Given this disrupted relationship, it is advisable to be cautious when dealing with or approaching animals. Sirach's rhetorical question is a compelling example: "Who pities a snake charmer when he is bitten, or all those who go near wild animals?" (Sir 12:13 NRSV).

In numerous instances, animals serve as the instruments of God's judgment. Their presence often signifies God's curse (Deut 32:24) and punishment (Ezek 14:21). This divine judgment is not limited to the people of Israel alone. These creatures also execute God's judgment on other nations, as exemplified by their role in the judgment of the Philistines (1 Sam 17:46) and the inhabitants of the earth (Isa 18:6).[6] Therefore, the presence of animals signifies God's punitive action. In some cases, it also indicates that the Almighty has forsaken the one who is enduring the punishment (e.g. Gen 40:19; 2 Sam 21:10).[7] According to the Old Testament (OT), the enmity between beasts and humans signifies that humanity is estranged from its Creator.

Nevertheless, some texts exhibit a positive tone. Certain passages highlight that the absence of animals is seen as a blessing from God (Isa 35:9; Ezek 34:25). An even more significant blessing when humans can exercise dominion over the animals (Jer 27:6; Ezek 31:6).[8] While the created order has been disrupted, the OT presents the possibility of restoration. This restoration includes the realization of harmony between humans and animals (Num 26:6; Isa 11:6–9; 35:9; Ezek 34:35).[9]

Special attention should be given to how Daniel addresses the concept of the beast. In Daniel, the mention of the beast is also viewed in the context of the fractured relationship between God and humanity. As demon-

6   R. Y. Liu, *The Background and Meaning of the Image of the Beast in Rev. 13:14, 15* (Diss. Andrews Uni.), Berrien Springs, MI 2016, 80–81.
7   W. Bauder, "θηρίον," *The New International Dictionary of New Testament Theology* (ed. Colin Brown), Grand Rapids, MI 1975, I 113–114.
8   Liu, *Rev 13:14,15*, 81.
9   Bauder, θηρίον, 113.

strated earlier in various parts of the OT, the appearance of the beast often symbolizes God's punitive action. However, in Daniel, God's judgment takes on an even more profound dimension, as godless rulers and kingdoms become akin to the beast.

A striking example of this transformation can be found in Daniel 4, where the self-glorifying Nebuchadnezzar is changed into a beast, or more precisely, an ox (Dan 4:22). According to Daniel 4, Nebuchadnezzar, intoxicated by his own authority, took on the appearance and behavior of a beast. Subsequently, he left his palace and lived in the company of animals ("μετὰ τῶν θηρίων" Dan 4:15[Theod.]). However, after Nebuchadnezzar attributed glory to God, he regained his human form (Dan 4:31). According to Goldingay, this depiction of the beast in Daniel 4 can be traced back to the Old Testament. Adam and Eve desired to become like God (Gen 3:5), and as part of God's punishment, they lost their authority over animals.[10]

Another noteworthy point is the presentation of Daniel 3:19. In this story, Nebuchadnezzar commands the people under his rule to bow down before the golden statue he has erected. According to Daniel 3:19[Theod.], when Daniel's friends refused to kneel before the golden statue, the countenance of the enraged king underwent a change (ἀλλοιόω). Also, significant is the chapter's use of the Aramaic word צְלֵם. Kim observes that צְלֵם is used in various senses here. It can refer to the statue (Dan 3:5, 7, 10, 15) or to the alteration of the king's image (אַנְפּוֹהִי וּצְלֵם) in Daniel 3:19. This choice of words gains special significance when considering that in Genesis 1:26, the Hebrew צֶלֶם expresses the creation of human beings in the image of God.[11]

It is worth noting Atkins's observation that the boundaries between the divine, human, and animal can be delineated through the themes of immortality and wisdom. The disparity between God and humans is evident in the fact that only God possesses immortality (Ezek 28:8–29). Furthermore, the Old Testament also emphasizes the mortality of animals, as seen in passages such as Ecclesiastes 3:18–21, Psalm 16:30 and Psalm 49:20. This contrast between humans and animals is indicative of wisdom (or rationality) or its absence, as highlighted in passages like Proverbs 30:2–3, Job 18:3, and Psalm 73:22.[12] From this perspective, Daniel 4 can

---

[10]   J. E. Goldingay, *Daniel* (WBC 30), Waco, TX 1989, 97.
[11]   D. N. Fewell, *Circle of Sovereignty: Plotting Politics in the Book of Daniel*, Nashville, TN 1991, 51.
[12]   Atkins, *Daniel 4*, 160–167.

also be seen. While God is explicitly described as living forever (Dan 4:31; cf. 6:27; 12:7), Nebuchadnezzar also arrogantly refers to himself as eternal in other parts of the text (Dan 2:4; 3:9). Atkins argues that the mention of the construction of Babylon can be interpreted as a reference to the king's ambition to establish an everlasting legacy (Dan 4:27). Since the king had laid claim to the divine attribute of eternity, he was subsequently stripped of his understanding and transformed into a beast-like state (Dan 4:13).[13] With Atkins's insight, it remains a sustainable interpretation, as discussed in the previous chapter. Particularly in Daniel 4, it is evident that Nebuchadnezzar, despite his humanity, became like a beast, driven by a desire to be like God (cf. Dan 4:22).

In addition to the narrative chapters (Dan 1–6), the motif of the beast recurs in the section containing Daniel's visions (Dan 7–12). Daniel 7 discusses the concept of the beast from a broader perspective, encompassing not only individuals but also empires (cf. Daniel 7:3). In Daniel 7:4, the story of the Babylonian king, Nebuchadnezzar, as depicted in Daniel 4, is encapsulated. Here, Nebuchadnezzar is symbolized as a lion with wings. The loss of the lion's wings signifies the king's loss of power. The verse concludes with Nebuchadnezzar regaining a human heart ("ἀνθρωπίνη καρδία"), indicating a turn of events akin to the narrative in Daniel 4.[14]

Daniel 7:3–7 portrays four kingdoms, representing them as predatory animals. The first beast is likened to a lion (λέαινα),[15] the second to a bear (ἄρκος), and the third to a leopard (πάρδαλις). However, it is the fourth beast that deserves special attention. This fourth beast is described as speaking against God, waging war against the saints, and exercising dominion over the entire earth (Dan 7:19–25). Numerous similarities can be drawn between Nebuchadnezzar and the fourth beast, including traits such as self-glorification and blasphemy (Dan 4:27, 31), persecution of the saints (Dan 3:15), and an extensive reign (Dan 2:37–38).

In Daniel 7:2–3, each beast emerges from the sea. It is worth noting that, in various contexts, the sea symbolizes the primordial chaos that existed before creation. The Old Testament also acknowledges the presence of ancient creatures inhabiting the sea (cf. Isa 27:1; 51:9). The sea's inhabitants, or the sea itself, can symbolize hostility. This concept is reflected

---

13   Atkins, *Daniel 4,* 170–181.
14   J. J. Collins, *A Commentary on the Book of Daniel* (Hermeneia), Minneapolis, MN 1993, 297.
15   Daniel mostly refers to the lion with λέων (e.g. Dan 4:33; 6, 8, 9, 13). Also, λέων is found in Revelation (Rev 4:7; 5:5; 9:8; 9:17; 10:3; 13:2).

in Canaanite mythology, where the sea god Yam is defeated by Baal, the chief god, underscoring this enmity. This conflict is also expressed in Daniel 7, as nations emerge from the sea in opposition to God.[16] Here, nations and rulers are mentioned, and they often claim divine authority (Dan 4:27).

Despite the frightening depictions, Daniel ultimately strikes a note of hope as it foretells the destruction of these beasts and the triumph of the Son of Man (Dan 7:11–14). However, this victory over the beasts is not confined to a future event alone. Even though Daniel 6 does not symbolize the beasts but presents them literally, in this chapter, God preserves Daniel, who remains faithful to him in the den of lions.

Daniel employs the symbol of the beast in a paradoxical manner. The beasts, in this context, do not symbolize desolation as seen in passages like Isaiah 13:21 or Ezekiel 31:13; 32:4, but rather represent great empires. Furthermore, despite God's mandate for humanity to rule over animals (Gen 1:26, 28), both the literal beasts, as seen in Daniel 6, and the symbolic beasts, as portrayed in Daniel 7, possess significant power. The symbolic beast not only symbolizes power (Dan 7:3–7) but also signifies the king losing his human essence (Dan 4:22). This transformation reflects a man or ruler who regards himself as God but ultimately forfeits his human nature, as seen in the case of Nebuchadnezzar in Daniel 4. Therefore, the term "beast" is not only paradoxical but also ironic. As Kim points out, according to Daniel 4, Nebuchadnezzar loses his *imago Dei* because his dominion extends to humans and not just to animals.[17] Certainly, in Daniel 4, it is evident that Nebuchadnezzar abused his power, but the passage clearly conveys that he was punished because he ascribed glory to himself rather than to God (cf. Dan 4:27). Therefore, it is more appropriate to assume that the focus in this passage is indeed on the boundaries between God, humanity, and the animal kingdom, rather than solely on the fact that Nebuchadnezzar extended his dominion to his fellow humans. This narrative underscores the consequences of human pride and the need to recognize divine authority.

---

[16] A. Frisch, *"Empires as Beastly Bodies,"* Four Kingdom Motifs Before and Beyond the Book of Daniel (eds. A. B. Perrin – L. T. Stuckenbruck) (TBN 28), Leiden 2021, 56–80, 63–64.

[17] D. Kim, *Biblical Interpretation in the Book of Daniel: Literary Allusions in Daniel to Genesis and Ezekiel* (Diss. Rice Uni.), Houston, TX 2013, 154.

The word "θηρίον" appears 46 times in the New Testament (NT), and particularly in Revelation, where it occurs 39 times.[18] Besides Revelation, there are also instances where the dominion of humans over animals is emphasized. In Acts 28:4–5, Paul is not harmed by the bite of a snake (θηρίον). During Jesus's forty days of fasting in the wilderness (Mark 1:13), he coexisted with wild beasts. This concept might also extend to the consumption of the meat of wild animals (Acts 11:6; Jas 3:7).[19] There are also instances, where θηρίον is personified. In Titus 1:12, Paul describes the Cretans as "evil beasts" (κακὰ θηρία).[20] Some interpret 1 Corinthians 15:32 as personification when Paul speaks of fighting with beasts (θηριομαχέω). As one can observe, θηρίον in the NT, outside of Revelation, is primarily not symbolic. Passages that describe the beast literally, often emphasize the authority of humans over animals.

However, the θηρίον is significant in the narrative of Revelation, with its 39 occurrences. The vast majority of these instances, with the exception of Revelation 6:8, employ θηρίον symbolically. The occurrences of θηρίον in Revelation are also notable for their irregularity. The word appears for the first time in Revelation 11:7, and in Revelation 13 and Revelation 17 θηρίον is used repeatedly, where the central figure is the beast (or beasts).

From a broader perspective, Revelation introduces several symbolic figures. Some of these figures are neutral or even portrayed in a positive manner. Notably, the four living creatures who stand before the throne and offer praise to God hold a special place (Rev 4). Another prominent figure is the Lamb, symbolizing Christ. Many scholars have pointed out that the beasts in Revelation can be seen as contrasting figures to the Lamb. This observation is supported by several key distinctions. 1. The beast emerges from the abyss, while the Lamb appears from heights of heaven (Rev 19:11). 2. The beast is slain, while the Lamb was slain. 3. The beast pretends to be resurrected (cf. Rev 17:8, 11), whereas the Lamb has conquered death and holds the key to it (Rev 1:18). 4. The Lamb rep-

---

[18] A. Strobel, "θηρίον," *Exegetical Dictionary of the New Testament* (eds. H. Balz – G. Schneider), Grand Rapids, MI 1991, II 148–149.
[19] Mark 1:13 proclaims that the Messiah brings reconciliation with nature (cf. Isa 11:6–9). R. Bauckham, *Living with Other Creatures: Green Exegesis and Theology*, Waco, TX 2011, 130.
[20] According to Clement of Alexandria, Titus 1:12 draws from Epimenides (Strom i. 59. 2.). Strobel, θηρίον, 148–149.

resents Christ, who draws near to humanity (Rev 1:5–7), while the beast symbolizes a person or kingdom who claims divine authority (Rev 13:12).

Although the word θηρίον is of neutral gender, there are some instances where the masculine gender refers to the beast. In Revelation 13:8, the masculine αὐτόν pronoun is used, not the neutral αὐτό. A similar phenomenon can be observed in Revelation 13:14, where the beast from the earth is designated by the masculine λέγων participle, even though grammatically the λέγον would be expected. Revelation 13:18, which concludes the narrative, reveals that the number of the beast is 666, and comments that "this is the number of a man" ("ἀριθμὸς γὰρ ἀνθρώπου ἐστίν").[21]

Besides these readings, the beast of Revelation can be seen from another perspective. The beast can also be understood to consider its place within the God-human-animal framework. It can be argued that the beast doesn't solely symbolize a person or an empire, but that the symbol of the beast carries intrinsic meaning in itself, without the necessity of elaborate decoding.

Θηρίον and εἰκών in Revelation 13

This paragraph will specifically focus on the connection between θηρίον and εἰκών. Apart from being used in the same context in passages such as Genesis 1:24–26, Daniel 2 and Daniel 7, and Revelation 13, these words carry a message concerning the God-human-animal boundary.

Several theological themes in Revelation have their origins in Genesis. Scholars often highlight the connections between Genesis 1–3 and Revelation 21–22. For instance, while Genesis 1:1 starts with the creation of heaven and earth, Revelation 21:1 narrates the appearance of a new heaven and a new earth. Both works address the role of the sun (Gen 1:16; Rev 21:23), the tree of life (Gen 2:9; Rev 22:1), precious stones (Gen 2:12; Rev 21:18), and the presence of God (Gen 3:8; Rev 21:3). Moreover, the influence of Genesis 1–3 can also be observed in various other chapters of Revelation. As this chapter primarily employs Revelation 13 to illustrate the nature of the beast, it is worth noting that there are

---

21   J. L. Resseguie, "Narrative Features of the Book of Revelation," *The Oxford Handbook of the Book of Revelation* (ed. C. Koester), New York, NY 2020, 37–52, 39–40.

several similarities between Genesis 1–3^{LXX} and Revelation 13. This resemblance can also be seen in identical words: θάλασσα (sea; Gen 1:10; Rev 13:1), γῆ (earth; Gen 1:10; Rev 13:11), θηρίον (beast; Gen 1:24; Rev 13:1, 11), εἰκών (image; Gen 1:26, 27; Rev 13:14), ποιέω (create/make; Gen 1:26; Rev 13:14), λέγω (speak; Gen 1:26; Rev 13:14), πνοή (breath; Gen 2:7) and πνεῦμα (breath; 13:15).[22]

Nevertheless, the contexts of Genesis 1–2 and Revelation 13 are vastly different. Genesis 1–2 portrays creation as good in the eyes of God, whereas Revelation 13 presents an extreme distortion. Among these disparities, one of the most significant is in the portrayal of the beast in Genesis 1–2 compared to Revelation 13. Beale argues that "the reason that the ungodly, satanic, earthly powers of the state are called beasts in Revelation, and in the OT, is to indicate that such rulers have so perverted the Genesis 1:26–28 commission—to reflect God's image and to rule over the beasts— that they have instead given themselves over to serving the earthly, beastly creation instead of the Creator."[23] The εἰκών in Revelation 13 carries a different sense. In Genesis, humanity was set apart from the beast by being created in the image of God (εἰκών; Gen 1:26–27), establishing the superiority of humans over the beasts. However, in Revelation 13, we witness a reversal of this order. While humans are called to rule over the beasts (e.g. Gen 1:26–28), all individuals are compelled to worship the beast and his image (εἰκὼν τοῦ θηρίου; Rev 13:14–15).

At first glance, it may appear that the use of εἰκών and θηρίον in Genesis 1–2 and Revelation 13 cannot be compared. In Genesis 1:26–27, εἰκών refers to the image of God that distinguishes humans from animals. In Revelation 13, on the other hand, εἰκών represents a statue. Although the word is the same, the meanings are quite distinct. Likewise, while θηρίον in Genesis 1:24–25, and 30 denotes earthly animals, in Revelation 13 it carries a symbolic meaning. Given these differences, one might argue that it is a coincidence that both texts use εἰκών and θηρίον.

However, two points can be made to confirm that there is indeed a connection between θηρίον and εἰκών in Genesis 1:26–27 and Revelation 13. First, there are numerous similarities between Genesis and Revelation, as indicated above. Second, it is possible that the words from Genesis 1:26–27 in Revelation 13 are viewed through the lens of Daniel 2 and

---

[22] Liu, *Rev 13:14,15,* 97, 103.
[23] G. K. Beale, *We Become What We Worship: A Biblical Theology of Idolatry,* Downers Grove, IL 2008, 258.

Daniel 7. Nevertheless, this second option presents the problem already described in the previous paragraph. In Daniel 2, εἰκών is associated with the statue, and in Daniel 7, θηρίον is used in a symbolic sense, which differs from the wording in Genesis 1:26–27.

Despite these differences, there are compelling arguments, as suggested by Seow, that confirm Daniel 2:38 echoes Genesis 1:26. Seow notes that "Humanity was created to represent divine presence on earth, just as a royal statue in an earthly domain might represent the presence of an imperial ruler." In Nebuchadnezzar's case, however, his dominion surpasses the scope outlined in Genesis 1:26, as the king ruled over both humans and animals. Kim, who also acknowledges this parallel, highlights that in Genesis 1:26, humanity was intended to have dominion solely over non-human creatures, whereas Nebuchadnezzar sought dominion over humans as well.[24] Németh's insight precisely underscores the boundary that this interpretation allows. According to his perspective, even though it may not be possible to definitively establish a literary connection between Genesis 1:24–31 and Daniel 2 and 7, there are notable similarities in the anthropological concepts presented in these two texts.[25]

Given the points discussed above, it is worth considering how Daniel assists us in understanding the meanings of θηρίον and εἰκών in Revelation 13. In Revelation, the influence of Daniel is evident in various aspects. However, in this subsection, we won't attempt to review the entire issue[26] but will concentrate on the specific words θηρίον and εἰκών.

As we have previously discussed, there is also a symbolic use of θηρίον in both Daniel and Revelation. Another similarity lies in the fact that the beast described in Revelation 13:1–2 is modeled after Daniel 7. In Daniel 7, we encounter four beasts emerging from the sea (Dan 7:3). These four beasts collectively possess seven heads and ten horns.[27] In Revelation 13:2, we observe that the Apocalypse amalgamates the characteristics of

---

[24] Kim, *Daniel*, 151.

[25] Á. Németh, "The Ideal and the Bestial Human: Anthropological Aspects of Dan 1–6," *Academia Letters* 836 (2021) 1–4, 1.

[26] G. K. Beale, *Use of Daniel in Jewish Apocalyptic Literature and in the Revelation of St. John,* Lanham 1984.

[27] In Daniel 7:3–7 there are four beasts. Since the fourth beast has four heads (Dan 7:6), we can speak of four beasts and seven heads in total. Furthermore, the fourth beast has ten horns (Dan 7:7). This explains the seven heads and ten horns in Revelation 13:1. R. Bauckham, *The Climax of Prophecy. Studies on the Book of Revelation,* Edinburgh 1993, 404.

the four beasts from Daniel. The sea beast in Revelation 13:1 stands alone with seven heads and ten horns (cf. Rev 12:3; 17:3, 7). This sea beast resembles a lion, a bear, and a leopard (similar to Dan 7:4–7), and it features ten horns, mirroring Daniel 7:7.

Apart from θηρίον, Daniel also uses εἰκών to refer to world empires. In Daniel 2, εἰκών is employed to describe the statue that Nebuchadnezzar saw in his dream (Dan 2:31, 32, 34, 35). In this dream, εἰκών symbolizes world empires. According to the dream, the successive world empires were represented in a single statue, yet each part was constructed from different materials. The most prestigious part of this statue is the head made of gold, symbolizing the empire of Nebuchadnezzar.

In the following chapter of Daniel, εἰκών also plays a significant role, referring to the golden statue erected by Nebuchadnezzar (Dan 3:1, 2, 3, 5, 7, 10, 12, 14, 15, 18). In contrast to Daniel 2, in Daniel 3, the whole statue is made of gold, not just the head. When Nebuchadnezzar finished the statue, he ordered his subjects to kneel before it. In the Greek translations of Daniel 3 (LXX; Theod.), the verb "προσκυνέω" is used to describe kneeling before the statue (Dan 3:5, 6, 7, 10, 11, 12, 14, 15, 18). In Revelation 13, we also encounter προσκυνέω (Rev 13:4, 8, 12, 15), where the image (εἰκών) of the beast is the object of worship. In addition to the identical wording, the two descriptions also align in that the rulers sought to compel everyone to worship them. In Daniel, Nebuchadnezzar commanded the worship of the statue, while in Revelation, the beast from the earth appeared in a similar role (Rev 13:12, 14).[28] Another similarity is that both texts contain an implicit or explicit call to the reader not to kneel before the statue, even at the risk of their life. In Daniel, only God could be worshipped (Dan 6:11), and in Revelation, worship is directed toward God (Rev 19:4) and Christ (Rev 5:14).

Thus, Daniel refers to world empires and their leaders as εἰκών (Dan 2–3) and θηρίον (e.g., Dan 4; 7). These words are used in a similar context in Daniel, where εἰκών and θηρίον can refer to several succeeding empires (Dan 2; 7). While Revelation borrows these words and concepts from

---

[28] In connection with εἰκών, we can consider the image found on the denarius coin featuring the likeness of the emperor, as mentioned in the New Testament (Matthew 22:20; Mark 12:16; Luke 20:24). This image was offensive to devout Jews for two primary reasons. Firstly, it was seen as a violation of the Ten Commandments. Secondly, it depicted a foreign ruler. O. Flender, "εἰκών," *The New International Dictionary of New Testament Theology* (ed. Colin Brown), Grand Rapids, MI 1976, II 286–288, 288.

Daniel, the emphasis is different. The key difference is that, unlike in Daniel, Revelation 13 does not use the two words in isolation; instead, εἰκών and θηρίον appear in the same context, even in the same phrase. Revelation 13:14–15 states:

> ¹⁴and by the signs that it is allowed to work in the presence of the beast it deceives those who dwell on earth, telling them to make an image for the beast [εἰκόνα τῷ θηρίῳ] that was wounded by the sword and yet lived. 15And it was allowed to give breath to the image of the beast [εἰκόνι τοῦ θηρίου], so that the image of the beast [εἰκὼν τοῦ θηρίου] might even speak and might cause those who would not worship the image of the beast [εἰκόνι τοῦ θηρίου] to be slain. (ESV)

As one can see, "εἰκὼν τοῦ θηρίου" is the central phrase in Revelation 13:14–15, repeated four times. It is argued that these verses combine elements from both Daniel 2 and Daniel 7. However, while Daniel uses these symbols in different contexts, Revelation interprets that Daniel 2 and Daniel 7 are attempting to convey a similar concept, albeit through different means, by merging these words.[29]

Revelation not only amalgamates the characteristics of the four Danielic beasts (cf. Rev 13:1–2), but also intertwines symbols used in Daniel by placing εἰκών and θηρίον in the same context. Moreover, in Revelation, εἰκών is never employed in isolation but is consistently paired with θηρίον. In addition to "εἰκὼν τοῦ θηρίου" (Rev 13:14, 15), the phrase "εἰκὼν αὐτοῦ" also appears (Rev 14:9, 11; 15:2; 16:2; 19:20; 20:4). This latter expression also aligns with this pattern, as the personal pronoun consistently refers to the θηρίον.

The idea that Revelation combines εἰκών and θηρίον, as found in Daniel, can be supported by examining the similarities between Revelation and 4 Ezra. The parallels between these two works deserves special attention because they were written in close proximity to each other, and the genre of apocalypse also serves as a bridge between them.[30] It is noteworthy that 4 Ezra 13:3–7 combines elements from Daniel 2 and Daniel 7 in a manner similar to Revelation. Given its significance, 4 Ezra 13:3–7 is also quoted:

---

[29] The phrase "χάραγμα τοῦ θηρίου" (Rev 16:2; 19:20) is also noteworthy.
[30] As is often noted, Revelation serves as an apocalypse, a prophecy, and an epistle simultaneously.

³And I looked, and behold, this wind made something like the figure of a man come up out of the heart of the sea. And I looked, and behold, that man flew with the clouds of heaven; and wherever he turned his face to look, everything under his gaze trembled, ⁴and wherever the voice of his mouth issued forth, all who heard his voice melted as wax melts when it feels the fire. ⁵After this, I looked, and behold, an innumerable multitude of men were gathered together from the four winds of heaven to make war against the man who came up out of the sea. ⁶And I looked, and behold, he carved out for himself a great mountain, and flew upon it. 7And I tried to see the region or place from which the mountain was carved, but I could not.[31]

This section of 4 Ezra incorporates numerous themes and symbols that stem from the Old Testament.[32] This is also another similarity between Revelation and 4 Ezra. Here, we focus on how 4 Ezra combines two motifs that can be traced back to Daniel 2 and Daniel 7. In 4 Ezra 13:6, a figure resembling the Son of Man (as seen in 4 Ezr 4:3) is described as having "carved out for himself a great mountain and flew upon it." This figure, akin to the Son of Man, also appears in Daniel 7:13. In Daniel, it is prophesied that after the power is taken away from the beasts (representing empires), the Son of Man will receive authority. The dominion of the Son of Man is distinct from that of the beasts, as his reign endures forever (Dan 7:14).

While the form may differ, the great mountain in 4 Ezra 13:6 conveys a similar concept, just as the dominion of the Son of Man does. This motif also finds its roots in Daniel. In the dream of Daniel 2:31–35 the statue is a symbol of successive empires. Along with empires following one another, the age of empires also comes to an end. This is symbolized in the dream where a massive rock descends from a mountain and crushes the statue (Dan 2:34, 45). According to Stone, the mountain in 4 Ezra 13:6 has its origins in Daniel 2:34.[33] Just as in the vision of the Son of Man in Daniel 7, Daniel 2:44 suggests that after the era of world empires, there will be a dominion that endures forever. It becomes evident that 4 Ezra 13:3–7 combines elements from both Daniel 2 and Daniel 7.[34] Remarkably, both

31   M. E. Stone – M. Henze, *4 Ezra and 2 Baruch: Translations, Introductions, and Notes*, Minneapolis, MN 2013, 72.
32   M. E. Stone, Fourth Ezra (Hermeneia), Minneapolis, MN 1990, 384–385.
33   Stone, *4 Ezra*, 385.
34   According to Beale and Gladd, 4 Ezra 13:3–7 establishes a connection between the stone in Daniel 2 and the figure of the Son of Man in Daniel 7.

the mountain and the Son of Man symbolize an everlasting divine dominion.

It is remarkable that both 4 Ezra and Revelation combine elements from Daniel 2 and Daniel 7. These connections arise from both works recognizing that the symbolic descriptions in Daniel express the same idea. This is evidenced by their use of imagery from both symbolic descriptions. Furthermore, it becomes apparent that the references in 4 Ezra and Revelation complement each other. 4 Ezra 13:6 speaks of the fulfillment of God's eternal reign through the mountain and the Son of Man,[35] while Revelation connects εἰκών and θηρίον, which symbolize the negative world empires. Εἰκών pertains to the statue in Daniel 2, which is destroyed by a stone rolling down the mountain, while θηρίον symbolizes the empires that rule temporarily in Daniel 7.

Indeed, the passage from 4 Ezra does not explicitly delineate the boundaries between God,[36] humans, and animals. However, the way it connects Daniel 2 and Daniel 7 creates a context that supports the idea of interpreting "εἰκὼν τοῦ θηρίου" in Revelation 13:14–15 with reference to Daniel.[37] While there have been various interpretations of this phrase in Revelation 13:14–15, to the best of our knowledge, none of them have highlighted the reading we are proposing.

G. K. Beale – B. L. Gladd, *Hidden But Now Revealed: A Biblical Theology of Mystery*, Downers Grove, IL 2014, 204.

[35] However, in addition to these positive motifs, 4 Ezra also refers to the four beasts (4 Ezr 11:39–40).

[36] 4 Ezra 7:62–74 suggests that the distinction between humans and beasts implies that humans are subject to judgment. Stone, *Fourth Ezra,* 123.

[37] The previous observation is further supported by several additional similarities in how the Revelation and 4 Ezra portray the beast. 1. As mentioned earlier, the beast in Revelation 13 combines the characteristics of the four beasts in Daniel 7, similar to how the eagle in 4 Ezra 11–12 symbolically represents the Roman Empire. 2. In both cases, these symbolic animals are representative of the Roman Empire. In Revelation 13:3, the description of a head wounded fatally and then healed is often interpreted in the context of the Nero *redivivus* (or *redux*) legends (cf. Tacitus, Hist. I, 2 and II, 8). Similarly, in 4 Ezra 11–12, the symbol of the eagle frequently represents the Roman Empire (cf. Josephus *BJ*, 3,123). 3. Both symbolic figures ultimately consume themselves and are subsequently destroyed (Rev 17:6; 4 Ezr 11:35; 12:3). 4. In both cases, there is an opposition between a messianic figure and the beast (Rev 17:14; 4 Ezr 11:45–46; 12:32). Frisch, Empires, 71–75.

Reflections

In Revelation, the symbolic beast indeed plays a significant role in the divine-human-animal boundary, just as in Daniel. While it is often noted that the beasts in Revelation cause distortion,[38] there is more to consider. The beasts in Revelation not only create distortion but also embody the deformation. The beast represents a person or empire that aspires to godlike status but, ironically, ends up becoming beastly themselves, akin to the transformation of Nebuchadnezzar in Daniel 4:13. They aim for more, but paradoxically, they become less. The symbolism of the beast can be seen as an irony. It is ironic that while a leader or empire seeks divine power and honor, they are compelled down a path contrary to their goal. As the name "beast" implies, their essence does not even touch on human qualities. The higher they rise, the deeper they fall, ultimately losing their *imago Dei*, as depicted in Daniel 4. Although this observation is particularly evident in Daniel, as we have highlighted earlier how Revelation draws from Daniel in various instances, it is not far-fetched to apply this concept to Revelation as well.

In light of this perspective, the character of the beast can be aptly described. It possesses the internal qualities of an animal but presents an external form similar to a human being.[39] The beast emerges from the underworld (as seen in Revelation 11:7) yet takes on an earthly appearance. As such, the beast represents an inhuman person or kingdom. The symbol of the beast effectively conveys a divided and conflicted nature.[40] In the words of Witherington, "The governing authority in Revelation is described as a brutal subhuman creature, a Beast."[41]

In Revelation, the beasts are depicted as being in the service of Satan. Various passages in Revelation make it clear that the θηρίον is dependent on the δράκων. For instance, Revelation 12:18 describes the dragon standing on the shore of the sea to bring forth the first beast, and Revelation 13:2 explicitly states that the beast receives its power from Satan. Throughout the narrative in Revelation, it becomes evident that it is Satan who is initially described as having seven heads and ten horns (Rev 12:3). Subsequently, the same characteristics are attributed to the beast that rises from

---

[38]   Liu, *Rev 13:14,15,* 133.
[39]   Gy. Takács, *A Jelenések könyve,* Budapest 2000, 290.
[40]   Resseguie, Narrative Features, 39.
[41]   B. Witherington, *Revelation,* Cambridge 2003, 186.

the sea in the next chapter (Rev 13:1). Furthermore, the beast is described as scarlet (κόκκινος; Rev 17:3, 7), while Satan is characterized as fiery red (πυρρός; Rev 12:3).[42] This demonstrates that the dragon is the primary force behind the beasts. As Bass succinctly puts it: "The greatest beast is the dragon."[43]

While the beasts are undoubtedly portrayed as a real threat in Revelation, they are not the root cause of the problem. According to Stevenson,

> Before depicting Rome as a monstrous beast (Rev 13), John introduces the dragon as the real enemy (Rev 12). By only then moving on to the beast and stating that the beast receives his power, throne, and authority from the dragon (13:2) does Revelation make it clear that Rome is merely one weapon among many that the dragon utilizes to wage its war on the followers of God.[44]

This becomes particularly evident in the final chapters of Revelation. After the beasts are cast into the lake of fire (Rev 19:20), Satan is depicted as going forth (ἐξέρχομαι) to deceive the nations (Rev 20:8). This passage clearly attributes the deception to Satan himself, emphasizing that the primary source of deceit is Satan rather than empires, rulers, or cults.[45]

In summary, the theological observation we can draw from this analysis is that while Daniel's perspective on the beast can also imply the loss of the *imago Dei* (as seen in Dan 4:13), Revelation presents the nature of the beast in a different light. As we have demonstrated, the beast in Revelation is intricately connected to Satan. Given the striking similarities in appearance and behavior between Satan and the beast, we can conclude that the beast is ultimately an image of Satan, the *imago Diaboli*. While the beast

---

[42] In addition to their visual similarity, they are also identical in their operation. Both deceive and persecute the elect (Rev 12:9). The beast makes the inhabitants of the earth worship the dragon (Rev 13:2). The beast from the earth speaks like the dragon (Rev 13:11), deceiving the inhabitants of the earth (Rev 13:14). The inhabitants of the earth also bowed down before the beast and the dragon (Rev 13:4). Just as the beast receives his power from the dragon (Rev 13:2), so he is able to transfer his power (ἐξουσία) to the beast from the earth (Rev 13:12).

[43] "The greatest beast is the dragon." M. Battle, *Heaven on Earth. God's Call to Community in the Book of Revelation*, Louisville, KY 2017, 39.

[44] G. Stevenson, "Perspectives on Evil in the Book of Revelation," *The Oxford Handbook of the Book of Revelation* (ed. C. Koester), New York, NY 2020, 275–290, 282.

[45] W. Tipvarakankoon, *The Theme of Deception in the Book of Revelation* (Diss. The Lutheran School of Theology), Chicago, IL 2013, 249–250.

from the earth compels worship of the image of the sea beast (Rev 13:14–15), the beast itself serves as an image. We propose the term *"imago Diaboli"* to describe the symbolic beast and, by extension, the nature of humanity, much like *imago Dei*. The *imago Dei* concept suggests that human nature is inherently related to God, as it is in the context of another being that humans find their place in creation and understand their essence. This interpretation is echoed in Revelation, where even if humanity has separated itself from God, it cannot exist without a pattern or point of reference. The strong emphasis in Revelation underscores that not even a world empire or its ruler can claim self-sufficiency in this regard. In this perspective, the beast becomes nothing more than an *imago Diaboli*, a symbol of separation from God that seeks to define itself according to a new point of reference, ultimately resembling Satan in both appearance and behaviour.

SYSTEMATIC THEOLOGY

Karl Barth's Interpretation of *Imago Dei* and Its Connection to the Covenant

Gyopárka Köves

1. The Concept of Covenant in Barth's Theology

The covenant in the Barthian theology is a covenant of grace made with Israel and fulfilled in Jesus Christ.[1] This concept itself is primarily Christological. Covenant is the "presupposition of reconciliation," and reconciliation is also the "restitution of the old fellowship, which was fulfilled in Christ."[2] Since we speak about the covenant of grace, it is not based upon the deserved merit of man, but it rises from the pure grace and freedom of the sovereign God.[3] However, God's grace is not a consequence of sin. His intent for covenant and grace is primary; it comes before sin. "The work of atonement in Jesus Christ is the fulfilment of the communion of Himself with man and of man with Himself which He willed and created at the very first."[4] Even the appearance of human sin does not stop him. The appearance of sin is merely an incident, an episode (*"Zwischenfall"*), and the redemption in Jesus Christ is "the contingent reaction" of this episode from God. God does not establish a relationship *because of* sin, but *in spite of* sin.[5] In the way his intervention takes place when he came as a human, we see a sign of God's "faithfulness," and that is the manifestation of the faithfulness of the covenantal God.[6] In Jesus Christ, therefore, this federal will is manifested as a reaction to sin, but the action he has begun

---

[1] E. Busch, "Der eine Gnadenbund Gottes. Karl Barths neue Föderaltheologie," *ThQ* 4 (1996), 345.
[2] K. Barth, *Church Dogmatics* IV, London 2009, 19.
[3] Barth, *Church Dogmatics* IV, 33.
[4] Barth, *Church Dogmatics* IV, 33.
[5] Barth, *Church Dogmatics* IV, 65. "Yet" and "Notwithstanding."
[6] Barth, *Church Dogmatics* IV, 33.

is in fact ongoing until he achieves his goal. This is God's true covenantal will, this is "his original covenant with man."[7] Due to this Christological emphasis, Barth's federal theology is separated from Orthodox Calvinist federal traditions in many places, but it does bring back a view of Protestant dogmatics that has been dormant since the 17th century. Therefore, Eberhard Busch rightly called the Barthian theology a "new federal theology."[8]

2. The Barthian Doctrine of Creation

In the four volumes of *Kirchliche Dogmatik* (Volume III),[9] the theology of creation is developed on both a noetic and an ontological approach, while the keynote is focused primarily on the teleological aspect, namely the covenant that is fulfilled in Christ. According to the noetic approach, creation is a creed and doctrine of faith, *"articulus fidei,"* it is "response" of the "divine self-witness."[10] Creation is, moreover, a factual event, it is grounded on the "objective reality," in which God acted "once and for all."[11] It differs from all other divine acts in that it has no analogy in the life of creatures, only in its own inner divine existence, and this analogy is "the eternal begetting of the Son by the Father."[12] The action of creation calls the "Creator-creature relationship" into being.[13] It "corresponds externally to the inner life of the Father, the Son and the Holy Ghost" and "it is the execution of the contingent decision of God in His predestination."[14]

The covenant appears among the basics of the doctrine of creation therefore, beyond the event (or rather before the event) of the divine decision, which is one of the secrets of the inner existence of the Trinity. What we learn about this is known in Jesus Christ, who is also "the key to the secret of creation."[15] On the one hand, the noetic exposition states that the centre of creation is the establishing of a relationship between

---

7   Barth, *Church Dogmatics* IV, 33.
8   Busch, "Der eine Gnadenbund Gottes," 341–354.
9   First editions in German: KD III/1: 1945; KD III/2: 1948; KD III/3: 1950; KD III/4: 1951. The full 13-volume work originally published by Theologischer Verlag in Zurich.
10   Barth, *Church Dogmatics* III/1, Edinburgh 1958, 3; 4; 22.
11   Barth, *Church Dogmatics* III/1, 5; 333; 13.
12   Barth, *Church Dogmatics* III/1, 14.
13   Barth, *Church Dogmatics* III/1, 16.
14   Barth, *Church Dogmatics* III/1, 16.
15   Barth, *Church Dogmatics* III/1, 28.

God and man. This relationship is the result of divine decision, and the reason for the determination is only the grace of God. This grace comes from the God who is "Lord and Ruler," and who in this relationship has "absolute authority and power."[16] God is the one who acts freely, by his will of his freedom, sovereign in both his decision and his action.[17]

On the other hand, Barth rejects the theory of *Creatio continua*. According to his freedom, God also limits his own created work. God is not an abstract spirit, working in perpetuity, but a personal, loving God.[18] The essence of the Christian doctrine of creation, according to Barth, is to show that God, the Creator, is also the Redeemer and the Saviour.

However, the ontic cause, the beginning, the fulfilment, and the purpose of creation are Jesus Christ himself. If a Christian view on creation is more than a general precept or theory of creation, then recognition of the fact of creation is a belief and therefore someone's "attitude and decision."[19] It is "necessary" to accept that God is the Creator, thereby acknowledging that He has the "right" and even the "power" to control us.[20]

3. The Connection Between Creation and Covenant

Although Barth originally planned to write *Kirchliche Dogmatik* IV under the heading "Doctrine of the Covenant," he later decided on the title "Doctrine of Reconciliation," but became convinced that the question of our relationship with God is focused around the concept of covenant. Finally, creation theology has gained a definite covenantal character, and it refers to this that its first main chapter, §41, is entitled "Creation and Covenant."[21] From three subchapters the two titles can be interpreted as theses: on the one hand, it states that "Creation is the external basis of the covenant"[22] and, on the other hand, "The covenant is the internal basis of creation."[23]

---

[16]   Barth, *Church Dogmatics* III/1, 44.
[17]   Barth: *Church Dogmatics,* III/1, 95.
[18]   Busch, "Der eine Gnadenbund Gottes," 353.
[19]   Barth, *Church Dogmatics* III/1, 32.
[20]   Barth, *Church Dogmatics* III/1, 32.
[21]   Barth, *Church Dogmatics* III/1, 42–329.
[22]   Barth, *Church Dogmatics* III/1, 94. ("Die Schöpfung als äußerer Grund des Bundes").
[23]   Barth, *Church Dogmatics* III/1, 228. ("Der Bund als innerer Grund der Schöpfung").

The main thesis states that creation can only stand before us in the form of a "saga," which shows that "the purpose and therefore the meaning of creation is to make possible the history of God's covenant with man."[24] The "beginning," the "centre" and the "culmination" of this covenant is "in Jesus Christ."[25] The purpose of the covenant is its story, and creation puts this story in motion, therefore Barth makes a very definite distinction between the teleological cause of creation and its temporality.[26] What follows in time – the other works of God – is already levelled to the establishing and keeping of the covenant of grace. In this covenant of grace, God "predestined and called man as his partner."[27] Regarding the scope of the history of the covenant of grace, covenant is prior to creation, says Barth, and creation itself creates the "basis and presupposition" of this history.[28] This world provides a place for the covenant of grace, which gains its comprehensive totality in Christ.[29]

Creation is therefore the "external" cause or "basis of the covenant."[30] It sets the preconditions for the realization of God's love within the covenant, in this way the "external cause" comes into being, namely the existence and nature of the creature with whom God makes the covenant.[31] Covenant "is the goal of creation and creation the way to the covenant."[32] So, it can only be considered as external cause. The "internal basis," by contrast, is expressed in several forms, according to Barth, as he seeks to express the complexity that is manifested in God's will for redemption, reconciliation, and new creation in Christ. Consequently, the "internal basis" of creation, or its source is "the free love of God, or more precisely the eternal covenant which God has decreed in Himself as the covenant of the Father with His Son."[33]

Creation, thus, establishes both the space and environment in which the covenant can play out and creates simultaneously the subject that will be a partner of God, namely a creature who can have a real connection

---

[24] Barth, *Church Dogmatics* III/1, 42.
[25] Barth, *Church Dogmatics* III/1, 42.
[26] Barth, *Church Dogmatics* III/1, 42.
[27] Barth, *Church Dogmatics* III/1, 43.
[28] Barth, *Church Dogmatics* III/1, 44.
[29] Barth, *Church Dogmatics* III/1, 44.
[30] Barth, *Church Dogmatics* III/1, 94.
[31] Barth, *Church Dogmatics* III/1, 96.
[32] Barth, *Church Dogmatics* III/1, 97.
[33] Barth, *Church Dogmatics* III/1, 97.

with God ("*verhandlungsfähig*") and is, therefore, able to have a federal relationship with him ("*bündnisfähig*").[34]

For Barth, the "internal basis," i.e. the real cause of the creation, is the covenant itself. Creation therefore precedes the covenant historically as a necessary circumstance to provide a formal condition for the covenant. The "material presupposition" is the covenant itself, and in material terms, the covenant takes precedence over the formal presupposition, i.e. the creation, since the main purpose of the story lies in the appearance of Christ and in the covenant with him.[35] Creation is "the threshold of the history of the covenant and salvation."[36] In the exegesis of Genesis 2, Barth points out that the narrative of man's creation in the Paradise is clearly supralapsarian, i.e. God's preliminary plan includes the possibility of sin. "But for the sake of completeness we must add at once that this picture of man's creation is used not only in a *supralapsarian* manner but in a *suprafederal* manner. That is to say, the creation of man is described in the light of the faithfulness of God confirmed on the far side of creation and the fall."[37] In fact, the federal story is about what the Paradise story speaks of in summary, that is, the covenant between God and man. On one side, it demonstrates how God turns to man and on the other side it depicts the "great gulf" that becomes a defining element in this story as a result of man's fall.[38]

Man is therefore called to be God's covenant partner, which will be at the heart of Barth's anthropology.[39] To prove this, he takes the concept of *imago Dei*, in which he interprets creation and covenant as interconnected. To do this, he carries out a very detailed exegetic examination of Genesis 1:27 and Genesis 2, although he applies different methods in discussing these two narratives. While in the exegesis of Genesis 1:27 he focuses primarily on key terms, in Genesis 2 he moves much more freely, even more so since in this chapter there is no explicit reference to *imago Dei*. In the second creation story, he emphasizes the sacramental accents of the text and thus his interpretation in this case is typological.

---

34 Barth, *Church Dogmatics* III/1, 184–185.
35 Barth, *Church Dogmatics* III/1, 231–232.
36 Barth, *Church Dogmatics* III/1, 239.
37 Barth, *Church Dogmatics* III/1, 244.
38 Barth, *Church Dogmatics* III/1, 275.
39 K. Barth: *Church Dogmatics* III/2, London 2009, 1–118. § 45 „Man in His Determination as the Covenant-partner of God."

The basic concept of Barth's *imago Dei* interpretation is that, based on the definitional sentence of Genesis 1:27, we must say that *imago Dei* is a "differentiation and relationship between man and man," i. e. "existence as man and woman."[40] The full context of the Old Testament confirms this, because the Old Testament saw the creation and their relationship as man and woman as an analogy to the covenant of grace.[41] Thus in the bond between man and woman, it is about a covenant, a union. "Hence Gen. 2 speaks of the covenant made and irrevocably sealed. [...] It was for the sake of this covenant that God first created man as male and female."[42] At the same time, Barth does not want to overstretch the analogy of marriage at this time. He invokes the philosophical term of personalism to represent the covenantal relationship, the relationship between God and man, in parallel with the relationship between woman and man, which is expressed in the relationship between "I and Thou."[43] He speaks about a dual and personal relationship: the human relation is repeated on a different level between God and man in the covenant. He therefore emphasizes (among others) in his *imago*-interpretation that we do not consider it as *analogia entis*, but as *analogia relationis*.

However, we cannot reduce the interpreting of the *imago Dei* to the exegesis of the biblical creation stories, and Barth continues it in the first volume of the doctrine of creation. The goal of creation is according to §42 not merely the covenant, but more precisely "the covenant of God with man fulfilled in Jesus Christ."[44] The final term of Barth's *imago-* interpretation receives an even deeper meaning in the second volume of the doctrine of creation, in the Christological anthropology.[45] God, who created the covenant, created man as his covenant partner to "correspond" with himself. Man's image of God foreshadows Jesus, who has become human. We also see that God did not create man as a solitary being, but as a community. This is exactly because God is not solitary himself, but is inherently connected and communed, "As the Father of the Son, as the Son

---

40 Barth, *Church Dogmatics* III/1, 195.
41 Barth, *Church Dogmatics* III/1, 312.
42 Barth, *Church Dogmatics* III/1, 313.
43 Barth, *Church Dogmatics* III/1, 184. This is the category of "directness" in the definition of personalism. In more detail see K. Stock, "Die Funktion anthropologischen Wissens in theologischem Denken – am Beispiel Karl Barths," *ET* 34 (1974), 533–535.
44 Barth, *Church Dogmatics* III/1, 330.
45 Barth, *Church Dogmatics* III/2, 117–118.

of the Father, He is Himself I and Thou, and yet always one and the same in the Holy Ghost."[46] Man's being created, however, does not automatically make him a covenant partner. Volume III/2 is already much more cautious in defining the covenantal relationship. Man is not immediately a partner because of his creaturely being, but he is determined to be this, which is fulfilled only if he receives the benefit of Christ, that is, he is "saved" by Christ, who, in this Barthian interpretation, is the real *imago Dei*.[47]

4. The Interpretation of Imago Dei by Barth

Barth further writes about the image of God in his Doctrine of the Word of God, where he defines it as a capability "of receiving God's Word."[48] The ability to receive the word is realized in faith, in which man is "in conformity to God."[49] However, this capability is not a hidden trait in man, but comes from outside, since it comes from our union with Christ in faith and thus cannot be translated into the language of anthropology.[50]

However, in the classical interpretations of *imago Dei* in Genesis 1:27, there are two aspects: the traditional "functional interpretation," which sees the essence of the image of God in the relationship between *mandatum Dei*, i.e. the *dominion terrae*, and the other is "the relational interpretation."[51] Barth consciously does not use philosophical and ethical definitions.[52] He seeks the meaning of *imago Dei* closely in verses 26–27, but also rejects the solution of Gunkel, who parallels the match of words between Genesis 5:3, which means for Barth that the meaning of image of God is not reduced to merely bodily existence.[53] He also rejects interpretations that equate *dominion terrae* with *imago Dei*.[54]

His basic thesis is, that the text offers us a definition, and according to this, the image of God is a "differentiation and relationship between man

---

[46] Barth, *Church Dogmatics* III/2, 118.
[47] Barth, *Church Dogmatics* III/2, 22–23.
[48] K. Barth, *Church Dogmatics* I/1, London 2010, 237.
[49] Barth, *Church Dogmatics* I/1, 237. He refers to the term *"Anknüpfungspunkt"* by Brunner.
[50] Barth: *Church Dogmatics* I/1, 253.
[51] N. Macdonald, "The *Imago Dei* and Election: Reading Genesis 1:26–28 and Old Testament Scholarship with Karl Barth," *IJST* 10 (2008), 304.
[52] Barth, *Church Dogmatics* III/1, 195–196.
[53] Barth, *Church Dogmatics* III/1, 193–194.
[54] Barth, *Church Dogmatics* III/1, 194.

and man," i.e. "existence as man and woman."[55] Because it is a relationship and not a quality, there is no point in researching where exactly the image of God is hidden in man and in which human peculiarities one can discover it.[56] It is a relationship, and therefore it is not an "intellectual and moral" talent or possibility of man.[57] What man can be in the world of creatures, i.e. the reign of man over the created world, his domination and dignity are already "consequences of the divine likeness."[58]

However, Barth further nuances the concept of divine likeness in a male-female relationship, when he points out that sexuality is not actually a measure of *imago*, it belongs to the "creatureliness," evidenced by the existence of sexual differences between animals.[59] The core of image of God is the relationship between I and Thou, which is an *analogia relationis* to the I–Thou relationship between God and man.[60] At the creation of humans, God not only creates man and woman, but also creates their "mutual relationship."[61] As Thorsten Waap points out, "the prototype of man is not the likeness to God, but also the fact, that their relationship determines their existence."[62]

Since *imago* is a relationship, there is also another aspect that has been debated for many centuries, and this relates to the fall. Was the *imago Dei* lost at the time of the fall and, if so, how was it forfeited? Was it forfeited completely or only partially, and if partially, what is left of it in man? According to the Reformation thesis *imago Dei* is the *rectitudo animae*, a man in the state of *status integritatis*, which was lost by sin. Barth definitely states, however, that there is no reference to this in the Scriptures, neither Genesis 1 nor Genesis 2 speaks of "an ideal man." [63] The image of God "is not lost by sin."[64] It could not have been lost, for it is a capability to stay in relationship with God, and consequently it is a possibility and a promise, so it cannot become the property of man, "it cannot

55   Barth, *Church Dogmatics* III/1, 195.
56   Barth, *Church Dogmatics* III/1, 184–185.
57   Barth, *Church Dogmatics* III/1, 185.
58   Barth, *Church Dogmatics* III/1, 187.
59   Barth, *Church Dogmatics* III/1, 196.
60   Barth, *Church Dogmatics* III/1, 196.
61   Barth, *Church Dogmatics* III/1, 298.
62   T. Waap: *Gottebenbildlichkeit und Identität. Zum Verhältnis von theologischer Anthropologie und Humanwissenschaft bei Karl Barth und Wolfhart Pannenberg*, Göttingen 2008, 225–226.
63   Barth, *Church Dogmatics* III/1, 200.
64   Barth *Church Dogmatics* III/2, 118.

be lost."[65] In fact, for being not lost, it shows that God's history with men would not only be "abrogated" by the fall, but it only begins. God and man can continue to address each other as I and Thou.[66] With his thesis that *imago Dei* cannot be lost, Barth "consciously and broadly breaks with a Reformation tradition." [67]

We have seen that the relationship between man and woman is a typological prototype of covenant. First in line is the "original image" of the relationship between God and his people, Israel.[68] However, the Old Testament image also points further, namely to the relationship between Jesus and "His community."[69] In connection with Paul's typology, Jesus Christ and the Church can be considered as man and woman.[70] Christ does not exist "isolated," but in communion with his "community," his Church, which includes us.[71] The analogy about the Church of Christ as a relationship between man and woman clearly shows that Barth's interest in the concept of covenant is allegorical and partly speculative.

Barth is much more able to break away from the male-female analogy in the second Volume of creation theology, and the definition *of imago Dei* becomes clearly and characteristically Christological. First, he refers to the relational aspect and says: "God is in relationship, and so too is the man created by Him. This is his divine likeness."[72] At the same time, Jesus, who is identical to God in his deity, is similar in his humanity to God.[73] The human Jesus is Godlike.[74] "The humanity of Jesus," that is, his human existence is "the image of God, the *imago Dei*"![75] Therefore, the real *imago Dei* is not an object, but a person, Jesus Christ himself, who became human.

65   Barth, *Church Dogmatics* III/1, 200.
66   Barth, *Church Dogmatics* III/1, 200.
67   T. Waap, *Gottebenbildlichkeit und Identität*, 234.
68   Barth, *Church Dogmatics* III/2, 91.
69   Barth, *Church Dogmatics* III/2, 93.
70   Barth, *Church Dogmatics* III/1, 203.
71   Barth, *Church Dogmatics* III/1, 203.
72   Barth, *Church Dogmatics* III/2, 118.
73   Barth, *Church Dogmatics* III/2, 16. Barth consistently talks about Jesus referring to Christ incarnate.
74   Barth, *Church Dogmatics* III/2, 16.
75   Barth, *Church Dogmatics* III/2, 16.

5. Critical Suggestions

a. Barth's Interpretation of Imago Dei

The reviews of the Barthian *imago Dei* interpretation first point to the methodological flaws of his exegesis. Nathan Macdonald, who analyses the Barthian *imago* approach primarily from a hermeneutic point of view, acknowledges that "the traditional Christian interpretation cannot be relinquished without a major reassessment of the structure and content of Christian dogmatics."[76] He is certainly right that, in the case of reception, the fundamental difference lies in the methodological differences between "critical exegesis and constructive theology."[77]

Nevertheless, we cannot ignore the unevenness and contradictions in Barth's exegetic solutions and conclusions. On the one hand, his translation of the words צֶלֶם and דְּמוּת with "*Urbild*"–"*Vorbild*" directs Barth to a very different field of interpretation than the original Old Testament definition. The translation as "original image" and "fore-pattern"[78] offers the use of analogies on a plate, which the text does not necessarily allow.

The analysis of the words זָכָר and נְקֵבָה is also problematic. Since there are other terms in Hebrew for the designation of "woman" and "man," which even more refer to their connectedness. After all, this word pair should have been examined not only based on the terms and phrases used in Genesis 1:27, but within the whole context of Scripture. Due to Barth's far-reaching conclusions, a deeper exegetic foundation would have been needed. Unfortunately, Barth did not produce a consistent exegesis of Genesis 1.

He sees in the most important "countertext" of Genesis 1:27, namely Genesis 5:3 not a conflicting argument, and he claims that the sequence of nouns and the exchange of their prepositions gives the same words a different meaning. However, researchers today can hardly accept this interpretation.[79] Therefore Thorsten Waap remarked, "Barth has indeed entered an exegetically quite controversial area with his own translation and explanation, [...] and evoked an explanation, that is hardly to surpass in systematic coherence, but which is imperfect in its exegetical accuracy."[80]

The questions raised in relation to the analogies set out below will be

---

[76] Macdonald, "The *Imago Dei* and Election," 303–304.
[77] Macdonald, "The *Imago Dei* and Election," 306.
[78] K. Barth: *Kirchliche Dogmatik* III/1, Zollikon–Zürich 1947², 205.
[79] Macdonald, "The *Imago Dei* and Election," 321.
[80] Waap: *Gottebenbildlichkeit und Identität*, 230.

explained in more detailed hereafter. Nevertheless, beyond that, there are several open questions about the Barthian *imago*-interpretation waiting for an answer. It is clear that Barth is starting from the primary thesis of God's sovereignty. It is new that his anthropology also starts from the divine, "from the top down." That is why Barth was accused of being an "antimodern or premodern thinker, since he overshadows the fundamental problem of modernism, namely the institution of freedom and autonomy."[81] Odo Marquard calls Barth straight a "Protestant variant of theological antimodernism."[82] Thorsten Waap resolves this, as he says, in such a way that Barth's anthropology is maybe not about the "destruction or deconstruction" of identity, but rather the reconstruction of it in the light of God."[83] "Man is free therefore only in his relationship with God, he is autonomous in the theonomy."[84] In doing so, Barth does not solve the issue of human freedom, "merely taking it to a higher level." [85] In my view, the covenantal idea itself is the key to the solution on the issue of human autonomy, since God chooses man as his partner for himself. In fact, he accepts this imperfect creature as his partner in such a way that he even accepts the possibility of the fall.

From the angle of contemporary theological anthropology, it is difficult to concede a theocentric or Christocentric approach such as the Barthian. Thorsten Waap expresses many doubts from the viewpoint of anthropology and is indeed right that if we build our anthropology solely on relation and, above all, on the relation between God and man, we cannot say everything about man, either on an empirical or philosophical basis. At the same time, when our only source is Scripture, and on this basis, we would like to formulate our dogmatic argument for *imago Dei*, we can simply conclude, like Barth, that our createdness as "man and woman" is indeed a community. In other words, the question is first of epistemological nature and concerns the main principles of our dogmatics, and only secondly becomes methodological as a result.

However, one point of Barth's *imago Dei* interpretation finds a common positive resonance in the theological reception to this day, and this is the Christological focus of his approach.[86]

---

[81]   Waap: *Gottebenbildlichkeit und Identität*, 176.
[82]   Waap: *Gottebenbildlichkeit und Identität*, 176.
[83]   Waap: *Gottebenbildlichkeit und Identität*, 177.
[84]   Waap: *Gottebenbildlichkeit und Identität*, 244.
[85]   Waap: *Gottebenbildlichkeit und Identität*, 244.
[86]   Waap: *Gottebenbildlichkeit und Identität*, 249–250.; K. Stock, "Die Funktion an-

b. Latent Natural Theology?

Barth often raises the suspicion that, although he has sharply argued against natural theology in the debate with Brunner, "Barth has a natural theology on the basis of a biblical core."[87] The charge first collapses at the point where Barth consistently starts from the sovereign election of God, who has free will for grace and election ("*Gnadenwahl*"), i. e. predestination.[88] Part of the same set of ideas is the supralapsarian idea of God's plan, since all fundamental decisions of man are part of this plan, and the fall (as we have seen) is merely an "incident." Thus, the question if it there had been no fall, one might as well be perfect, becomes completely meaningless since the fall is not a contingent event.

My second argument is the Christological nature of Barth's doctrine of creation. In the traditional view of creation, when it is regarded as the work of the Father alone, it is possible to speak of man as a being left to himself after creation. This is how deism will be possible, and consequently, this leads to a subjective image of man, that we can support with different philosophical anthropologies. Yet the closed system of Christology with a special aim, in which the covenant of grace is effective, excludes the widespread speculation about man's nature. Barth does not wish to pursue a theology that seeks its foundation and causes in human religious consciousness and experience. If a human being is interpreted in the light of the election of Christ, it is possible "to develop an anthropology that places less weight upon some generic description of 'nature' or 'human nature'." [89]

My third argument concerns the covenant. The very moment, when Barth interprets creation as part of the covenant of grace, he eliminates possible traces of a covenant of nature or natural theology from the history of creation. Creation is also part of prevenient grace, and it is the work of the same covenantal God throughout, who later enters a relationship with

---

thropologischen Wissens in theologischem Denken – am Beispiel Karl Barths," *ET* 34 (1974); Macdonald: "The *Imago Dei* and Election," 326.

[87] C. Brown, "Karl Barth's Doctrine of the Creation," *Churchman* 76 (1962) 2, 104. Such criticisms of Barth are detailed by N. Arner: "Precedents and prospects for incorporating natural law in Protestant ethics," *Scottish Journal of Theology* 69 (2016) 4, 375–388.

[88] Barth, *Church Dogmatics* IV, 63.

[89] K. Oakes, "The Question of Nature and Grace in Karl Barth: Humanity as Creature and As Covenant-partner," *Modern Theology* 23(2007) 4, 600.

man over and over again in history. That is why there is no point in an idea of man without a relationship with God.[90]

c. Created as Man and Woman – The Issue of Analogies

I presume the most serious and legitimate criticism lies in the problem of analogies. On the one hand, Barth is consciously avoiding any *analogia entis*. He has good cause for this, not only in order to evade the traps of natural theology, but also to develop to the extreme the principles of personal partnership and reciprocity – that is, the covenantal idea. On the other hand, analogies offer themselves, as they appear in well-known Old Testament and New Testament images. The relationship between man and woman is already appearing in the Old Testament and frames the metaphor by which Scripture illustrates the story of the covenant. Paul's image of Jesus Christ as a man and his Church as a woman is also well known.[91] Scripture is open to speak the language of typology, one of the classic examples of this is the covenant. But while Scripture can prescind from them, Barth often pulls the pattern of analogy on concepts that are bit suitable for this purpose. For example, the relationship within the Trinity, which is such a serious element, that I will discuss the subject in more detail in an additional point.

The *analogia relationis* is by Barth "a strictly dual and personal principle." Even if we interpret a relationship between a man and a woman as merely a community relationship, it is problematic that not all relationships are "dual" (let alone a relationship of love). In fact, postmodern network theory now proves the immeasurability of social formations. Nevertheless, Barth goes beyond that in some places, and he understands the male-female relationship not only as an analogy to the relationship between God and man as I and Thou, but also at the level of sexual relations. He talks about how the relationship between Yahweh and Israel in Scripture *horribile dictu* is depicted as "an erotic relationship."[92]

At first sight, it seems an internal contradiction that, while Barth clearly sees the relationship between man and woman as a relationship of love, he denies that the story of the creation of man includes the prototype

---

[90] K. Barth, *Church Dogmatics* III/3, London 2006, 49–51.
[91] Barth, *Church Dogmatics* III/1, 190.
[92] Barth, *Church Dogmatics* III/1, 322.

of marriage.[93] He also denies that the story of Paradise legitimates monogamy. In my view, Barth is right on these issues, indeed the text does not speak implicitly or explicitly about marriage or the rules of marriage.

However, Barth is no longer so consistent in correcting the principle of analogy on the basis of revelation, and not the other way around, so he could have avoided getting involved in strange self-contradictions even in relation to the man's supremacy. [94] He stresses in vain, that the dual is "the presupposition" of the "plural,"[95] yet it cannot show the qualitative difference of community from the individual.

d. The Issue of the Covenant within the Trinity

Barth sees in the relational analogy the antitype of the covenantal relationship between God and man the divine existence within the Trinity. The eternal decree comes into being within the Trinity, and that decides on the whole covenant of grace. Thus "the inner basis of the covenant is [...] the eternal covenant which God has decreed in Himself as the covenant of the Father with His Son."[96] The question also comes up within exegesis, since Barth refers in case of the plural in Genesis 1:26 ("Let us") to the Old Church interpretation, which clearly considers the Trinity to be the subject of the plural verb. Barth is more cautious, talking about a joint act, but at the same time refers to the joint action of the persons of the Trinity, which manifests itself in the I-Thou relationship.[97]

However, the duality of the I-Thou relationship in the case of the Trinity raises serious concerns, which Thorsten Waap points out in detail.[98] Barth uses the term "modes of being" instead of "person," which does not solve the question, but the Holy Spirit is degraded to a principle that connects the Father and the Son. This seems to be justified by Barth's summary of the idea of the relationship between *imago Dei* and the covenant, in which he states that God created man not as a solitary being, but as functioning in a community – because he is not unique himself, but

---

93   Barth, *Church Dogmatics* III/1, 328–329.
94   Waap: *Gottebenbildlichkeit und Identität*, 237.
95   Barth, *Church Dogmatics* III/2, 41.
96   Barth, *Church Dogmatics* III/1, 97.
97   Barth, *Church Dogmatics* III/1, 192.
98   Waap, *Gottebenbildlichkeit und Identität*, 226.

inherently connected and commune "as the Father of the Son and the Son of the Father He is Himself I and Thou, confronting Himself and yet always one and the same in the Holy Ghost."[99]

When Barth so arbitrarily draws the pattern of dual personalism in the doctrine of creation to the divine relationship within the Trinity, he is in serious contradiction with his later thoughts stated in the doctrine of reconciliation. Barth bids farewell to several Calvinist theological traditions in the Church Dogmatics IV, with a comprehensive criticism of 17th century federal theology. Thus, he touches on the thesis by Cocceius about the inner divine covenant, the so called *pactum salutis*, which is the plan or covenant for salvation.[100] The idea of a decree between the first and second person within the Trinity, the Father and the Son, he quite simply calls a "mythology," "for which there is no place in a right understanding of the doctrine of the Trinity as the doctrine of the three modes of being of the one God, which is how it was understood and presented in Reformed orthodoxy itself."[101] In addition, there is a high risk of "dualism," as if two separate parties were playing a role in a contract.[102]

We know very well that the relationship between the persons of the Trinity is an extremely delicate area, and even one bad phrasing can result in the denial of the Trinity. In addition, the divine existence, decisions, and processes within the Trinity are a secret for man, in which we have little insight. Therefore, of the two approaches of Barth I certainly consider this latter, clearer idea acceptable.

6. Conclusions

Karl Barth includes *imago Dei* into God's plan for the entire covenant of grace. The covenant of grace is a covenant that is present throughout the relationship between God and man. For this relationship, God creates man to become his covenant partner. Therefore, man's image of God is expressed as a relationship. Barth sees multiple relationships through *analogia relationis* within the Trinity, which decision is the creation of man, the further history of the covenant and Christ and his Church. The basis

---

[99] Barth, *Church Dogmatics* III/2, 118.
[100] Barth, *Church Dogmatics* IV, 61–63.
[101] Barth, *Church Dogmatics* IV, 62.
[102] Barth, *Church Dogmatics* IV, 62.

for comparing of the analogy, the *tertium comparationis*, is always the personal relationship between two partners.

However, this *imago Dei* interpretation cannot go beyond the principle of personality and, above all, duality, and the main obstacle of that is that he seeks in everything that parallels with the male-female createdness, the I–Thou relationship. Therefore, Barth's covenantal approach has difficulty showing the community perspectives of the covenant. At the same time, we must take into account that the personalistic philosophy was born along the lines of very important demands at the time of the writing of *Church Dogmatics*, and that the conjuncture of contemporary philosophy with the theological language also filled a void, i.e. it was a current and modern formulation. Today, in theology, as well as in liberal arts, in postmodern thinking a broader community relationship system receives more emphasis. This idea meets a centuries old Federal Tradition of Calvinism.

Human Work as an Important Dimension of the Likeness of God

Zoltán Balikó

Introduction

We live in a complex society, and the world around us changes at an accel-erated pace. There is a constant need for reflection on how to respond to old-new phenomena from the perspective of Christian theology. Are we able to speak in a relevant manner? Can we engage in a dialogue with those disciplines that examine these social phenomena in ways declared to be objective, while being influenced by their own ideological frame-works that are often mistakenly or intentionally presented as scientific approaches? The lecture reflects on a phenomenon using the tools of Chris-tian systematic theology, which is old and new at the same time. Worka-holism has always been a part of human existence, even if the term was coined by Wayne Oates in his book (Confessions of a Workaholic) in 1971.[1] When we link this to hybrid office work, where one can work flexibly from home and in the office in positions where it is naturally possible, we already deal with a topic that is very relevant to many employees. If we consider the church related aspects, we can find quite some similarities to the pastoral service in congregations. Therefore, we can trust that our re-flection can be helpful in finding the right work-life balance, which is both actual and trendy today. We will then describe the phenomenon we have taken as an example, to reflect on it, but our elaboration will be more gen-eral compared to it, as we examine human work as an important aspect of *imago Dei*.

---

[1] Wayne Oates, *Confessions of a Workaholic. The Facts About Work Addiction*, New York 1971.

1. Workaholism in a Hybrid Office Environment

First, let us examine the phenomenon of workaholism, which is well characterized by the following statement: when someone takes pride in being mentally ill. Clearly, there are societal reasons for this, just as there are for the societal acceptance of alcoholism or other phenomena that we tend to embellish for ideological reasons rather than show them the red card immediately. The good news is that younger generations (e. g., Gen Z) place much greater importance on work-life balance than previous generations, although it is a good question if the labour market conditions in our region, where there are more opportunities to keep this balance, would remain favourable to the employees.

Let us first look at the phenomenon through the lens of psychologists. For example, Robinson defines it as follows: "an obsessive-compulsive disorder that manifests itself through self-imposed demands, an inability to regulate work habits, and an overindulgence in work to the exclusion of most other life activities."[2] In this definition, we can see the imbalance that manifests as an overriding and consuming compulsion in the life of the impacted individual. It is worth noting that workaholism has different degrees, so it is a longer journey until a person's lifestyle becomes practically unsustainable, leading to the disintegration or permanent breakdown of their social relationships.

Not all positions can reach such extremes. Rasmussen provides us with guidance in this regard: "most of them are found within the so-called knowledge-intensive professions. Within these professions, working hours are often not fixed, and it is the actual tasks rather than the clock that dictate when it is time to go home."[3] Therefore, autonomy can come at a great cost if a person lacks the internal controls that can balance periods of inevitably increased workload. Project-based work, for example, is typically like this.

The development of workaholism is not only determined by the type of occupation but also by the worldview that families can pass down from generation to generation. Barbara Killinger, for example, attempts to trace its roots back to the Calvinist foundations of American society. "The roots of workaholism lie in the old Calvinistic philosophy that work redeems the believer and that indulging in pleasure, especially the pleasures of the

---

[2] Bryan E. Robinson, *Chained to the Desk* (Kindle ed.), New York 2007, 7.
[3] Pernille Rasmussen, *When Work Takes Control* (Kindle ed.), London 2008, 90–91.

flesh, will bring eternal damnation."[4] It is not quite clear where this profound statement originated; perhaps she also read Max Weber, but it does not have much relevance to what Calvin wrote on the subject, as we will explain later. Nevertheless, family patterns can be very strong and contribute to the development of workaholism. Epigenetics has become a burgeoning field in psychology in recent years. We can read from Orvos-Tóth Noémi about how strongly these patterns influence us. "The experiences, memories, fears, and passions of our parents, grandparents, and even unknown ancestors influence our destiny as a burdensome inheritance." [5]

The term "workaholic" was coined by Wayne Oates in his book "Confessions of a Workaholic," where he also used his own life as an example. He also created a theological reflection on the phenomenon by this. An important observation from this perspective in his book is as follows: "Something less than God is treated and valued as if it were God; [...] The end result is to turn one's life over to the demonic, to become possessed – in this case by one's job."[6]

Next, we describe the development of hybrid work, which means that someone can work from home while also going to the workplace within the framework of a flexible schedule. Obviously, this is not possible in many positions. However, the COVID period has shown that many companies were able to sustain their operations using this method. This type of work has become so ingrained in these positions that it is highly questionable to advertise such positions in the labour market without the possibility of hybrid work. The graph below shows that even in 2019, several EU countries had already reached significant levels of this type of work, while there were other countries where it was not significant. However, the 2020 data show a significant increase in this level everywhere. During days of working from home, employers have much less control, which can be motivating for many individuals, but at the same time, supervision provides a sense of protection, for example, in enforcing rest breaks. Therefore, for those already prone to workaholism or those who are close to it, the risk of exacerbation increases. In the case of pastors, the strict employer control described earlier does not exist, so its positive effects that prescribe the scheduling and protection of the workforce also do not apply.

[4]   Barbara Killinger, *Workaholics. The Respectable Addicts*, New York 1992, 14.
[5]   Orvos-Tóth Noémi, *Örökölt sorsok*, Budapest 2018, 12.
[6]   Oates, *Confessions of a Workaholic*, 88.

The COVID pandemic significantly increased remote work, but there are significant differences between countries as well.[7]

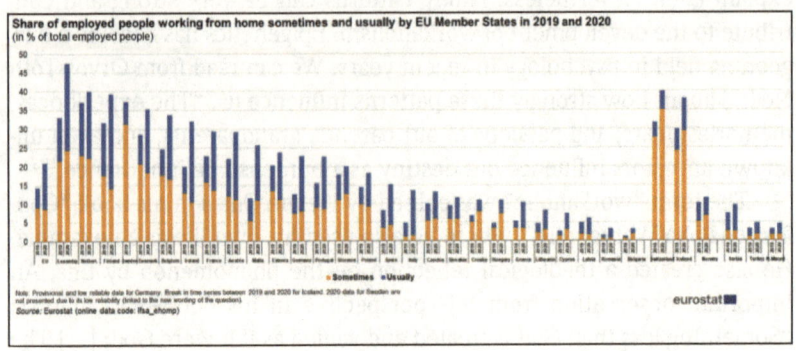

Share of employed people working from home sometimes and usually by EU Member States in 2019 and 2020 (in % of total employed people)

The following table presents the summarized results of a survey conducted in the United States.[8] It is clearly visible that workaholism has only a positive impact on a person's career, while it has very negative effects on other dimensions such as mental and physical health, and interpersonal relationships. Perhaps in many workplaces, this type of behaviour is still commendable, and short-term interests often override long-term risks. However, it is evident that workaholism has particularly detrimental effects on mental and physical health, as well as interpersonal relationships. In the next part of the study, we will argue for the statement in our title, namely, that work is an important aspect of our *imago Dei*. We will do this by also reflecting on the negative effects that hybrid work has had on the risk of workaholism.

2. Why is Human Work an Important Aspect of Imago Dei?

If we give the common response in Protestant theology, it is because of "order of creation." However, it is important to be cautious before generalizing too much, as we immediately find ourselves dealing with the question of the relevance of natural theology and a major theological debate of

7 Eurostat, *Share of employed people working from home sometimes and usually by EU Member States in 2019 and 2020.*
8 *InsuranceQuotes, The Inner Workings of a Workaholic,* https://www.insurance-quotes.com/business/the-inner-workings-of-a-workaholic (accessed: 03.03.2023.).

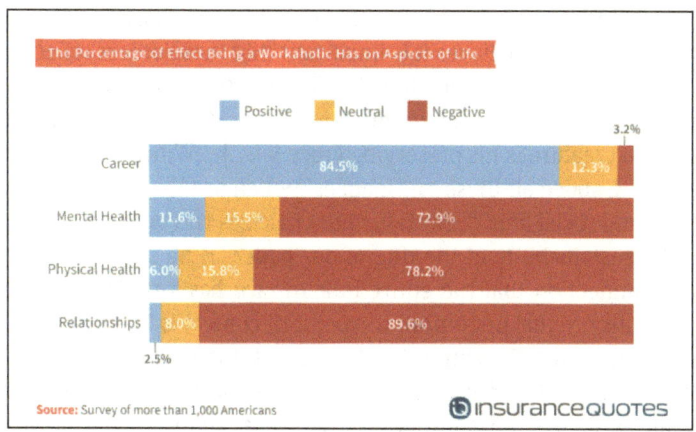

the previous century (Barth versus Brunner). As Brunner formulated, although these orders are severely damaged due to the Fall, they still reflect God's will, such as marriage, work, or the state, and must be approached accordingly. "They must be preserved – so far as their content is concerned [...] All the orders, the created orders no less than the sinful 'orders,' are, in their historical form also revelations of human sinfulness and godlessness."[9] Focusing on work, we can read the following: "It is a God-given 'calling' for the service of our neighbour. In this service the creator is honoured and only in obedience to His will does labour really become service."[10]

Barth connects human work to God's providence in the usual way, in which man is a "co-worker." We can consider this parallelism as one aspect of *imago Dei*, although we will see later that Barth did not write with this intention. "As God sees to His creature, and cares for it, in order that it may not cease as the object of His love, He requires of man the action corresponding to this care and providence."[11] We can also find his definition of work as an activity that arises from existence. "Work simply means man's active affirmation of his existence as a human creature."[12]

During the unfolded debate between them, Barth fundamentally questions who would be capable of defining these "orders." "Who among us,

---

[9]   Emil Brunner, *The Divine Imperative*, Philadelphia 1937, 216.
[10]   Brunner, *The Divine Imperative*, 388.
[11]   Karl Barth, *Church Dogmatics – III.4. The Doctrine of Creation*, Peabody 1951, 517.
[12]   Barth, *Church Dogmatics – III.4. The Doctrine of Creation*, 518.

who are 'sinners through and through' decides what they are?"[13] On the other hand, Brunner believes it is important that these orders reflect God's presence, showing that even after the Fall, He does not abandon His creation but preserves it through them. "The manner in which God is present to his fallen creature is his preserving grace." [...]. "Within this preserving grace belong above all those 'ordinances' which are the constant factor of historical and social life."[14] Barth further criticizes this which raises doubts about the sustainability of the title of our paper, as he questions the very point of connection that the entire human race has lost. "Thus, Brunner returns to his original definition: the point of contact is 'the formal' imago Dei which not even the sinner has lost, the fact that man is man, the humanitas."[15] In his Church Dogmatics, he links work ordained by God to Christian existence and not in a general sense, and work has no general interpretation or necessity outside of this. "The work of man is in fact commanded by God in the context of his true and essential service as a Christian." [...] "No independent meaning of work, no intrinsic necessity, can be proved in the framework of Christian ethics."[16] Barth's experiences with Nazism may have influenced this debate, particularly regarding the role of the state. However, Bonhoeffer insists that we can talk about these orders and does so in a strongly Christocentric way, using the term "mandate" instead of "order." He also emphasizes "Not the Christians who shape the world with their thoughts, but Christ who shapes people to be like Himself."[17] "The world exists in its relationship with Christ, whether it knows it or not [...] This connection is concretized in certain God-given mandates [...] work, marriage, authority, and the church."[18] This Christocentric approach is also evident when focusing on work. "Work is divine solely because God gave the command and His promise regarding work in relation to Christ."[19] So, we must be cautious when connecting work to imago Dei, but we can also be bold, like Bonhoeffer, in looking to Christ, which helps us overcome the trap of the relevance of natural theology.

[13] Karl Barth – Emil Brunner, *Natural Theology*, Eugene 2002, 86–88.
[14] Barth – Brunner, *Natural Theology*, 28–29.
[15] Barth – Brunner, *Natural Theology*, 86–88.
[16] Barth, *Church Dogmatics – III.4. The Doctrine of Creation*, 523.
[17] Dietrich Bonhoeffer, *Etika*, Kolozsvár 2021, 68.
[18] Bonhoeffer, *Etika*, 48.
[19] Bonhoeffer, *Etika*, 49.

3. Let Us Examine the Janus-faced Nature of Work!

In connection with Bonhoeffer, using the concept of "mandate," but at the same time we confront the general theological belief that the world of work has been and will always be distorted due to the Fall. The first thought is that work itself is not a punishment for the Fall, as Richardson states: "It must be emphasized that work is God's intention for mankind entirely apart from sin."[20] We can connect this with Westermann's explanation based on Genesis 2, where the connection of work to the *imago Dei* is strongly articulated. On the one hand, this represents humanity's responsibility towards the created world, and on the other, it reflects the blessings that unfold as the world of work becomes complex: "It is meant rather in the sense of the other classic form of dominion, that of kingship. It means the full responsibility of the ruler for the welfare of the people and country entrusted to him."[21] And also states: "God's blessing, active in success, accompanies this branching out, and all human work can participate in it."[22]

Volf, on the other hand, speaks about alienation in relation to work and defines it as follows: "... significant discrepancy between what work should be as a fundamental dimension of human existence and how it is actually performed and experienced by workers."[23] It is important to mention that, unlike Marxism, he sees the cause of alienation not in work itself but in the deterioration of man's relationship with God. "The fundamental form of alienation cannot be alienating work, but alienation from God."[24]

Moltmann tries to put work in perspective by considering the development of human societies, which has brought about the possibility for work to become a means of self-realization. However, it has also been a burden and a tool of exploitation for large masses of people. For example, he writes about premodern societies: "Meaningful life existed only outside of work [...] Work did not liberate; it enslaved."[25] In modern societies, there is a kind of identification with work that can cause serious psychological trauma if that possibility is somehow compromised. "It is also un-

---

[20] Alan Richardson, *The Biblical Doctrine of Work,* London 1963, 23.
[21] Claus Westermann, *Elements of Old Testament Theology,* Atlanta 1982, 98.
[22] Westermann, *Elements of Old Testament Theology,* 99.
[23] Miroslav Volf, *Work in the Spirit. Toward a Theology of Work,* Eugene 2001, 157.
[24] Volf, *Work in the Spirit,* 163.
[25] Jürgen Moltmann, *On Human Dignity,* Minneapolis 2007, 487.

derstandable that for many people life becomes meaningless when they are unemployed or must do work to which they cannot relate."[26] In current social conditions, the possibility of meaningful work becomes important. However, this relationship often reflects the peculiar situation of the intellectual class, as many still work on assembly lines despite automation. For them, self-realization may not come from work itself, but rather from the financial security and leisure time it provides, allowing them to engage in activities that are meaningful and liberating for them.

4. The Usability of the Approach to "Vocation" and New Possibilities

In relation to work, the Reformation brought about a changed understanding of vocation, and after the primary focus on the calling of priesthood, a more general interpretation of vocation emerged that could provide a sense of calling to many occupations. Let us examine this through the thinking of Luther and Calvin!

In the case of Luther, the usage of terminology undergoes changes, but according to Althaus, we can say that "After 1522 he also uses Beruf synonymously with station (Stand), office or function (Amt), and duty (Befehl)."[27] Accordingly, his relationship to the calling of priesthood, especially the monastic vocation, changes, as "His doctrine of vocation presupposes that the monastic ideal has already been overthrown from within."[28] God demands different life paths from different people, in which they can fulfil goals corresponding to their calling and build God's kingdom, whether in ecclesiastical or other occupations. "The same works are not required of everyone; rather, each has different works according to his station and vocation."[29]

Calvin affirms that in choosing work, the Christian individual obeys the word of God, as summarized by Biéler: "A person's work is nothing but a futile restlessness as long as he has not accepted God's call addressed to him or her."[30] They must find this calling for themselves based on God's word, and in this, Calvin introduces an expressed new aspect, as he questions the monopoly of transmitting parental vocation. "It is possible to

---

26 Moltmann, *On Human Dignity,* 493.
27 Paul Althaus, *The Ethics of Martin Luther,* Minneapolis 2007, 39.
28 Gustav Wingren, *Luther on Vocation,* Eugene 2004, viii.
29 Althaus, *The Ethics of Martin Luther,* 40.
30 André Biéler, *Calvin's Economic and Social Thought,* Geneva 2005, 356.

change station and calling."[31] Parents should not divert their children from "a truly spiritual choice of occupation."[32]

However, since Luther and Calvin, societal conditions have changed significantly, leading individuals' choices in different directions, and it is becoming increasingly difficult to speak of vocations. Instead, we see a multitude of scope of activities of jobs that exist for only a few years before transforming, and individuals bring their skills to the labour market, which is then utilized by employers in various ways and in circulation at an ever-accelerating pace. Jürgen Moltmann, with keen insight, saw this earlier: "In a working society of interchangeable workplaces and jobs, that vocational ethos disappears. At its best this society gives people a multiplicity of opportunities for change. At its worst it forces people constantly to re-learn. It requires flexibility, adaptability, willingness to change, and imagination, but not loyalty to vocation and employer."[33]

By looking through a Christian lens, we can raise questions about the direction and goals of societal change. Beyond the fact that we must always live out our individual and communal belonging to Christ within the context of a given society, there is still something special about how Christians choose to apply their individual abilities, which are correlated with the charisms received for service. In this regard, we can connect with Moltmann's thinking: "In its works worldwide Christianity follows its divine cáll and fills the whole world with the charismata of the new creation; reformation is the beginning of the eschatological reformatio mundi."[34]

It is also crucial that individuals' self-evaluation or worthiness should not be monopolized by their current situation in the world of work, whether they are students, active individuals, or temporarily inactive for some reason. "No one has to justify himself through work. No one has to demonstrate her right to existence through work!"[35] Workaholism narrows the individual's perception of reality and measures everyone solely based on their current job or work capacity. Alternatively, we can understand that people can participate in societal processes in various ways, and work is one aspect of this. "Work shall be understood as 'active participation' in the social process."[36]

---

[31] Ronald Wallace, *Calvin's Doctrine of the Christian Life,* Eugene 1997, 154.
[32] Biéler, *Calvin's Economic and Social Thought,* 356.
[33] Moltmann, *On Human Dignity,* 628–629.
[34] Moltmann, *On Human Dignity,* 596–597.
[35] Moltmann, *On Human Dignity,* 698–699.
[36] Moltmann, *On Human Dignity,* 724–725.

If we follow this line of thought, we can also turn to one of Moltmann's disciples, Miroslav Volf, who dedicated a whole book to the theology of work. In this book, he states: "Charisma is not just a call by which God bids us to perform a particular task, but also an inspiration and gifting to accomplish that task."[37] It is worth noting that we receive our talents from God for the benefit of others as well.[38] In modern terms, we can refer to them as soft skills. It is essential that using these charisms (grace gifts), they can become actions that follow God's will. Volf makes a bold statement, assuming a connection between the multitude of available job positions and the simultaneous presence of various charisms given by God to Christians. Undoubtedly, they facilitate experiencing work as a renewed calling and address the issue of alienation described earlier. However, their fundamental significance is derived from the new creation, not from their applicability to the current social context. "Paul presupposes both a diachronic and synchronic pluralism of charisms ... The diachronic plurality of charisms fits the diachronic plurality of employments or jobs in modern societies."[39]

Witherington, drawing from Moltmann and Volf, further explores the possibilities given by charisms. He correctly distinguishes between these gifts and work/vocation, describing them as a kind of capacity. "The Spirit gives gifts to everyone, and these gifts equip people for various forms of service ministry, and work. But the gifts are not the work or vocation."[40]

In agreement with Volf, he concludes, "The Spirit Christianizes work." "This automatically eliminates certain jobs for Christians."[41] The question of which jobs can be performed by Christians has accompanied ethical history, excluding certain occupations for them (e. g., warfare) or being less prominent in a particular era. From the perspective of workaholism, we can also ask whether it is acceptable for a Christian to engage in work that has a detrimental effect on their mental well-being. However, in the example provided, many people work in those job positions without be-

---

37 Volf, *Work in the Spirit,* 114.
38 Ferenc Szűcs, *Teológiai Etika,* Budapest 1993, 168. "First and foremost, it is important to emphasize the primacy that our talents are gifts from God, not only for our own benefit but also for the benefit of the smaller and broader community."
39 Volf, *Work in the Spirit,* 116.
40 Ben Witherington III, *Work. A Kingdom Perspective on Labor,* Grand Rapids 2011, 37.
41 Witherington, *Work,* 37.

coming workaholics. Therefore, the crucial factor in this regard is not primarily the nature of the job but the attitude towards it and the relationship experienced within it.

5. Life is More Than Just Work

This may be the most important message in reflecting on workaholism. While work is an important aspect of the *imago Dei,* despite all its contradictions as seen in the Barth-Brunner debate, it is also a mandate, in agreement with Bonhoeffer, that highlights its significance in relation to Christ. However, human redemption does not depend on work, but as Moltmann notes, "This means that man has been liberated from the coercive power of works (*necessitates operum*). Man does not have to make himself. Rather he demonstrates his new being out of God by doing free works."[42] At this point, it resonates with Barth's opinion as well. "Such a total life of work is not only not commanded but actually forbidden. For work can have in life only secondary significance. Its only meaning can be to set men free to participate in the service of the Christian community."[43]

Therefore, let us encourage those who overload themselves and their surroundings with workaholism to seek healing for themselves. As Christians, they can find tasks that align with their calling and liberate themselves from the compulsions associated with work.

[42] Jürgen Moltmann, *Theology of Play,* New York 1972, 46.
[43] Barth, *Church Dogmatics – III.4. The Doctrine of Creation,* 518.

PRACTICAL THEOLOGY

Imago Dei in Preaching
Theological Warrant for More Active Involvement of the Listeners[1]

Enoh Šeba

Preaching is typically an integral part of almost every church service – and for some Christian traditions, it is the focal point of their public worship and ecclesial identity. As such, its purpose has always been to communicate in order to edify, encourage, and enlarge the positive effects of congregating together as a people of God. Why, then, is the subjective perception of the listeners sometimes so different, if not completely opposite from its intended goals? This inconsistency is even more intensified by its relative invisibility – the congregants attend the service Sunday after Sunday, and as they bring their expectations along, they listen to sermons that create impressions and evoke responses that are usually not easily expressed, especially if they are not too positive.

These and similar concerns were often based on observable facts and regular preaching practices in different church traditions and began to dominate the homiletical discussion and continued to do so during the larger part of the 20th century. Roughly speaking, around the mid-20th century, the majority of preachers, especially those within Protestantism still followed the Barthian standpoint that the Word of God comes only from above and cannot arise from below.

Barth is very straightforward when he says: "Revelation is a closed system in which God is a subject, the object, and the middle term."[2] Within this system, a preacher faithfully reproduces the Word he or she hears, but there is no place for invention since "… it [Word of God] owes

---

[1]   Significant portions of this paper have been previously published as a part of the monograph *Sermon Listening. A New Approach Based on Congregational Studies and Rhetoric* (Carlisle: Langham Monographs 2021) and are here reproduced by permission of Langham Publishing.
[2]   Karl Barth, *The Preaching of the Gospel*, Philadelphia 1963, 12.

nothing to man's ingenuity; he can only bear witness to it."[3] The proclamation of God's truth does not require "vain images" or "outpourings of sentimental eloquence" on the preacher's part.[4] Preaching cannot be seen as "a joint action by two collaborators. It is the exercise of sovereign power on the part of God and obedience on the part of man."[5] The sole purpose of preaching is to confess the Word of God.

Yet the empirical reality showed that such a clean, fully theological approach to preaching was impossible because sermons are always and inevitably embodied. The dwindling church attendance was visible evidence. Thomas Long suggests that at this point many preachers have rediscovered the argument that Emil Brunner used in his dispute with Barth. He believed that the gospel can meet a human being *only* in its particularity and in specific situations.[6] And this encounter requires a much stronger attention paid to the listeners. This is a key reason why the major homiletical trend in the latter part of the previous century became generally known as the "turn to the listener."

Put briefly, scholars have accurately identified the lack of dialogue and the inferior position of the listeners as the root of sermons' inefficiency, experientially and repeatedly detected by both preachers and hearers in various contexts. A number of authors have suggested different homiletical reconstructions that have often been consolidated by insights from other disciplines, such as human communication theory, psychology, or literary criticism. Some of these contributions have effectively helped to build a new paradigm for preaching, one that respects the listeners by creating inductive movement in sermons, by incorporating dialogical principles, or by placing a stronger emphasis on acquiring a "thick" understanding of the actual listeners' world. It also has become clear that in taking this turn, homiletics can not only still learn from its ancient ally, rhetoric, but also receive valuable lessons from younger disciplines, such as congregational studies.[7]

---

[3]   Barth, *Preaching*, 82.
[4]   Barth, *Preaching*, 12–13.
[5]   Barth, *Preaching*, 16.
[6]   T. G. Long, "And How Shall They Hear? The Listener in Contemporary Preaching," *Listening to the Word: Studies in Honor of Fred B. Craddock*, in G. R. O'Day – T. G. Long (eds.), Nashville 1993, 167–188.
[7]   Within the scope of this paper, it would be impossible to elaborate on all of those authors and their contributions. Nevertheless, I will mention only several of them whose work has proven to be ground-breaking or stimulative for further developments in the field: D. G. Buttrick, *Homiletic: Moves and Structures*, Philadelphia

Over time it became clearer that the prospects of closing the gap between preachers and their hearers can improve only insofar as the hearers are allowed to voice their concerns, convictions, and perspectives *by themselves*. And as various researchers then began to conduct empirical studies focused on those on the receiving end of sermonic communication, it has become evident that the preaching practice can experience qualitative transformation only when the input from the listeners is earnestly taken into account within its particular context.[8] Therefore, the contemporary homiletics largely relies on a descriptive approach that focuses on a particular *Sitz im Leben* of the preaching practice in question.

However, my purpose in this paper is to show that this redefinition of the listeners' role can also be supported by substantial theological and scriptural authentication. Preaching is essentially a Christian practice and, by definition, an exercise of Christian faith enacted within (although not exclusively) and by a Christian congregation. If, on the other hand, theology is a conceptual discourse with a threefold task that Elaine Graham and others have termed as helping the *"formation of character,"* "building and maintaining the *community of faith*," and "relating faith-community's own

---

1987; F. B. Craddock, *As One without Authority*, Nashville 1979; R. L. Eslinger, *A New Hearing: Living Options in Homiletic Method*, Nashville 1987; L. L. Hogan – R. Reid, *Connecting with the Congregation: Rhetoric and the Art of Preaching*, Nashville 1999; R. L. Howe, *Partners in Preaching: Clergy and Laity in Dialogue*, New York 1967; J. Jeter – R. J. Allen, *One Gospel, Many Ears: Preaching for Different Listeners in the Congregation*, St. Louis 2002; J. S. McClure, *The Four Codes of Preaching: Rhetorical Strategies*, Louisville 2003; R. D. James, *The Renewal of Preaching*, Philadelphia 1969; C. H. Reid, *The Empty Pulpit: A Study in Preaching as Communication*, New York 1967; L. T. Tisdale, *Preaching as Local Theology and Folk Art*, Minneapolis 1997.

[8] Although space does not allow for a detailed overview of all these studies, a very useful guide can be found in D. Rietveld, "A Survey of the Phenomenological Research of Listening to Preaching," *Homiletic* 38/2 (2013), http://dx.doi.org/10.15695/hmltc.v38i2.3867. Interestingly enough, the geographical location of these studies is highly diverse. For example, one is done in Denmark – M. R. Lorensen, *Dialogical Preaching: Bakhtin, Otherness And Homiletics*, Göttingen 2013, another in Madagascar – H. Austnaberg, *Improving Preaching by Listening to Listeners Sunday Service Preaching in the Malagasy Lutheran Church*, New York 2012, a third one in Holland – T. Pleizier, *Religious Involvement in Hearing Sermons: A Grounded Theory Study in Empirical Theology and Homiletics*, Delft 2010, and yet another in the USA – J. M. Martin, "Preaching for the Listener: Does Vineville Baptist Church in Macon, Georgia, Prefer Logos, Pathos, or Ethos in Connecting with Sermons?" (Diss. Mercer University; 2011), http://search.proquest.com/pqdt/docview/864740931/abstract/CEA9F964C1C24725PQ/1.

communal identity to the surrounding culture,"[9] then proving that such theological warrant can be provided and sustained would mean that the whole practice of preaching might be reinvented as a vital dimension of congregational life, with formidable unifying and formative potentials. For that purpose, I will focus on the well-known doctrine of *imago Dei*.[10]

Imago Dei – Introduction

If we accept that every sermon is essentially an effort to establish and maintain a communication between God and human beings, then the pressing issue is: What does it take to turn this effort into a meaningful contact between the Divine and those made in the divine image? This becomes even more intriguing if the listeners are perceived as embodied, visible images that nonetheless refer to something beyond them that is invisible. If we expand the initial question, then it can be asked: What are the consequences of the fact that those who are to be addressed by God through a sermon are already created in the image of that same God and are the bearers of His likeness?

The biblical motif of the human as created in the image and after the likeness of God is mentioned only at three places in the Old Testament: Genesis 1:26–27; 5:1–3; 9:6. Yet, it caused a number of heated issues among distinguished theologians and biblical scholars since the earliest days of Christian theology: Is the "image of God" to be understood as a reference to the primary human condition and "likeness" as a description

---

Special attention should be given to the study *Listening to Listeners*, conducted in the USA and resulting in four volumes: R. J. Allen, *Hearing the Sermon: Relationship, Content, Feeling* (Channels of Listening), St. Louis, MO 2004; J. S. McClure – L. S. Bond – D. P. Moseley – G. L. Ramsey – R. J. Allen – D. P. Andrews, *Listening to Listeners: Homiletical Case Studies* (Channels of Listening), St. Louis, MO 2004; M. A. Mulligan – D. Turner-Sharazz – D. Ottoni Wilhelm, *Believing in Preaching: What Listeners Hear in Sermons* (Channels of Listening), St. Louis, MO 2005; and M. A. Mulligan – R. J. Allen, *Make the Word Come Alive. Lessons from Laity* (Channels of Listening), St. Louis, MO 2005.

[9] E. L. Graham – H. Walton – F. Ward, *Theological Reflection. Methods*, London 2005, 10.

[10] Elsewhere I argued that there are other two doctrines – namely, the doctrine of the priesthood of all believers and Incarnation – that contribute to the same theological backup for a stronger involvement of listeners. E. Šeba, *Sermon Listening. A New Approach Based on Congregational Studies and Rhetoric*, Carlisle 2021, 219–230.

of the ultimate state at the end of history? Was this image just corrupted or utterly annihilated by the Fall? What else, apart from baptism, can help its restoration?

A significant amount of ink has been used in identifying that single point of likeness between God and humanity that defines this image. Of course, scholars have also been keen to determine what this image consists of. In the past, they usually pointed to some of the human faculties – be it reason, conscience, or freedom – or particular endowments, such as dominion over other creatures. More recently, though, authors such as Daniel Migliore question those traditional insights. For instance, the longstanding emphasis on human reason (he says) "fostered an intellectualization of Christian anthropology," resulting in a "depreciation of the emotional and physical dimension of human existence." On the other hand, the concept of dominion over the creation corresponds to the worldview of hierarchical relationships whose consequence can be exploitation, especially of nature. And the stress on human freedom as the content of that image, says Migliore, in this contemporary culture too often coincides with mere independence from others or even with sheer self-gratification.[11] So, my intention here is to offer a brief overview and account of the doctrine that both incorporates insights from more contemporary theologians and suggests some solid homiletical implications.

Imago Dei – Relational Model

To start with, let me point to the interesting grammatical detail: in Gen 1:26–27, God's decision to create humans is accompanied by an abrupt change to a grammatical plural ("Let us make man in our image, in our likeness"). Also, the very first biblical reference to *imago Dei* underlines the fact that humanity is created "male and female." This reality moved Plantinga and others to signalise that the 20th-century "theologians such as Barth, Brunner, and Bonhoeffer took this gendered qualification of humankind as a key interpretive principle in order to emphasize a more social and relational theological anthropology."[12] In this view, claims

---

[11] D. L. Migliore, *Faith Seeking Understanding. An Introduction to Christian Theology* (3rd edition), Grand Rapids 2014, 144–145.
[12] R. J. Plantinga – T. R. Thompson – M. D. Lundberg, *An Introduction to Christian Theology*, Cambridge 2010, 186.

Migliore, human existence inevitably "reflects the life of God who eternally lives not in solitary existence but in communion."[13] Furthermore, this male-female duality could (and perhaps should) be read as a paradigm for the diversity of relationships defined by our race, gender, gifts, or ethnic identities. The *imago Dei* thus implies certain mirroring of ways in which the divine Persons relate to each other. *Imago Dei* also holds a capacity for living a life with the "other" being the chief interest of our actions and behaviour.

Pannenberg reasons in a similar way when discussing the notion of human personhood as related to the *imago Dei*: "We can attain to the totality of our own lives, notwithstanding its fragmentary form, only in the relation to our Creator. But we achieve our particularity in our encounter with others. Both types of relations are in their own ways constitutive for our individual personhood."[14] The divine immanence is thus profoundly involved in and tied to our relationships with our fellow humans. This relational concept then invites humanity to a life of mutuality and dialogue that is initiated and propelled by God's act of creation. What is even more significant, it also results in an active responsibility of the bearers of *imago Dei*: "humanity is called to reflect God's likeness and character in the range of its relationships – not only to be the visible image of God (noun) in creation, but also to image God (verb) concretely in all of its tasks and activities."[15] By creating human beings in his image, God addressed them and entangled them in this God-relationship.

Imago Dei – Representational Model

However, this line of interpretation is not the only viable reading. It can perhaps be complemented with another model, the one that brings the representational dimension to the forefront. Plantinga and others understand the image of God in Gen 1:26–27 as referring to the custom of Near-Eastern rulers who would erect statues with their image in the territories under their rule. Thus, human beings are to be viewed as God's living statues with a representational function. Their reading of the passage suggests that the image can only be understood as including the entire human

---

[13] Migliore, *Faith*, 145.
[14] W. Pannenberg, *Systematic Theology II*, Grand Rapids 1994, 200.
[15] Plantinga – Thompson – Lundberg, *Introduction*, 190.

being (and not some of its capacities) and implying that "the general human vocation has a sacramental quality about it, pointing beyond itself to the reality of God." Equally important, the bodily aspect of human existence is not to be ejected from the image of God "since the function of an 'image' resides in its visibility."[16]

This interpretation goes along almost perfectly with Moltmann's idea of humanity's double identity.[17] In Moltmann's reading of the Genesis creation account, human beings are certainly given a transcendent identity by virtue of being created in the image of God. But humans also have an immanent identity as creatures made in the image of the earth. These identities make humanity distinct from the rest of creation and yet humans still share enough creatureliness with the nonhuman creatures so as not to have a basis for dominating or exploiting nature. In addition, this location at the intersection of immanence and transcendence turns human beings into priestly mediators between God and the creation. We represent God to the creation through the *imago Dei*, but we also represent the earth to God through the *imago mundi*.

Imago Dei – New Testament Perspective

Naturally, this actualises the necessity to introduce the New Testament perspective on the Genesis material. The epistles, especially those from the Pauline corpus, repeatedly depict Jesus Christ as the image of God (2 Cor 4:4; Col 1:15; also Heb 1:3). He is presented as the true and exact image to which human beings, although bearers of the *imago Dei* by creation, must conform (Rom 8:29; Col 3:9-10; 2 Cor 3:18; Eph 4:22-24; 1 Cor 15:49). The New Testament clearly underscores that the restoration of the image of God is absolutely necessary and possible only through Jesus Christ. The question is: What is the nature of the relation between Christ's perfect likeness to God and our likeness imprinted on us by creation? In other words, what is the relationship between our creation and our redemption? Of course, the necessity of redemption derives from the reality of human sin and its effects on the *imago Dei*.

Throughout history, theologians have offered various answers – usually by describing the different degrees of damage caused by the Fall. For in-

---

[16]   Plantinga – Thompson – Lundberg, *Introduction*, 184–185.
[17]   J. Moltmann, *God in Creation*, Minneapolis 1993, 185–190.

stance, Calvin agrees with Augustine in his assessment that man's natural gifts (such as the soundness of mind and the integrity of heart) were corrupted by sin, while his supernatural gifts (such as "the light of faith and righteousness") were entirely withdrawn. Drawing both on the history of human thought and the biblical witness, Calvin affirms that the human mind continues to seek the truth "to which it never would aspire unless some relish for truth antecedently existed." He also acknowledges the existence of diverse gifts, as expressed in the manual and liberal arts, which are distributed to all human beings by their Creator. Although these "have ceased to be pure to polluted man," they cannot be "polluted in themselves in so far as they proceed from God." And in their diversity, continues Calvin, "we can trace some remains of the divine image distinguishing the whole human race from other creatures." On the other hand, in matters of spiritual discernment – the knowledge of God, the way of salvation, and the righteous conduct of life – human beings are left blinded as a result of the Fall and are in a need of enlightenment by the Spirit. So, even though the proper knowledge of God requires supernatural intervention ("when the Spirit ... forms the ear to hear and the mind to understand"),[18] Calvin still seems to imply that this act of God includes the *renewal* of human capacities that are already present in every person, albeit corrupted and inadequate in their present state.

Of course, there are also other, more radical interpretations. Perhaps Karl Barth's reasoning is a suitable example. When discussing the knowability of God and man's readiness for God,[19] he maintains that man has lost the "conformity to God," that is, that there is no point of contact between God and man, and hence no possibility of receiving God's Word. The reason for that is, according to Barth, the fact that "the image of God is not just ... destroyed apart from a few relics; it is totally annihilated." Therefore, a person may be open to God, but that does not mean he or she is ready for God. Given that, as a result of the Fall, a human being always keeps "an indivisible remainder of enmity against the grace," the only possibility for knowing God opens up in Jesus Christ, a real man and Son of God – in Him, God is knowable to Himself and also to human beings. In his campaign against the natural theology of his time,[20] Barth is

---

18 J. Calvin, *Institutes of the Christian Religion*, Peabody 2008, 165, 168, 169, 170.
19 K. Barth, *Church Dogmatics* I.1 (2nd edition), Peabody 2010, 239–241.
20 Natural theology, in his words, begins and ends with "the affirmation that even apart from God's grace, already preceding God's grace, already anticipating it, he

anxious to demonstrate the superiority of the theology of revelation. Hence, the Word of God comes to us only when "the knowability of God which is bestowed upon us in His grace is received and accepted as such by us."[21] By faith, people can then participate in Christ's person and work. In that sense, it could be maintained that, for Barth, the *imago Dei* is defined almost exclusively in christological terms:

> The image of God in man of which we must speak here and which forms the real point of contact for God's Word is the *rectitudo* which through Christ is raised up from real death and thus restored or created anew, and which is real as man's possibility for the Word of God.[22]

Also, theologians have tended to explain the Fall by employing the doctrine of original sin, as maintained by Augustine. Thus, all sins have their shared source in the Fall and all humans receive that sin, as Migliore explains, "by virtue of the common stock into which they are born (i. e., human nature)."[23] However, some contemporary scholars have tried to revise this doctrine by arguing that the *imago Dei is* affected both by "propensity" toward sin, shaped by our being born into a sinful world corrupted by structural and societal sins, and by our actual sins.[24]

At the same time, other scholars also show that the Bible never implied that the Fall distorted this perfect first estate or that the *imago Dei* ever included immortality. Some of them indicate on exegetical grounds that Paul "ascribes immortality only to the second eschatological man."[25] According to their understanding, the fullness of the image of God historically occurs only with Christ as the end of an ongoing process. Believers can then participate through character formation and a transformation into the likeness of Christ that not only restores the *imago Dei*, but also places them into a new, unprecedented relationship of intimacy with God. This agrees with the relational model according to which the *imago Dei* describes human life as the totality of its relationships. Consequently, the distortion of the *imago Dei* through sin corrupts three basic human rela-

---

[the human being] is ready for God, so that God is knowable to him otherwise than from and through Himself." Barth, *Church Dogmatics* II.1, 135.

[21] Barth, *Church Dogmatics* II.1, 161.
[22] Barth, *Church Dogmatics* I.1, 239.
[23] Migliore, *Faith*, 198.
[24] Plantinga – Thompson – Lundberg, *Introduction*, 194–203.
[25] Pannenberg, *Systematic Theology II*, 213.

tionships – with God, with one another, and with nature. Basically, these corruptions can then be seen as consequences of the sinful attitudes: "our acts of sin express attitudes of either excessive self-love or stultifying self-loathing. That is to say, we sin both 'above ourselves' and 'beneath ourselves'."[26]

From the New Testament perspective, the remedy for all sin thus can be seen in the fullness of the image of God that historically occurs only with Christ. Believers can participate in that fullness through character formation and a transformation into the likeness of Christ. This process not only restores the original *imago Dei*, but also places them into a new, unprecedented relationship of intimacy with God, leading to eternal life. This agrees with the relational model according to which the *imago Dei* describes human life as the totality of its relationships. But more importantly, it proves the continuity between the *imago Dei* inscribed in human beings at the point of creation and the likeness of Christ which is to be educed in every believer until the very end.

Imago Dei – Its Homiletical Implications

Perhaps there is no need to follow Barth's distinct division between creation and redemption. Perhaps we were created for communion and communication with God in the first place, so the restoration of the human ability to hear and respond to the Word of God through Christ's redemption is not an *utterly different* act of the *same* God. Also, if we decide that the *imago Dei* can be seen as a work of "preliminary" grace bestowed upon humans in the act of creation, then human experience as the point of contact does not need to be located outside God's grace. Similarly, the reality of creation can be conceived as the initial act of God's revelation to be followed by revelation in Jesus Christ. Having said all that, I am inclined to agree with Pannenberg as he comments on the NT perspective by saying that, in Paul's statements about Christ as the image of God,

> ... the Christian doctrine of the divine likeness must see an elucidation of our general destiny of divine likeness. But in so doing it may not expunge the differences between the fulfilling of our divine likeness in and by Jesus Christ on the one hand, and the OT statements about Adam's divine likeness on the

[26] Plantinga – Thompson – Lundberg, *Introduction*, 201.

other. To do this is to miss the point that our destiny as creatures is brought to fulfilment by Jesus Christ.[27]

Now, what can be made of these theological considerations? I believe that several answers are relevant for my purposes here.

First of all, unless understood in terms of total depravity, the doctrine of *imago Dei* always reveals something in humans that effectively points to God. As a result, the act of preaching has a potential for meaningful communication because there is an inherent possibility of contact between God and human beings. Given that the *imago Dei* encompasses the entire human being, the listeners' experience is a fully-fledged candidate for being the location in which this contact will be established. Nowadays several studies are showing the importance of identification or recognition on the part of listeners as that key ingredient for a successful homiletical communication.[28] And that ingredient is usually found when the preacher manages to strike a chord with something in his hearers' personal experience. Thus, the listeners' experience should never be considered as something subjective, volatile, or nugatory. Instead, it should be viewed as a realm in which momentary glares of the *imago Dei* can be seen as they fall on the soil of the *imago mundi* and from which numerous sermons could find their beginnings, points of contact, or cruxes.

Secondly, the relational character of *imago Dei* affects both preaching and listening in manifold ways. For example, there are qualitative studies conducted among sermon listeners that show how for some participants sermon listening is a fundamentally communal experience, during which a sense of connectedness (or its absence) with fellow believers and the preacher decisively shapes their involvement with the sermon.[29] This phenomenon can be better understood by referring to this social constitution of the image of God in those listeners.

Also, if the diverse nature of humanity is carved into an *imago Dei* at the point of creation, then human beings can hope for the restoration of

---

[27] Plantinga – Thompson – Lundberg, *Introduction*, 210.
[28] For instance, C. A. Loscalzo, *Preaching Sermons That Connect. Effective Communication through Identification*, Downers Grove, IL 1992. His argument is largely based on Kenneth Burke's rhetoric concentrated around the idea of identification – see K. Burke, *A Rhetoric of Motives* (new edition), Berkeley 1969.
[29] See, for instance, my study conducted among Croatian Baptists: E. Šeba, *Sermon Listening*, 141–147, but also the very extensive study *Listening to Listeners* (especially the Mulligan – Allen, *Make the Word*).

that image only when they live in dialogue and exchange with other humans. With that in view, it is easy to realize where the basic human need to be heard and understood comes from. Taking their seats on Sunday morning, the listeners come to listen in order to hear that they have been taken seriously and to have their questions, fears, and hopes recognised by their preachers, but also by God. I doubt that any of that can happen unless the preachers infuse their preaching with a dialogical attitude.

And this is why Don Browning, a practical theologian, is right when he qualifies listening as the most evident expression of love and terms it "an act of descriptive theology – an act that in itself witnesses to God's grace in creation and redemption."[30] This is also why preachers should take to heart Lori Carrell, human communication scholar, and her assessment that studying the "text" of the listeners is equally important as studying the biblical text[31] and intensify their deliberate efforts in the former activity. This is also a reason why Leonora Tubbs Tisdale's invitation to preachers to exegete their congregations by employing congregational analysis in their daily involvement with the congregants aims at developing a listening stance that will allow them to get to know their listeners better and to incorporate the world of their listeners into their sermons.[32]

At the heart of all preaching should be an awareness that every hearer has been created after God's likeness, and the appreciation of this reality should be manifested in the preacher's practice of preaching. Sharing the image of God with her hearers, a preacher will show her closeness to them by preaching in a way that discloses her honest work of hearing and understanding them. In other words, the preacher's respect for common participation in *imago Dei* with their listeners should take the form of careful listening to them *before* preaching to them.

Thirdly, an earnest acknowledgement of the *imago Dei* adds to the eschatological aspect of preaching. The history of God's dealings with humanity, which reached their climax in Jesus Christ as the perfect image of God, represents a continuous movement of God's promises and salvific ac-

---

[30] D. S. Browning, *A Fundamental Practical Theology. Descriptive and Strategic Proposals*, Minneapolis 1991, 286.

[31] L. Carrell, *The Great American Sermon Survey*, Wheaton 2000, 209–210.

[32] L. T. Tisdale, "Exegeting the Congregation," *Teaching Preaching as a Christian Practice: A New Approach to Homiletical Pedagogy* (eds. T. G. Long – L. T. Tisdale), Louisville 2008, 75–89 and L. T. Tisdale, *Preaching as Local Theology*.

tions whose ultimate purpose was to re-establish God's blessing of the creation. And that blessing was originally intended to take place through that "general human vocation" derived from the *imago Dei*. Correspondingly, preaching should acknowledge the image of God in the listeners and encourage them to continue their journey toward their eschatological destiny which is the full actualization of the *imago Dei*. To reach that destiny, however, the sermon listeners must experience a need to have their character reformed in order to conform to the character of Christ.

Fourthly, the very practice of preaching and listening at once testifies that the preachers' speaking and the listeners' hearing are surely cognitively impaired by sin. But that same practice also reveals the redemptive grace of God at work in preaching that uplifts and intensifies the present transformation as a precursor of the eschatological full conformation to *imago Christi*. This spiritual and moral betterment of all participants in the preaching practice seems to be in direct correlation to the homiletical give and take between the hearers and their preachers, no matter how flawed it may be in our present circumstances. Their mutual collaboration is therefore an expression of their anticipation of the time when their perfected characters will be capable of perfect communication. Until then, the preachers should help this process of character formation by their vigorous integration of the listeners' perspectives, by treating their listeners' experiences seriously, and by allowing their various voices and concerns to be heard and evaluated, believing that this is their joint participation in the re-establishment of God's original blessing of all peoples.

Conclusion

I believe that the doctrine of the *imago Dei*, as exposed above, lends a plausible theological validation of the more active involvement of the listeners in preaching practice. This doctrine requests a proper appreciation of the believers' present state, which is made possible by God's act of creation, and of their individual experience of life as a result of this divine image still being operative in them. What follows is that *imago Dei* endorses preaching that respects the hearers' experience and acknowledges their worlds as spaces where they, as bearers of the image of God, will most successfully co-create the meaning of sermons. On top of that, whenever the listeners come to listen with the expectation to be changed, we can be reminded that through the formation of their characters, they will have their *imago Dei* renewed and *imago Christi* fostered on their way to taking the fullness of the image of God. In that sense, dialogue and interaction as a part of preaching service stands as a harbinger of future full communion and perfect relationships with one another, creation and God.

Restoring the Image of God?
A Theological Perspective on Pastoral Care

Theo Pleizier

Introduction

In Christian theology the idea of *imago Dei* captures something of the uniqueness of human beings. Humans are created in the image of God. Not surprisingly, it often plays an important role in theological proposals.[1] However, *imago Dei* is not the only theological idea; its cognate is the "soul." In Western theology both ideas became intrinsically linked, the soul was conceived of "as the seat of the likeness to God."[2] In contemporary theology, however, this identification of the image of God and the soul has become highly problematic. Not in the least because the very idea of the soul has become problematic.

In this paper I explore the relationship between these two theological ideas. There is an intriguing connection between soul and *imago Dei*. About the soul we could say that the soul is wounded, stained or bruised. In mystic spirituality there is the experience of the dark night of the soul (John of the Cross). Likewise, in post-Fall humanity we acknowledge that the image of God is severely damaged, the mirror is broken, the likeness is gone. "Soul" as well as the "image of God" share the same theolog-

---

[1] In his theological studies, the Dutch theologian Gerrit C. Berkouwer summarized theological anthropology with the notion "Image of God;" see Gerrit C. Berkouwer, *De mens het beeld Gods*, Kampen 1957 (Translated into English as *Man. The Image of God*, Eerdmans 1962). Emile Brunner likewise starts his theological anthropology with the theme of the mystery of humanity and refers to creation and its contrast by referring to the image of God, cf. Emil Brunner, *Der Mensch im Widerspruch. Die christliche Lehre vom wahren und vom wirklichen Menschen*, Zürich 1965, 85–167.

[2] Kevin Vanhoozer, "Human Being, Individual and Social," in Colin E. Gunton (ed.), *The Cambridge Companion to Christian Doctrine*, Cambridge 1997, 164.

ical diagnosis of brokenness and failure. To explore this connection between soul and *imago Dei* I turn to the field of pastoral care and counselling. There are two reasons for this approach. First, the discipline of pastoral care and counselling could be helpful to understand the distinction between the theological ideas. Pastoral care can be conceived of as religious practice that is specifically interested in *restoring* the image of God. Second, in pastoral care and counselling the "soul" is a more prominent idea. In contemporary German we still have the term "Seelsorge" (soulcare) which refers to the traditional practice of *cura animarum*. Pastoral care is one of the central practices in Christian communities. Workers in churches are often designated as "pastors" and the pastoral vocation has many facets, with respect to multiple actors involved in pastoral activities and with regard to the many forms of pastoral care in local churches. The focus in this paper is therefore on the restorative function of pastoral care as an ecclesial practice. This function is resembled in the older term "cure." *Cura animarum* has the double meaning of "care" and "cure." There is something in us humans that needs to be cured. This "something" does not only concern our physical and mental health and wellbeing; the cure of souls has to do with the mystery of being human: made in the image of God.

In the paper I proceed as follows. First, I present a few practical-theological thoughts on human reparation. Next, two contemporary approaches in pastoral care literature are introduced to explore how contemporary pastoral care and counselling deals with human repair. Finally, these two approaches are contrasted with an approach that aligns with a theology of retrieval.

Are Humans in Need of Repair?

The world is full of evil. Most of it is of human making. There is something wrong with humans living together and humans engaging with the non-human world. Wrong-doing and evil, however, do not involve moral categories only. Christian theology speaks about the need for a religious restoration. The restoration involved concerns the relationship between God and humans. The analytic theologian Eleonore Stump uses a medical term like "healing" to explain what is needed for repairing post-Fall humans.[3]

---

[3] Let us refer to this state of "being damaged" as to the post–Fall conditions of hu-

It may be the case that the "image of God" is only a marginal concept in the Biblical creation story, it does play quite a central role in the Pauline understanding of salvation. To be saved is to be taken into the restorative work of the Spirit who restores us in the likeness of Christ. As it often is the case with "healing," the reparation of the marred image of God in us requires something or someone beyond ourselves. In Christianity, Christ is the one who embodies the relatedness in the most unique and alienable way. In the words of the apostle Paul: Christ is the image of God from the beginning (Col 1:15). And as Paul proceeds, he explains that we are called to take on the new humanity, to be renewed in the image of our Creator, to become Christ-like (Col 3:15). In other words, for Paul our created humanity, Christology and the renewal of human beings are intrinsically linked.[4]

At these Pauline crossroads of post-Fall humanity, the story of Jesus, and salvation as the renewal of humans, I locate my practical theological contribution. Practical theology is concerned with religious practices. Religious practices are empirical realities. They belong to the created world. They consist of actions of humans, patterns of behaviour in communities and traditions that have a long history. Preaching is such a tradition, as well as pastoral care. In religious practices, creation, Christ and salvation come together. The empirical world reflects creation, the world that is willed by God and shaped by humans. Practices are rooted in human existence. Yet there is more to religious practices.

Christian religious practices are grounded in a narrative that defines their ultimate meaning. Jan-Olav Henriksen talks about the story of Christ.[5] He uses the language of memory: our practices recall the story of Jesus. For example, celebrating the Lord's Supper always evokes the memory of Christ's death and resurrection. Preaching the gospel reminds us of the good news and Christ who is at its centre. If practices could be understood as *meaningful* and *collaborative* actions in relation to the *material* world, the story of Jesus relates to all three aspects. The actions are meaningful because they refer in some way to the life, death and resurrection of Christ: the breaking of bread, the coming together as disciples of Jesus

---

mankind. For the post–Fall condition and the need for repair in medical terms as "healing," see Eleonore Stump, *Atonement*, Oxford 2018, 178–180.

4   Chris Kugler talks about "Christological monotheism" in Paul; see Chris Kugler, *Paul and the Image of God*, Lanham 2020.

5   Jan-Olav Henriksen, *Christianity as Distinct Practices. A Complicated Relationship*, London 2019.

and the reading of the Scriptures that testify about Jesus. These actions are collaborative in the sense that they are expressions of the body of Christ and they shape a new community that comes together in the name of Jesus. They are embedded in the material world: church buildings tell the history of the community of Christ and express both in the exterior and the interior how the story of Jesus is connected to this space, and celebrating the Lord's supper involves sharing the materiality of bread and wine, the symbols of Christ's life-giving death.

Third, religious practices serve a salvific purpose.[6] This aspect especially emerges from ecclesial practices: the preaching of the Word, the sacraments, worship, and practices of care.[7] Those are the practices that are believed to communicate God's forgiveness; they bring us into the realm of atonement, grace and the promise of renewal. In other words, religious practices have a restorative function, the aim for healing of the divine-human relationship.

In sum, practices can be understood as aiming for repair, being grounded in creation and the material world and in the story of Jesus. In the second part of the essay I exemplify this for one particular ecclesial practice: pastoral care and counselling, or even better: the care of souls.

Pastoral Care as Restorative Practice: Contemporary Examples

Churches engage in restorative practices. Restorative practice is a wider-used term and it includes practices that foster reconciliation and peace making. I take it in this broad sense but in view of the central anthropological idea of humans being created in the image of God. It goes beyond the scope of this essay to reflect on restorative practices in relation to restorative justice and reconciliation within societies, and I confine myself to contribute to a further understanding of the interface of theological anthropology and pastoral theology in relation to restoration.

---

6   James Nieman uses the concept of "purpose" to analyse the dimensions of practices, cf. James R. Nieman, "Why the Idea of Practice Matters," in Thomas G. Long, Leonora Tubbs Tisdale (eds.), *Teaching Preaching as a Christian Practice. A New Approach to Homiletical Pedagogy*, Louisville 2008, 18–40. In his theory of religion, Martin Riesebrodt points to this salvific purpose of religious practices, see Martin Riesebrodt, *The Promise of Salvation. A Theory of Religion*, Chicago 2010.

7   I use the term "ecclesial" to denote a specific set of Christian practices.

Pastoral care addresses the fundamental brokenness in human existence and aims to contribute to healing and restoration. The relationship between pastoral care and restorative practice, however, is a complicated one that is related to the fundamental problem in practical theology involving the theory-practice relationship.

We should be aware of two different directions in the theory-practice relationship. The first direction is *theoretical*. A theological theory on human brokenness, such as hinted at above in the introduction, expresses a certain understanding of what this brokenness entails. For instance, in her book on atonement Eleonore Stump uses a term from Thomas Aquinas, the "stain of the soul."[8] Likewise, theological theories on original sin, on shame and guilt or on suffering provide different, sometimes but not always mutually excluding understandings of human brokenness. Pastoral care practices then are designed and performed to address these kinds of brokenness. When brokenness is theologically understood as guilty behaviour that is in need of forgiveness, the resulting practice will be that of private confession and absolution. The second approach, however, takes its lead from those practices. Its direction is *practical*. Practices themselves also embody understandings of brokenness. In other words, the practise itself is theory-loaden. Practical theology is less interested in dogmatic groundings of the practice. Its interest is in lived faith, lived religion or actual ecclesial practices. Hence, the actual practice itself entails a reconstruction of brokenness and restauration. Understandings and experiences of restoration are embedded in the practice. For instance, when pastoral care consists of practices of confession and absolution, this calls forth a theology of guilt and forgiveness.

Hence, pastoral care practices can be generated by specific theological convictions, but they also generate their own theologies. This is a given ambiguity in the theory-practice relationship. Literature that describes pastoral care practices often entails a certain understanding of care as restorative practice. I test this suggestion by comparing two different approaches in pastoral care and counselling. I take my starting point in a pastoral care classic, Howard Clinebell's *Basic Types of Pastoral Care and Counselling* (first edition 1966). Second, I look at a contemporary proposal, Carrie Doehring's postmodern approach in her work, *The Practice of Pastoral Care* (first edition 2006). These two examples exemplify the shift in pastoral care paradigms from therapy to narrativity.[9] Supposedly, they provide

---

[8]   Stump, *Atonement*, 40.

[9]   These paradigms are further discussed in Theo Pleizier, "Psychologie en narra-

different reconstructions of pastoral care as restorative practice by providing different reconstructions of the wrong that is in need of repair. In the analysis I focus on the question how these approaches view change, transformation or improvement in pastoral care practices.

Therapy: Pastoral Care as Counselling in Crises (Howard Clinebell)

As one of the fathers of the counselling movement, Howard Clinebell is known for his *Basic Types of Pastoral Care and Counselling*, written in the sixties of the 20th Century, revised and reprinted many times.[10] Being aware of the secular times that were emerging in the western world, Clinebell wrote about the need of the church to be relevant. This had implications for his understanding of pastoral care: "the only relevance that really matters is relevance to the *deep needs of persons* – relevance to the places in their lives where they hurt and hope, curse and pray, hunger for meaning and thirst for significant relationships."[11]

For Clinebell, pastoral care and counselling contributes to healing and growth of human beings. To explain this, Clinebell introduces the notion of change. Pastoral care aims "to integrate intrapsychich and interpersonal healing and growth with constructive change in the wider structures and institutions of people's lives."[12] Clinebell explicitly locates pastoral care and counselling in the Christian church. He calls his model a "holistic liberation growth model" and applies it in three directions by distinguishing between pastoral care ("the broad, inclusive ministry of mutual healing and growth within a congregation and its community"), pastoral counselling ("a variety of healing [therapeutic] methods to help people handle their problems and crises more growthfully") and pastoral psychotherapy ("long-term, reconstructive therapeutic methods when growth is deeply diminished by need-depriving early life experiences or by multiple crises in adult life.")[13]

---

tiviteit in het pastoraat. Overwegingen bij de terugkeer van de ziel," *Kerk en Theologie* 70 (2019), 118–130.

[10] Quotations are from the first edition of his work, Howard John Clinebell, *Basic Types of Pastoral Counselling*, Nashville 1966.

[11] Clinebell, *Basic Types*, 14.

[12] Clinebell, *Basic Types*, 18.

[13] Clinebell, *Basic Types*, 26.

In his work, Clinebell often refers to biblical sources to understand the specific role of pastoral ministry in the church and he takes a client-centred approach when it comes to the spirituality of those who are being offered pastoral support. In his own words: "pastors serve the valuable function of helping people fathom and appropriate personally their religious traditions' wisdom about life's meaning."[14]

Though the therapeutic approaches focus upon needs, problems and crisis, in one of the chapters of his book, "Facilitating Spiritual Wholeness" (Chapter 5), Clinebell also addresses the pastor in his or her role as a theologian: "as theological counsellors – the function of pastors is to nurture the growth of persons toward a more mature (in tune with spiritual reality) faith and a more vitalizing, growthful relationship with God." At this point in his work, Clinebell seems to leave a more crisis-oriented approach to pastoral care.[15] At the same time, however, he remains within a therapeutic paradigm, with a preference to growth-language. Growth is a positive counterpart of restoration. Rather than stressing the deficient, Clinebell focusses upon the potential. Potential meaning in his view an inner feature of the human psyche.

At the end of the day, however, it remains to be seen whether the relationship with God is also in need of repair. Yet Clinebell hesitates. He is deeply impressed by what he calls the "inner crippledness and interpersonal destructiveness that flourish in individuals, in relationships and in society." But he rejects the theological idea of the "fall," understood as "some deep irreparable flaw in our humanity that irreparably sabotages all our strivings toward wholeness" and points at the same time at the limits of pastoral care counselling in those situations in which it seems "totally ineffective." Clinebell thus provides a very realistic approach to the limitations of pastoral counsellors, however skilled they might be. Other professions have skills for those situations. In Clinebell's framework, however, there does not seem to be conceptual space for redemption or salvation as an act of God that transcends therapeutic skills and competencies. From the practices described by Clinebell and the pastoral practice he envisions, growth is the counterpart of repair. The dominant framework is positive psychology. The pastor's role does not seem to deal with a broken image of God that is in need of repair beyond human making.

---

[14]   Clinebell, *Basic Types*, 104.
[15]   About the notion of "crisis" in pastoral care theory, see Theo Pleizier, "Ordinary Pastoral Care. Deconstructing the Concept of 'Crisis' in Practical Theology," *International Academy of Practical Theology. Conference Series* 3 (2023).

What about the current developments in pastoral care? Does pastoral care aim to contribute to the restoration of human beings in relation to God? In her work titled *A Practice of Pastoral Care. A Postmodern Approach* Carrie Doehring adopts a narrative approach.[16] Just as drama, literature, and film use images, metaphors, and symbols artistically to convey what is unique yet also universal about life and death, storytelling in pastoral care often searches for ways to connect with God, humanity, and creation amidst pain, suffering, and the everyday trials of life.[17] Storytelling is the main method. Besides narrativity, however, two aspects are particularly relevant in Doehring's work: "intercultural care" and "caregiving relationships." First, she puts intercultural care against confessional care. Pastoral care aims at the creation of meaning which relies upon the culturally embedded and appropriated practices and values. Further, she stresses important features of the caregiving relationship: compassion, power dynamics, reflexivity, confidentiality, relational boundaries. For Doehring, the two aspects of intercultural care and caring relationships are intertwined: "[W]hen care seekers trust that caregivers will respect what is unique about their religious beliefs, values, and spiritual practices then cocreation of meanings and practices can begin."[18]

What does this mean for our question to understand the nature of restoration and the contribution of pastoral care practices? Here Doehring's reflections on change in the pastoral care relationship is important. Change is understood in the widest possible sense; it includes individuals, communities, structures, and – depending upon one's theology – even God. More specifically, though, intercultural spiritual care is about identifying the lived theologies embedded in care seekers' stories. How is this theology live-giving or life-limiting? What theology – emotionally charged values, beliefs, and spiritual practices – do care seekers want to live out?[19]

Ultimately, its goal is "liberative integration of the care seeker's core values, ultimate beliefs, and spiritual practices, which emerge from the

---

16   References concern the second edition of Doehring's book, Carrie Doehring, *The Practice of Pastoral Care. A Postmodern Approach*, Louisville 2015.
17   Doehring, *Practice of Pastoral Care*, xiv.
18   Doehring, *Practice of Pastoral Care*, 1.
19   Doehring, *Practice of Pastoral Care*, 8.

care seeker's narrative."[20] "The goal of spiritual care is liberative spiritual integration that aligns practices, beliefs, and values in ways that liberate persons, families, and communities."[21] This understanding of change works with an "action-reflection-action" method and change happens when "pastoral relationships help people integrate and embody *spiritual practices* that foster goodness and compassion with *beliefs* and *values* complex enough to account for suffering – one's own and the world's."[22]

In her book, Doehring proposes a model for planning care that consists of three phases: building trust through compassion, mourning losses and fostering accountability, reconnecting with the goodness of life.[23] These three phases reflect the importance of stories as a meaning making process and point to the centrality of relationships, when dealing with loss, violence or stress. It is in the final phase that Doehring points to "moments of experiencing goodness," often "theologically interpreted as glimpses of eternal life or epiphanies."[24] (185). She concludes that one of the roles of caregivers is to help the care seeker recognize and cherish such moments and find strategies to experience them increasingly through spiritual and religious practices, individually and within communities of faith.[25]

Doehring's method offers a fresh, contemporary approach to pastoral care. She offers a theological perspective by integrating the religious beliefs and the moral values that are relevant in pastoral situations. In doing so, she continues to operate within a therapeutic paradigm of care givers and care seeker, and pastoral care practices are concerned with troubling situations in human lives (loss, violence and stress). She emphasises the importance of the relationship between care giver and care seeker with help of notions such as trust, compassion and safety. More importantly, theology is a source for guidance and coping. Yet the relationship between a human being and God is not assessed in personal and relational terms. Though not of conceptual necessity, her construction of the intercultural and the confessional seems to contribute to not opening up this dimension.

---

20 Ibid.
21 Doehring, *Practice of Pastoral Care*, 15.
22 Doehring, *Practice of Pastoral Care*, 17–18.
23 Doehring, *Practice of Pastoral Care*, 173–186.
24 Doehring, *Practice of Pastoral Care*, 185.
25 Doehring, *Practice of Pastoral Care*, 186.

The two examples of Clinebell and Doehring represent two paradigms of pastoral theology. The paradigms of therapy and narrativity hardly offer an integrated perspective on Christology and theological anthropology. More specifically, they do rarely provide a perspective on a type of restoration that concerns the divine-human relationship. To put it more theologically, if Christ came to save us by restoring our humanity in relation to God, it seems that contemporary pastoral approaches have little to offer. However, that does not mean that the paradigms of therapy and narrativity should be rejected. For decades, they have proven that they add important tools to the pastoral wisdom of the church. Yet as any other paradigm, they have their own limitations. From a theological point of view, these limitations easily run into reductions. To put it less in terms of deficiency, the church has pastoral wisdom beyond therapeutic and narrative approaches. So, we may need to turn to different pastoral sources to understand how pastoral care practices contribute to restoring the blurred, marred, broken, or lost image of God in human beings.

A methodical note will be helpful here. What does justify the jump from contemporary, modern sources into the history of pastoral care? If a jump at all, it should not be an uncritical jump. Two motifs are relevant. The first methodical motif goes against reductionism. If contemporary sources do not address issues that have been dealt with in the rich history of pastoral theology, this could point to at least two directions. First, the issues are not relevant anymore and bypassed by current knowledge. Second, the issues may be relevant, but contemporary authors select other topics to engage with. With respect to a pastoral interest in restoring the image of God in humans, it seems that the second direction fits the contemporary literature. As any practical theological discipline, pastoral care and counselling is a very contextual discipline. The issues at stake and the topics authors address are very much connected to the contextual situation that they engage with. Modern pastoral approaches find themselves in a very intercultural context. This accounts for the selected topics. If this is a sound analysis, sources that address other topics should not be neglected. It would be a sign of methodical reductionism to leave aside sources, both contemporary and historical, that address different issues. Hence, going back to historical sources may be in order.

The second methodical motif takes its lead from the current literature on the so-called "theology of retrieval." Bushart and Eilers use "retrieval" for a style of theological discernment "that looks back in order to move forward." They cite John Webster who talks about "an attitude of mind."[26] This attitude of mind has to do with response, a theology that puts itself in the position of *responding* to God's grace that is always prior to our thinking and doing. Or as Buschart and Eilers put it:

> while the moment at hand faces the theologian with challenges and opportunities, her response is generated by unembarrassed recourse to the doctrinal, liturgical, and spiritual assets of the Christian tradition. Such recourse is many times not uncritical, but it is nonetheless caused by the theologian's mindfulness of her place in the middle of a tradition of faith from which forgotten, lost or unappreciated resources wait to be recruited.[27]

The motif of retrieval opens a dialogue with the past and challenges the pastoral theologian to look for resources that may have been neglected. The call for a pastoral theology that seeks to restore the image of God would be a candidate for retrieval.

The literature on pastoral care occasionally moves out of the boundaries of modern paradigms. Though its style is a bit polemic, Thomas Oden opens up the history of pastoral care in his *Care of Souls in the Classic Tradition*.[28] He mentions 19th century authors such as Alexander Vinet and Washington Gladden but his main argument is to go back to the times of the Early Church: Cyprian on patience, Tertullian on the soul, Chrysostom on priesthood, Ambrose on responsibility and the many pastoral works of Augustin. Another type of window to the history of pastoral care is opened by the German practical theologian Jürgen Ziemer. In his work titled *Seelsorgelehre*, Ziemer describes the changes in pastoral care and counselling through the Christian ages. "Changes" could suggest progress, but that is not how Ziemer refers to the pastoral past. He describes pastoral care as "war against sin" (Early Church), "sacrament of confession" (Middle Ages), "comfort" (Luther), "shepherding" (Swiss Reformation), "edification" (Pietism), and "formation" (Enlightenment), respectively. Rather than leaving behind the previous phases in the fog of history, Ziemer proposes that "every epoch emphasizes an important aspect of the entire understanding of pastoral care." He stresses that "none of these aspects is

---

[26] W. David Buschart, Kent Eilers, *Theology as Retrieval. Receiving the Past, Renewing the Church*, Downers Grove 2015, 12.

[27] Ibid., 13.

[28] Thomas C. Oden, *Care of the Souls in the Classic Tradition*, Philadelphia 1984.

just history."[29] Another reassessment of pre-modern practices of pastoral care is offered by Andrew Purves in his *Pastoral Theology in the Classical Tradition*.[30] I take Purves' approach as an example for a retrieval of the pastoral wisdom of the Church. Andrew Purves reads the Patristics and the Reformers in order to rediscover ancient practices of the church without copying them. "That option," Purves writes, "is hardly realistic or legitimate." In his small book he presents five classical texts, ranging from Gregory of Nazianzus, the Cappadocian Father, to Richard Baxter, the Puritan theologian.

Purves' journey in the past is a journey of retrieval. He considers the history of pastoral care as a source for theological wisdom in the present. This does not entail a move away from the 21st century to the 4th or the 15th century at the expense of losing the wisdom and insights from contemporary sources, such as the turn to the subject, the conversation skills learned from psychotherapy and the importance of narrativity. Purves' journey has two additional features. First, his choice of authors reflects a broad orthodoxy. Obviously, other voices and authors should be included in the small selection he offers. But the direction is clear: his going back to the past is not going back to Calvin or to Thomas Aquinas only; it is a retrieval of the broad Christian tradition which can easily be extended to many authors as sources of wisdom. One might ask whether something as "the classical tradition" (as the title of the book reads) exists. Yet, Purves' intuition seems plausible: there is a rich tradition of the practices of the church that approach pastoral care from the perspective of "its specific Christian identity."[31] That this tradition in fact contains *many* Christian traditions does not disqualify Purves intuition of an existing body of pastoral wisdom.

Textbooks put the therapeutic and narrative paradigms against the background of the dialectic theology in the early 20th century. The German theologian Eduard Thurneysen is often mentioned as representative of the so-called "kerygmatic paradigm" in pastoral care. The kerygmatic paradigm can also be reconstructed as a version of confessional pastoral care. We already came across the opposition between confessional and intercultural pastoral care in Carrie Doehring's work. Purves' proposal reconnects to the confessional tradition(s) of Christian pastoral care practice. To some

---

[29] Jürgen Ziemer, *Seelsorgelehre*, Göttingen ⁴2015, 50.
[30] Andrew Purves, *Pastoral Theology in the Classical Tradition*, Louisville 2001.
[31] Ibid., 2.

extent, this is a provocative aspect of a theology of retrieval, especially in the light of some interreligious and intercultural approaches. It reminds us that specific religious approaches to pastoral care do have confessional aspects indeed.

Though Purves' proposal does include a variety of Christian authors, the major issue his approach addresses is the issue of the divine-human relationship. First, Purves sounds rather critical when he writes:

> pastoral theology and pastoral practice have become concerned largely with questions of meaning rather than truth, acceptable functioning rather than discipleship, and a concern for self-actualisation and self-realisation rather than salvation.[32]

On the positive side, however, he continues by stating that the most important and provocative conclusion to come from a thoughtful reading of the classical tradition in pastoral theology is the discovery of theological realism. The classical pastoral writers really did believe that theological statements made truthful reference to God, and these statements had primary consequences for the understanding of human life and its healing and well-being.[33]

What does it mean for our theme of change and restauration? Let us listen to one of Purves classic voices, the Cappadocian Father, Gregory of Nazianzus:

> The scope of our art (namely pastoral ministry) is to provide the soul with wings, to rescue it from the world and give it to God, and to watch over that which is in His image, if it abides, to take it by the hand, if it is in danger, to restore it, if ruined, to make Christ dwell in the heart by the Spirit: and, in short, to deify, and bestow heavenly bliss upon, one who belongs to the heavenly host.[34]

Here we find a pastoral care practice that tries to do justice to the restoration of *imago Dei* in humans. Gregory's discourse is very specific. It is about giving wings to the soul, to give the soul to God, to watch over "that

---

[32]   Ibid., 3.
[33]   Ibid.
[34]   Gregory of Nazianzus, *Oration 2.22* as cited in Purves, *Pastoral Theology in the Classical Tradition*, 9.

which is in His image." He summarizes the goal of pastoral care as deification. Purves provides the following commentary on Gregory's position: "the final goal of the Christian life that pastors must have in view for their people, the purpose for which they were created, from which they have fallen away, and for which they have been recreated by Christ – is a direct and dynamic relationship with God in the life to come."[35] In other words, soulcare that aims to restore the broken image of God in human beings, is soulcare that is primarily interested in the divine-human relationship, both in the present and in the world to come.

Let me summarize the previous argument in two statements. First, *current pastoral theology has a different interest than caring for the divine-human relationship*. Change, transformation and restoration are framed within the assumptions of therapeutic counselling or intercultural narrative care. Second, *the anthropological idea of the image of God is ultimately about restoring the lost, broken or hampered connection between God and humans*. Soulcare is one of the ecclesial practices that aims for this. Ecclesial practice not only means that it is done within a faith community. It also opens up a theology of retrieval because the church is a more extended body than the current set of faith communities. To engage in restoring the broken image of God is framed within a theology that acknowledges the story of Jesus or the Christ-event as a source for healing and restoration.

Conclusion

Eleonore Stump uses the notion "union" in her account of atonement.[36] Repair of a human being in relation with God is restoring the union with God. In presenting Aquinas' view, Stump writes the following:

> The greatest good for a human being is to be in a relationship of love in union with God. [...] It is hard to see what could be a greater state for a human person than being made like God. And so full or complete union with God is an intrinsic upper limit on human flourishing.[37]

---

35   Ibid., 14.
36   Stump, *Atonement*, 115–142.
37   Ibid., 41.

This is only one way to represent the classic tradition in which reparation of the relationship with God was among the chief goals for pastoral ministry. In this essay I have argued that a "theology of retrieval" as outlined above opens up a new way to reflect upon these positions, not only for the sake of a philosophy of religion or doctrinal theology but also for practical theology. What does it mean for the church to engage in soulcare, when the soul is "stained" (again, Stump in summarizing Aquinas)[38] and when the image of God is in need of repair. The method of retrieval, however, is not an uncritical dismissal of recent practical theological approaches. Hence, two final thoughts sketch a way forward. They incorporate the insights of contemporary pastoral approaches, while taking into account a Christian understanding of reparation that takes its lead from Paul's Christocentric view of restoring the image of God; this we find reflected in the classical pastoral sources as well.

First, the counselling model that we encountered in Clinebell uses conversation skills to be sensitive to the needs of people. These skills help to listen deeply and attentively. This is a kind of priestly listening. Rather than staying on the surface of the Self and even moving deeper than the level of relational ethics, listening eventually touches upon humans' relatedness to God. Being with someone in the name of Christ may simply mean to ask "what happens or might happen between God and you in this situation." The counsellor asks for the presence of God, and the theologian in the counsellor realises that the presence of God and closeness of God is related to restoring the union between God and a human being.

Second, narrative care rediscovered the healing power of stories. These approaches often speak about the "story of God" as if God could be anyone or anything within the frame of reference of the care seeker. Thinking along with Doehring, one could say: storytelling in pastoral care searches for ways to connect with the story of Jesus. When the story of Jesus remains silent, Paul's connection between creation, Christ and salvation remains unoperative in the cure of souls. On the other hand, when the story of Jesus enters a pastoral encounter, it provides opportunities to communicate the union with God in a concrete, personal way. For in the story of Jesus, God and humans come together.

The restauration of the damaged image of God cannot be orchestrated by humans. It depends upon God. More precisely, on what God has done

---

[38]   Ibid., 40.

in Christ, in his death on the cross and in his resurrection. By attesting to the Jesus story, we may expect the dynamics of divine primacy. While such an expectation requires an attitude of faith, only in this way can we sensibly talk about souls to be cured and humans being restored in the image of God.

PHILOSOPHY, CULTURE, AND SCIENCE

Ist der Mensch ein Triebwesen?

Bernhard Kaiser

Es ist eine grundlegende Frage für die Ethik, ob der Mensch über sein Handeln frei bestimmen kann oder ob er aus welchen Gründen auch immer determiniert ist, mithin also, ob Ethik als Besinnung auf das, was der Mensch tun soll, sinnvoll ist. Ich sehe drei Faktoren, die für die (scheinbare) Unfreiheit des Menschen sprechen:

(1) Der philosophische Determinismus, dem zufolge Freiheit nicht begründbar ist, sondern bestenfalls als Idee zu stehen kommt.

(2) Der neurobiologische Determinismus, eigentlich eine Sonderform des philosophisch-wissenschaftlichen Determinismus, der einem streng naturalistischen beziehungsweise materialistischen Ansatz folgt und demzufolge alles menschliche Handeln neurochemisch determiniert ist.

(3) Der theologische Determinismus, der von der absoluten Souveränität Gottes ausgeht und seine Allwirksamkeit so auffaßt, dass der Mensch keine Freiheit hat.

Die Frage, ob der Mensch ein Triebwesen sei, mithin also die Frage, ob der Mensch von seinen Trieben oder Begierde gesteuert wird, oder ob er die Freiheit hat, über sein Handeln zu entscheiden, betrifft in unterschiedlichem Ausmaß den philosophischen und neurochemischen Determinismus. Letzterer folgt einem atheistischen und evolutionären Weltbild, demzufolge es keinen Gott oder keine geistige Dimension gibt, die in irgendeiner Form auf die materielle Dimension wirken könnte. Im Rahmen dieses Denkens steht auch das Menschenbild Freuds und seiner Schule. Das aber beinhaltet, dass die Triebhaftigkeit des Menschen Resultat einer evolutionären Entwicklung ist und also dem Menschen angeboren ist.

Ich skizziere zunächst das, was die heilige Schrift über die Triebe im Menschen sagt. Im zweiten Teil behandle ich die Aussagen Freuds und seiner Schule und gebe abschließend eine zusammenfassende Würdigung.

1. Was die Bibel sagt

Es gehört zum biblischen Realismus, den Menschen in seiner Komplexität zu sehen. Der Mensch ist einerseits Gottes Geschöpf, im Bilde Gottes geschaffen, andererseits aber in Sünde gefallen und in der Lage, seiner geschöpflichen Berufung und der geschöpflichen Ordnung zuwider zu handeln. Eignet ihm aufgrund seiner Gottesbildlichkeit Würde und Wert, so beinhaltet seine Sündhaftigkeit die Neigung zum Bösen. Ich gehe davon aus, dass die Triebhaftigkeit des Menschen zur ursprünglichen geschöpflichen Ausstattung des Menschen gehörte und vor dem Sündenfall nicht auf Böses gerichtet war, sondern dem Design des Schöpfers entsprach und gemäß der geschöpflichen Ordnung wirksam war. Mit anderen Worten, der Mensch konnte und wollte seine natürlichen Bedürfnisse im Einklang mit dem Willen seines Schöpfers stillen. Zu denken ist hier an den natürlichen Impuls zum Essen und Trinken, an den Geschlechtstrieb, an das Interesse zu gelten oder auch das Interesse, etwas zu schaffen. Mit dem Sündenfall jedoch begann der Mensch seine Begierden auch entgegen dem Willen Gottes zu stillen. Hochmut und Selbstüberschätzung, Besitzgier, Rachsucht, Vielweiberei, Völlerei und Süchte unterschiedlichster Art wurden zu Faktoren, die das Handeln des Menschen bestimmten und bestimmen, Faktoren, die im "Herzen" des Menschen angelegt wurden und die als "Gedanken" im Bewußtsein zu finden sind, um anschließend das Handeln zu steuern.

Die heilige Schrift zeigt deutlich, dass der Mensch Triebe hat. Sie spricht ausdrücklich von den Begierden des Fleisches, den *epithymiai sarkos*.[1] Mit dem Begriff Fleisch bezeichnet Paulus in der Regel die sündige Konstitution des Menschen. Man muß indes ausdrücklich unterscheiden zwischen einer gnostischen Abwertung des Leibes und dem, was unter den Begierden des Fleisches zu verstehen ist. Es wäre ein Mißverständnis, hier vornehmlich die leibliche Dimension zu sehen. Das "Fleisch" im Sinne des Paulus befindet sich im Aufstand gegen Gott; die fleischliche

---

[1] S. Galater 5,16; Epheser 2,3; man beachte die häufige Erwähnung der *epithymiai* im NT.

Gesinnung ist "Feindschaft gegen Gott."[2] Ich werde die entsprechenden Aussagen der Bibel nicht alle besprechen, sondern nur die folgende zitieren, die zeigt, auf welche Gegenstände die Begierden des Fleisches gerichtet sind: "Offenkundig sind aber die Werke des Fleisches, als da sind: Unzucht, Unreinheit, Ausschweifung, Götzendienst, Zauberei, Feindschaft, Hader, Eifersucht, Zorn, Zank, Zwietracht, Spaltungen, Neid, Saufen, Fressen und dergleichen. Davon habe ich euch vorausgesagt und sage noch einmal voraus: Die solches tun, werden das Reich Gottes nicht erben."[3]

Bekanntlich lautet das 10. Gebot: "Du sollst nicht begehren (*ouk epithymeseis; lo tachmod)*." Um den Begriff der *epithymia* näher zu bestimmen, schauen wir auf einige weitere Aussagen des Neuen Testaments. Ganz offensichtlich haben wir es mit sexueller Begierde zu tun, wenn Paulus sagt: "Wenn sie sich aber nicht enthalten können, sollen sie heiraten; denn es ist besser zu heiraten, als sich in Begierde zu verzehren."[4] Damit ist ein breiteres Verständnis des Begriffes nicht verneint. Das dürfte aus der rückblickenden Aussage des Paulus hervorgehen: "Unter ihnen haben auch wir alle einst unser Leben geführt in den Begierden unseres Fleisches und taten den Willen des Fleisches und der Sinne und waren Kinder des Zorns von Natur wie auch die andern."[5] Geht man davon aus, dass Paulus hier sein Leben als Pharisäer einschließt, dann ist der Begriff der Begierde sicherlich breiter zu fassen. Indem Paulus auf die Natur *(physis)* des Menschen Bezug nimmt, macht er deutlich, dass die Sündhaftigkeit des Menschen nicht eine akzidente und austauschbare ist, sondern eine wesensbestimmende. Ansonsten wären die folgenden Aussagen nicht wirklich verständlich.

Sehr deutlich verneint die Schrift ein Leben, das den Begierden verfallen ist, wie aus folgenden Aussagen deutlich wird: "Die aber Christus Jesus angehören, die haben ihr Fleisch gekreuzigt samt den Leidenschaften und Begierden."[6] – "So tötet nun die Glieder, die auf Erden sind, Unzucht, Unreinheit, schändliche Leidenschaft, böse Begierde und die Habsucht, die Götzendienst ist."[7] – "Denn es ist genug, dass ihr die vergangene Zeit zugebracht habt nach heidnischem Willen, als ihr ein Leben führtet in Ausschweifung, Begierden, Trunkenheit, Fresserei, Sauferei und

---

[2] Römer 8,7.
[3] Galater 5,19–21.
[4] 1. Korinther 7,9.
[5] Epheser 2,3.
[6] Galater 5,24.
[7] Kolosser 3,5.

gräulichem Götzendienst."[8] Das aber heißt, dass der Christ nachgerade nicht seiner Triebsteuerung folgen soll, sondern dem Anruf des Heiligen Geistes.

Die heilige Schrift hat also vor Augen, dass der Mensch nicht nur Triebe hat, sondern auch seinen Trieben verfallen ist. Er ist ohne den Heiligen Geist in größerem oder geringerem Maße triebgesteuert. Ziel der Triebsteuerung ist die *hedone,* also das süße Leben. Offensichtlich sieht die heilige Schrift die *hedone* kritisch.[9] Der Begriff *hedone* hat ein insgesamt recht breites Bedeutungsspektrum.

Paulus nimmt in seinem Brief an die Römer auf die Begierden des Menschen Bezug: "Darum hat Gott sie in den Begierden ihrer Herzen dahingegeben in die Unreinheit *(en tais epithymiais ton kardion auton eis akatharsian),* sodass ihre Leiber durch sie selbst geschändet werden, sie, die Gottes Wahrheit in Lüge verkehrt und das Geschöpf verehrt und ihm gedient haben statt dem Schöpfer, der gelobt ist in Ewigkeit. Darum hat sie Gott dahingegeben in schändliche Leidenschaften *(eis pathe atimias);* denn ihre Frauen haben den natürlichen Verkehr vertauscht mit dem widernatürlichen; desgleichen haben auch die Männer den natürlichen Verkehr mit der Frau verlassen und sind in Begierde *(en te orexei)* zueinander entbrannt und haben Mann mit Mann Schande getrieben und den Lohn ihrer Verirrung, wie es ja sein mußte, an sich selbst empfangen."[10] Seine Ausführungen sind Teil seiner Argumentation, mit der er die Sündhaftigkeit der Menschen aufweist – hier besonders betreffs der Nichtjuden. Die Aussagen des NT ergeben, dass der Mensch sich als Sünder vorfindet. Er muß zugeben, dass er mit seinen Trieben auf die *hedone* gepolt ist.

Aus den Paränesen des Neuen Testaments geht aber ebenso klar hervor, dass der Christ im Heiligen Geist lebt, mithin also im Glauben, und in diesem den Begierden widersteht, ja sie "kreuzigt." Paulus schreibt an Titus: "Denn es ist erschienen die heilsame Gnade Gottes allen Menschen und nimmt uns in Zucht, dass wir absagen dem ungöttlichen Wesen und den weltlichen Begierden und besonnen, gerecht und fromm in dieser Welt leben."[11] Die Begierden werden dabei nicht ausgelöscht, aber sie werden in ihrer Wirkung auf das Leben gehindert. Das aber heißt, dass

---

[8] 1. Petrus 4,3.
[9] S. 2. Timotheus 3,4; Titus 3,3; Jakobus 4,1.3; 2. Petrus 2,13.
[10] Römer 1,24–27.
[11] Titus 2,11–12.

die Begierden nicht weiter zum Lebensprinzip gehören. Sie sind da, aber der Christ hat mit dem Evangelium von Jesus Christus die Software und durch den Glauben die Kraft, gegenüber dem Anruf der Begierden Nein zu sagen, sofern sie sich gegen das Gebot Gottes richten. Mit anderen Worten, die Erfüllung der Begierden kann nicht das Lebensziel des Christen sein, ohne damit den Genuß der geschöpflichen Gaben zu verneinen. Positiv heißt dies, dass der Christ besonnen lebt, Zucht übt, auch seinem Leib die nötige Aufmerksamkeit zukommen läßt, aber doch so, dass er nicht seinen Begierden verfällt.

Martin Luther hat schon in seiner Römerbriefvorlesung 1515/1516, die ich für vorreformatorisch halte, die aber von Augustins Antipelagianismus beeinflußt ist, im Gegensatz zur römischen Lehre vom Menschen die menschliche Sündhaftigkeit in großer Klarheit gesehen. Augustin hatte bekanntlich sehr ausführlich von der *concupiscentia* gesprochen, sie als das Motiv für die Weitergabe der Sünde (Erbsünde) gesehen[12] und deren Kraft am eigenen Leibe erfahren. Luther nimmt auf die mittelalterliche Anschauung des *fomes* (Zunder) Bezug, indem er sagt: "Also ist die Tatsünde (wie sie von Theologen genannt wird) richtiger Sünde im Sinn von Werk und Frucht der Sünde, die Sünde selbst aber ist eben jene Leidenschaft, der Zunder, die sündhafte Begehrlichkeit oder der Hang zum Bösen und der Widerwille gegenüber dem Guten ..."[13] Die katholische Lehre hingegen hält den *fomes,* diese Neigung zur Sünde, nicht eigentlich für Sünde.[14] Sie betrachtet die Sünde als ein Akzidens, das nicht das Wesen des Menschen kennzeichnet, und nimmt eine quasi-intakte Geschöpflichkeit des Menschen an.

2. Freud und seine Schule

Sigmund Freud (1856–1939) beschäftigte sich mit der Erforschung von Neurosen und kam anhand der Äußerungen seiner Klienten zu der Annahme einer Sphäre des Unbewußten, die dann in den Mittelpunkt seines Interesses – der Psychoanalyse – rückte. Wesentliche Aussagen dazu finden sich in seiner Schrift *Das Ich und das Es* (1923)[15] sowie in seinen *Drei*

---

[12] Augustin, *De nuptiis et concupiscentia* I, XXIV.27 (Migne PL 44, Sp. 429).
[13] M. Luther, *Vorlesung über den Römerbrief* 1515/1516; (MüAErgBd 2, 150, WA 56,271).
[14] *Katechismus der Katholischen Kirche*, München 1993, 1264.
[15] S. Freud, *Das Ich und das Es* (Gesammelte Werke [= GW]), Köln 2014, 829–872.

Abhandlungen zur Sexualtheorie.[16] Das Es als die unbewußte, aber das Ich stets beeinflussende Schicht im menschlichen Seelenleben wurde zum Ort des Triebes. "Das Ich repräsentiert, was man Vernunft und Besonnenheit nennen kann, im Gegensatz zum Es, welches die Leidenschaften enthält."[17] Das Ich pflegt "... den Willen des Es in Handlung umzusetzen, als ob es der eigene wäre."[18]

Zur Bestimmung des Begriffes "Trieb" sagt Freud: "Unter einem Trieb können wir zunächst nichts anderes verstehen als die psychische Repräsentanz einer kontinuierlich fließenden, innersomatischen Reizquelle, zum Unterschiede vom Reiz, der durch vereinzelte und von außen kommende Erregungen hergestellt wird. Trieb ist so einer der Begriffe der Abgrenzung des Seelischen vom Körperlichen. Die einfachste und nächstliegende Annahme über die Natur der Triebe wäre, daß sie an sich keine Qualität besitzen, sondern nur als Maße von Arbeitsanforderungen für das Seelenleben in Betracht kommen. Was die Triebe voneinander unterscheidet und mit spezifischen Eigenschaften ausstattet, ist deren Beziehung zu ihren somatischen *Quellen* und ihren *Zielen*. Die Quelle des Triebes ist ein erregender Vorgang in einem Organ, und das nächste Ziel des Triebes liegt in der Aufhebung dieses Organreizes."[19]

Ferner: "Eine weitere vorläufige Annahme in der Trieblehre ... besagt, daß von den Körperorganen Erregungen von zweierlei Art geliefert werden, die in Differenzen chemischer Natur begründet sind."[20] Wir beachten die naturalistische Sichtweise, dass der Trieb im Somatischen wurzelt, mithin also nicht eine geistige Wurzel hat, aber als etwas Seelisches beziehungsweise Psychisches wahrgenommen wird.

Freud sagt: "Mit diesen Vermutungen über die chemische Grundlage der Sexualerregung stehen in guter Übereinstimmung die Hilfsvorstellungen, die wir uns zur Bewältigung der psychischen Äußerungen des Sexuallebens geschaffen haben. Wir haben uns den Begriff der *Libido* festgelegt als einer quantitativ veränderlichen Kraft, welche Vorgänge und Umsetzungen auf dem Gebiete der Sexualerregung messen könnte ... In der Sondierung von libidinöser und anderer psychischer Energie drücken wir die Voraussetzung aus, daß sich die Sexualvorgänge des Organismus durch einen besonderen Chemismus von den Ernährungsvorgängen un-

16   S. Freud, *Drei Abhandlungen zur Sexualtheorie* (1924). 2. Aufl., Hamburg 2015.
17   Freud, *Das Ich und das Es* (GW), 844.
18   Freud, *Das Ich und das Es* (GW), 845.
19   Freud, *Drei Abhandlungen zur Sexualtheorie*, 48.
20   Freud, *Drei Abhandlungen zur Sexualtheorie*, 48.

terscheiden."[21] Der französische Freud-Interpret und Psychoanalytiker Jacques Lacan (1901–1981) kommentiert dazu: "Die Libido ist bei Freud eine Energie, die einer Quantimetrie *[quantimétrie]* fähig ist, die sich um so leichter in die Theorie einführen lässt, als sie ohne Nutzen ist, weil in ihr allein gewisse Konstanz-Quanten *[quanta de constance]* anerkannt werden."[22] Gleichwohl muß man zugeben, dass die Quantisierung der Libido nicht wirklich meßbar ist. Sie ist eben ein geistig-psychisches Phänomen.

Der Mathematiker Tobias Finis (1975–) kommentiert, dass Freud zwar auf eine biologische Fundierung der Triebtheorie hoffte, aber diese Fundierung sei immer problematisch geblieben.[23] Das hängt damit zusammen, dass die Kräfte, die den Trieb kennzeichnen, nicht meßbar sind. Zwar hat Freud versucht, die Libido zu quantisieren, doch eine wissenschaftlich belastbare Aussage über die Kraft der Libido ist nicht möglich. Finis kommentiert: "Lacan fasst den Trieb als eine für die unbewusste Subjektkonstitution grundlegende Struktur auf."[24] Der Trieb ist eine konstante Kraft.

Freud unterscheidet in *Triebe und Triebschicksale* vier Aspekte des Triebs: Quelle, Drang, Ziel, und Objekt.[25] Über den für ihn höchst bedeutsamen Sexualtrieb sagt Freud: "Der Geschlechtstrieb ist wahrscheinlich zunächst unabhängig von seinem Objekt und verdankt wohl auch nicht den Reizen desselben seine Entstehung."[26] "Es ist durchaus unaufgeklärt geblieben, woher die Sexualspannung rührt, die bei der Befriedigung erogener Zonen gleichzeitig mit der Lust entsteht, und welches das Wesen derselben ist."[27] Es ist auffällig, dass Freud regelmäßig im Konjunktiv redet und Mutmaßungen oder Wahrscheinlichkeiten ausspricht. Demensprechend stellt Dirk Quadflieg fest, dass der Status des Triebes und seiner Repräsentation nach wie vor undurchsichtig bleibt: "Vieles deutet darauf hin, dass mit dem Trieb ein zutiefst innerspsychisches und im Grunde narzisstisches Phänomen gemeint ist, das nach Abfuhr drängt und dem

---

[21] Freud, *Drei Abhandlungen zur Sexualtheorie*, 101.
[22] J. Lacan, „Über den Trieb bei Freud und das Begehren des Psychoanalytikers", *Lacan. Trieb und Begehren*, Berlin 2007, 13.
[23] T. Finis, "Trieb-Strukturen". Zu Trieb und Subjekt der Wissenschaft in Lacans Seminar XI," *Lacan. Trieb und Begehren,* Berlin 2007, 33.
[24] Finis, "Trieb-Strukturen", 38.
[25] Finis, "Trieb-Strukturen", 37.
[26] Freud, *Drei Abhandlungen zur Sexualtheorie*, 26.
[27] Freud, *Drei Abhandlungen zur Sexualtheorie*, 97.

sich die Objekte der Außenwelt entweder als Erfüllungsgehilfen oder als Hindernis darbieten."[28]

Freud hat ja seine Triebtheorie bekanntlich aus den Auskünften abgeleitet, die ihm im Zuge der Psychoanalyse geäußert wurden. Er sagt zum Beispiel: "Es ist auf diese Weise (scil. durch Psychoanalyse, BK) in Erfahrung gebracht worden, daß die Symptome (scil. der Neurose, BK) einen Ersatz für Strebungen darstellen, die ihre Kraft der Quelle des Sexualtriebes entnehmen."[29] Doch man bedenke, dass dies Schlußfolgerungen sind, die Freud anstellt, aber nicht wissenschaftlich bewiesen werden können. Sie sind Projektion, nicht Faktum. Ich weise darauf hin, dass Freud im Laufe seiner Arbeit nicht nur die Libido als Grundtrieb ausmachte, sondern auch den Todestrieb, der sich im Sadismus und im Masochismus äußert. Daneben stehen sogenannte "Partialtriebe," "als Bringer neuer Sexualziele," "der Trieb der Schaulust und der Exhibition und der aktiv und passiv ausgebildete Trieb zur Grausamkeit."[30]

Zu Freuds Triebtheorie gehört auch die Annahme, dass ein Trieb etwa durch schöpferische oder kulturelle Leistungen sublimiert werden könne. Er konstatiert: "Die Kulturhistoriker scheinen einig in der Annahme, daß durch solche Ablenkung sexueller Triebkräfte von sexuellen Zielen und Hinlenkung auf neue Ziele, ein Prozeß, der den Namen *Sublimierung* verdient, mächtige Komponenten für alle kulturellen Leistungen gewonnen werden."[31]

Der Freud-Schüler und Mitarbeiter Carl Gustav Jung (1875–1961) postuliert ebenfalls eine Sphäre, die er das Unbewußte nennt, und spaltet dieses auf in das persönliche und das kollektive Unbewußte. Das persönliche Unbewußte sind vergessene Kenntnisse, Gedanken, und Bilder, verdrängte Inhalte und Grundannahmen, die ein Mensch in Laufe seines Lebens gleichsam abgespeichert hat und die ihn in seinen Entscheidungen ständig beeinflussen, ohne daß der Mensch sich deren bewußt ist. Daneben steht das kollektiv Unbewußte, das die Menschheit Jung zufolge in ihrer langen Geschichte angesammelt hat und jedem Menschen angeboren ist (daher die Gleichheit der Verhaltensmuster oder der Reaktion auf bestimmte Sachverhalte). Im kollektiv Unbewußten sind die Archetypen zu lokalisieren. Sie sind archaische Überreste oder Urbilder, eine angeborene, dynamische

[28] D. Quadflieg, "Die Sprache des Triebes. Hegel, Freud, Lacan", *Lacan. Trieb und Begehren*, Berlin 2007, 64.
[29] Freud, *Drei Abhandlungen zur Sexualtheorie*, 44.
[30] Freud, *Drei Abhandlungen zur Sexualtheorie*, 46.
[31] Freud, *Drei Abhandlungen zur Sexualtheorie*, 56.

Tendenz beziehungsweise psychische Energie,[32] bewußte Motivbilder (Träume, Phantasien) zu formen,[33] weshalb sich Analogien zwischen den Traumbildern der unterschiedlichsten Menschen und Kulturen aufweisen lassen. Sie seien Folgen starker emotionaler Erlebnisse, mithin beruhen sie auf der Erfahrung der Menschheit, und sie leiten das Unbewußte. Sie äußern sich daher neben dem Bild auch in der Emotion. Sie seien autonom.[34] Die Archetypen produzieren Mythen, Religionen und Philosophien; sie charakterisieren ganze Nationen und geschichtliche Epochen (cf. Heldenmythos).[35] Jung weist mit seiner Archetypenlehre in eine Schicht der Seele, in der begriffliche Differenzierung angeblich nicht mehr möglich ist und die sich damit der Identifikation entzieht.[36] Die Archetypen seien eben verborgene Mächte, die sich nur deutend erschließen lassen. Sie werden innerpsychisch vorgestellt, indem sie personifiziert werden, so etwa unter den Begriffen „Mutter Erde" oder „unser Vater," oder sie sind als Animus/Anima wirksame Bilder im Zueinander der Geschlechter.

Die Anschauungen Freuds verfolgend fordert Wilhelm Reich (1897–1957) eine neue Sexualökonomie als politisch-gesellschaftliches Ziel. Er stellt fest: "Die Sexualökonomie lehrt jedoch, daß das unbewußte Triebleben des heutigen Menschen, soweit es in der Tat asozial ist und nicht bloß als solches von Moralisten beurteilt wird, ein Produkt der moralischen Regulierung ist und nur mit ihr fortfallen kann. Nur sie kann den Widerspruch zwischen Kultur und Natur aufheben, indem sie mit der Triebunterdrückung auch den perversen und asozialen Trieb beseitigt."[37] Im Gegenzug fordert er: "Das Wesen der sexualökonomischen Regulierung besteht gerade darin, daß man das Setzen absoluter Vorschriften oder Normen vermeidet und die Interessen des Lebenswillens und der Lebenslust als Regulatoren des menschlichen Zusammenlebens anerkennt."[38] Dazu stellt er Forderungen auf, die das Zusammenleben in der Gesellschaft unmittelbar betreffen.[39]

---

[32] C.G.Jung, "Zugang zum Unbewußten", *Der Mensch und seine Symbole* (1968), aus dem Englischen übers. v. K.Thiele-Dohrmann, 12. Aufl., Olten/Freiburg i. Br., 98.
[33] Jung, "Zugang zum Unbewußten", 67.
[34] Jung, "Zugang zum Unbewußten", 83.
[35] Jung, "Zugang zum Unbewußten", 79.
[36] Jung, "Zugang zum Unbewußten", 96.
[37] W. Reich, *Die sexuelle Revolution* (1936). 16. Aufl., Frankfurt 2004, 43.
[38] Reich, *Die sexuelle Revolution*, 50.
[39] S. B. Kaiser, "Die Instrumentalisierung der Sexualität zur Veränderung der Gesell-

Herbert Marcuse (1898–1979), einer der herausragenden Vordenker der Achtundsechziger, nimmt den Ansatz Freuds in durchaus breiter gesellschaftlicher Dimension auf. In seinem Buch *Triebstruktur und Gesellschaft* kritisiert er die patriarchalische Ordnung: "Die vom Vater auferlegte Einschränkung der Triebbefriedigung, die Unterdrückung der Lust, war somit nicht nur die Folge der Herrschaft, sondern schaffte auch die psychischen Vorbedingungen für das fortdauernde Funktionieren der Herrschaft."[40] Demgegenüber fordert Marcuse eine Kultur ohne Unterdrückung und Verdrängung. Eine solche "… tendiert auf eine neue Beziehung zwischen Trieben und Vernunft hin. Die kulturelle Moral wird durch die Harmonisierung von Triebfreiheit und Ordnung aufgehoben und ersetzt: befreit von der der Tyrannei repressiver Vernunft richten sich die Triebe auf freie und dauerhafte existentielle Beziehungen – sie schaffen ein neues Realitätsprinzip."[41] Mit dieser Forderung akzeptiert Marcuse die grundlegende Triebhaftigkeit des Menschen als neues Realitätsprinzip, als Grundannahme für das gesellschaftliche Zusammenleben.

Unter einer naturalistischen Weltdeutung, die versucht, ohne Gott, den Schöpfer, auszukommen, ist der Mensch als Resultat der Evolution für sich genommen gut, einfach deswegen, weil er so ist, wie er ist. Das aber heißt, dass auch seine Triebhaftigkeit im Grundsatz als positiv anzusehen ist und infolgedessen die Befriedigung des Triebes nicht nur Handlungsziel, sondern auch rechtmäßig sein soll. Franz M. Wuketits (1955–2018), österreichischer Biologe und Wissenschaftstheoretiker, verweist auf die evolutionäre Vorgeschichte des Menschen und hält eine Erziehung, die die menschliche Natur ändern möchte, für illusorisch, ebenso wie den Gedanken der Willensfreiheit. Der Mensch ist im Grunde ein Gefangener seiner Natur. Im Blick auf den Geschlechtstrieb kommt er zu dem Schluß: "Aus biologischer Sicht ist heute nur die Meinung vertretbar, dass jede Unterdrückung der Sexualität grundsätzlich falsch ist und Verbote fehl am Platze sind."[42] Ferner sagt er: "Die Vorstellung vom freien Willen ist eine Illusion. Aber Illusionen sind durchaus nützlich. Sie können als Resultate der Evolution durch natürliche Auslese gedeutet werden und haben ihren

schaft", (2019), in: https://irt-ggmbh.de/?ngt=w7e2c0a0e2c24d2069027123346 11817 (11.04.2022)

[40] H. Marcuse, *Triebstruktur und Gesellschaft. Ein philosophischer Beitrag zu Sigmund Freud* (1955), Frankfurt 1979, 64–65.

[41] Marcuse, *Triebstruktur und Gesellschaft*, 195.

[42] F. Wuketits, *Der Affe in uns. Warum die Kultur an unserer Natur zu scheitern droht*, Stuttgart 2002, 189.

Sinn im Dienste des Überlebens."[43] Das bedeutet, dass eine sexuell ent-
schränkte Kultur gleichsam wesensnotwendig ist.

3. Schluss

Der Trieb ist für Freud ein Grundbegriff der Psychoanalyse. Finis kommentiert: "Die Triebe sind mythische Wesen, großartig in ihrer Unbe-
stimmtheit."[44] Freud sieht die Triebhaftigkeit als unbewußte Grundlage
und als das eigentlich Charakteristische des Menschseins an. Sie äußert
sich in den vordergründig einander widersprechenden Trieben Libido und
Todestrieb. In gleicher Weise teilen die Freud-Schüler die Annahme einer
im Unbewußten verankerten Triebhaftigkeit des Menschen. Hier sei jedoch darauf verwiesen, dass die Annahme einer solchen Sphäre unbe-
gründet und experimentell nicht nachweisbar ist. Es sei zugestanden, dass
es ein persönlich Unbewußtes im Sinne Jungs gibt, das aber erinnert und
ausgesprochen werden kann. Die Annahme einer unbewußten Sphäre im
Sinne Freuds und des kollektiv Unbewußten bei Jung, die als nicht be-
stimmbarer Trieb zu fassen ist, bedeutet, dass dieses Menschenbild den
Mythos der unhinterfragbaren und nicht kritisierbaren Triebhaftigkeit des
Menschen kreiert. Dem steht die biblische Aussage entgegen, dass das
Wort Gottes auch Seele und Geist des Menschen beurteilt und dass vor
ihm nichts verborgen ist.[45] Auch der von seiner Begierde geleitete Mensch
folgt nicht einem irrationalen und unwiderstehlichen Impuls, sondern er
kann wissen und sagen, aus welchem Grund und mit welchem Ziel er
handelt, auch wenn Grund und Ziel des Handelns fragwürdig und seine
Triebe mächtig sind.

Der amerikanische Physiologe Benjamin Libet[46] (1916–2007) hat –
wohl unter anderem motiviert durch seine jüdische Herkunft – zu zeigen
versucht, dass der Mensch auch in neurochemischer Hinsicht frei ist.
Seine vielbeachteten Versuche führten indes zu dem Ergebnis, dass der
Impuls zu einer Tat etwas weniger als eine halbe Sekunde früher stattfin-
det, bevor er dem Menschen ins Bewußtsein tritt. Wuketits hat diese Be-

---

[43]   F. Wuketits, *Der freie Wille. Die Evolution einer Illusion.* 2. Aufl., Stuttgart 2008,
7.
[44]   Finis, "Triebstrukturen", 32.
[45]   Hebräer 4,12–13.
[46]   B. Libet, *Mind Time. Wie das Gehirn Bewusstsein produziert*, Frankfurt 2005.

obachtung zur Rechtfertigung seiner quasi deterministischen Sicht des Menschen herangezogen. Er nahm jedoch nicht zur Kenntnis, dass Libet dem Menschen die Fähigkeit zuschrieb, vor einer dem neurochemischen Impuls folgenden Tat zu dieser Nein zu sagen.

Die bewußte Opposition Freuds und seiner Nachfolger gegenüber dem christlichen, von Vernunft und Besonnenheit geleiteten Denken des Abendlandes ist offensichtlich. Das neuere Menschenbild, das im Denken des Neumarxismus der Achtundsechziger-Bewegung aufgenommen wurde, hat mittlerweile weite Teile der westlichen Gesellschaften geprägt und zu einem verbreiteten Hedonismus geführt.[47] Es trägt bei allen psychologischen Einsichten einerseits einen stark irrationalen Zug und ist darüber hinaus von einem deterministischen Naturalismus geprägt. Es zeigt sich besonders in der Bewertung und Handhabung der Sexualität, die zu einem wesentlichen Element menschlicher Selbstwahrnehmung avanciert ist. Es liegt auf der Hand, dass das skizzierte Menschenbild eine kulturbestimmende Bedeutung hat. Es prägt gegenwärtig die Dimension des Rechts, der Pädagogik, der Wirtschaft und der Kultur und hat allemal auch eine maßgebliche Bedeutung für die persönliche Lebensführung des Menschen.

Ich identifiziere diese von Freud und seinen Nachfolgern angenommenen Triebe als Aspekte dessen, was die heilige Schrift *epithymia* oder *orexis* nennt. Es ist im Licht der heiligen Schrift nicht zu bestreiten, dass der Mensch Triebe hat. Sie sind aus schöpfungstheologischer Sicht anerschaffen. Aus hamartiologischer Sicht sind sie in den Sündenfall hineingezogen und richten sich auch auf Objekte jenseits der vom Schöpfer durch die Zehn Gebote verfügten Grenzen. Damit ist auch klar, dass die Triebhaftigkeit des Menschen nicht auf den Sexualtrieb beschränkt werden kann. Allerdings wird man den Menschen nicht auf seine Triebhaftigkeit reduzieren können, so dass die Aussage, der Mensch sei ein Triebwesen sehr vereinseitigend und im Grunde entwürdigend ist.

Aus soteriologischer Sicht steht im Raum, dass der Christ durch den Glauben besonnen leben kann, mithin also seine Triebe in den vom Gebot des Schöpfers gesetzten Schranken leben kann, ohne damit an Lebensqualität zu verlieren, sondern das (irdische) Leben zu gewinnen. Es ist ein Ausdruck der wiedergewonnenen Menschenwürde, wenn er nicht dem Impuls seiner Triebe folgt. Damit ist auch klar, dass der Christ in der Spannung zwischen Geist und Fleisch steht und zeit seines Lebens herausge-

---

[47]   Vgl. Kaiser, "Die Instrumentalisierung der Sexualität zur Veränderung der Gesellschaft".

fordert ist, den Kampf gegen die Sünde in der Begierde zu führen. Das Leben in Weisheit und Zucht ist für den Christen kein unerreichbares Ideal, sondern Lebenspraxis, ohne damit sagen zu wollen, der Christ sei ethisch vollkommen. Er wird vielmehr der sündigen Begierde in seinem Herzen gewahr, aber er sagt Nein zu deren Verwirklichung in der Tat. Er wird sich darüber freuen, dass er durch Christus ein Stück des heilen Lebens gewonnen hat. Im übrigen gibt es einen rechten Gebrauch der geschöpflichen Gaben, der Sexualität, des Besitzes und der Macht, der nicht von erzwungenem Triebverzicht und Heuchelei geprägt ist, sondern von der Freiheit in Christus und von der Freude an dem, was Gott dem Menschen gibt. Eine christliche Kultur wird die Triebhaftigkeit des Menschen anerkennen, aber es als Würde des Menschen ansehen, um einen Gebrauch der geschöpflichen Gaben mit Vernunft und Besonnenheit zu ringen und einen solchen zu praktizieren.

In His Own Likeness, After His Image
Self-Propagating Parodies of Life

Jaap Doedens

Master and Emissary

In his seminal work, *The Master and His Emissary: The Divided Brain and the Making of the Western World*, Iain McGilchrist[1] describes how within western culture the brain's left hemisphere has taken the lead and impresses its worldview upon society, science, and culture. He describes how the right hemisphere of the human brain is oriented outwards, toward the "Other," is always attentive to the world around us, and understands metaphor and humor. The function of the left hemisphere is to systematize the input coming from the right hemisphere, and after doing its task of sorting everything out, give back the results to the right hemisphere so that people can take their proper place in their surrounding reality. As it turns out from this description, the right hemisphere should be dominant, while at the same time the left hemisphere should serve as its helper. McGilchrist assigns the role of "master" to the right and that of "emissary" to the left hemisphere. However, in the view of McGilchrist, within the dominant western culture, the "emissary" gradually learnt to despise its "master" and succeeded in taking over leadership, seeing its own attribution as the one and only valuable. He traces this development within philosophy, art, and literature, from pre-Socratic philosophy until modernity and post-modernity.

According to McGilchrist, in order to acquire leadership, a left-brain approach has resulted in at least four myths. The first myth is that all science has a kind of uniformity, as if science did not consist of several disci-

---

[1]   Iain McGilchrist, *The Master and His Emissary. The Divided Brain and the Making of the Western World*, New Haven 2012.

plines, all with their own different methodology that does not necessarily work in other disciplines. The second myth is the thought that this scientific mode of strict logical operating is sovereign above everything else – thus failing to acknowledge that much of scientific advance was reached by accidental observations, the tenacity of skilled local enthusiasts, or mere serendipitous spin-off from trying to invent something totally different. This left-hemisphere scientific myth definitely would react with indignation to the science-limiting statement that there exists not only an *ignoramus* (we do not know), but also an *ignorabimus* (we will never know) within our knowledge of the world.[2] The third myth is the notion that science is the only reliable source for morality and decent living. This myth, of course, dismisses the fact that science not only alleviated human suffering, but also often caused or even aggravated it, sometimes by associating with corrupt political regimes. Moreover, science may be able to describe reality to a certain extent, but cannot prescribe how humans should behave. An "is" cannot be turned into an "ought" so easily. The fourth myth is that science is a kind of freedom fighter against all dogmatism – usually directed against a simplified picture of the Church and Christian doctrine – as if only science is a bias-free endeavor.[3] Ironically, adherents to this last myth defend their fight against dogmatism with a most dogmatic *rigueur*.

Self-Propagating Parodies of Life

According to this analysis, the results of the Industrial Revolution arise as the temporary climax of the above-mentioned left-hemisphere-driven myths. McGilchrist describes the Industrial Revolution as the left hemisphere *outflanking* the right. Since the right hemisphere deals with the

---

[2] As coined by Emil du Bois-Reymond, *Über die Grenzen des Naturerkennens. Die sieben Welträthsel*, Leipzig 1891, 51: "Gegenüber den Räthseln der Körperwelt ist der Naturforscher längst gewöhnt, mit männlicher Entsagung sein *'Ignoramus'* auszusprechen. Im Rückblick auf die durchlaufene siegreiche Bahn trägt ihn dabei das stille Bewusstsein, dass, wo er jetzt nicht weiss, er wenigstens unter Umständen wissen könnte, und dereinst vielleicht wissen wird. Gegenüber dem Räthsel aber, was Materie und Kraft seien, und wie sie zu denken vermögen, muss er ein für allemal zu dem viel schwerer abzugebenden Wahrspruch sich entschliessen: *'Ignorabimus'*." For critical reactions to this *ignorabimus*, see Du Bois-Reymond, *Über die Grenzen des Naturerkennens*, 70–72.

[3] See McGilchrist, *The Master and His Emissary*, 385–386.

"between-ness" of the outside world and human consciousness, the left-brain could overtake the right by producing its own reproductions within the outside world. Thus, the right hemisphere could hardly escape a kind of hall full of mirrors reflecting the left hemisphere's reality beyond the human mind within the outside world. During the Industrial Revolution, the left-brain not only began to grasp power over the natural world, but it also *created* a world in the image of its own left hemisphere approach.[4] In McGilchrist's words:

> The mechanical production of goods ensured a world in which the members of a class were not just approximate fits, because of their tiresome authenticity as individuals, but truly identical: equal, interchangeable members of their category. They would be free from the 'imperfections' that come from being made by living hands. The subtle variations of form that result from natural processes would be replaced by invariant forms [...]. It would above all make tools, mechanisms, the sort of inanimate objects preferentially dealt with by the left hemisphere, and it would make machines that make machines, self-propagating parodies of life that lack all the qualities of the living. Its products would be certain, perfect in their way, *familiar* in the 'iconic' sense (preferred by the left hemisphere), not in the sense of 'special things that have value for me' (preferred by the right): identical entities, rectilinear in shape, endlessly reproducible, mechanistic in nature, certain, fixed, man-made.[5]

It would be difficult to deny McGilchrist's observations on the effects of the Industrial Revolution. In his view, the right hemisphere's approach theoretically still might escape from this industrially designed replica of reality. "Through the fact of our embodied nature, through art and through religion, the right hemisphere might still be able to make a comeback."[6] Yet, as McGilchrist views it, in the twentieth and twenty-first centuries, the left hemisphere successfully has blocked this emergency exit.

---

[4]   See McGilchrist, *The Master and His Emissary*, 386.
[5]   McGilchrist, *The Master and His Emissary*, 386–387.
[6]   McGilchrist, *The Master and His Emissary*, 388.

All these developments culminating in the Industrial Revolution and subsequently the digital revolution had an almost irreversible effect on how we humans tend to see ourselves. As a result, we tend to think that the world of identical and "perfect" forms produced in factories is how reality should be. In the meantime, organic, living, non-rectilinear shapes became looked down upon as inferior, even when applied to our own human bodily existence. Plastic surgery with its botox-treatments and silicone implants is only the tip of the iceberg here.

Summing up what happens to people, McGilchrist observes: "an excess of consciousness and an over-explicitness in relation to what needs to remain intuitive and implicit; depersonalization and alienation from the body and empathic feeling; disruption of context; fragmentation of experience; and the loss of 'betweenness'."[7] People gradually have lost the feeling that their lives have meaning and thus end up in boredom. As an illustration, McGilchrist quotes a 1990 French research according to which 23 percent of French men and 31 percent of French women reported being bored while making love.[8] Consequences of this boredom can be seen in a culture of entertainment, in which speech has to be evermore hyperbolic, music loud, ideas fantastic, and emotions borderless and shameless.[9]

As the left hemisphere prefers abstractions and also *things*, for the sake of how they can be *used*, left-brain worldview is per definition materialistic. And, as McGilchrist paradoxically observes: materialists are not people who *overvalue* matter, but, on the contrary *undervalue* it by only seeing it from the angle of its usefulness.[10] Concrete things are represented by abstract concepts and subsequently these concepts become the new things. As if a map of the world is replacing the world itself.[11] Yet a map is only a schematic reproduction, something in a low resolution, leaving out

---

[7] McGilchrist, *The Master and His Emissary,* 397.

[8] McGilchrist, *The Master and His Emissary,* 400.

[9] McGilchrist, *The Master and His Emissary,* 400, referring to Anton van Zijderveld's study of the cliché.

[10] McGilchrist, *The Master and His Emissary,* 401.

[11] See McGilchrist, *The Master and His Emissary,* 401–403. Jorge Luis Borges describes in his short story "On Exactitude in Science," how cartographers, searching pure perfection of their profession, built a map of an empire with exactly the same size as the empire itself. See Jorge Luis Borges, *A Universal History of Infamy*, New York 1972.

all that is unnecessary for its aims. Interestingly, leaving out unnecessary details is the way in which our brain functions, allowing us to find our way in the world. Yet not allowing for the *possibility* to concentrate on these uncontrollable aspects of life, deprives us from the chance that the world still can surprise us.

At the end of his book, McGilchrist depicts what a world totally ruled by the left hemisphere would look like, and he concludes that western culture has almost reached that culmination. He sums up a list of the effects of the left-brain taking the lead, among other things:[12]

- increasing specialization and technicalizing of knowledge
- substituting information for experience-based knowledge
- appreciating of knowledge above wisdom
- increase of bureaucracy, work overtaken by documenting tasks or supposed tasks at the expense of the real job
- growing governmental control of society
- tendency towards reification: if humans are like machines, society wants to know how much they can do, how fast they can do it, and in what measure of precision
- diminishing of individuality, instead people being determined by their group-identity of socioeconomic groups, races, sexes, gender, etc.
- family relationships become suspicious
- skilled functions in society, like priests, teachers, and doctors are looked upon with suspicion
- growing need for controlling unpredictable aspects of life, like accidents, illnesses, and "wild" nature
- death, as the ultimate uncontrollable factor will become a taboo, while sex would become explicit and omnipresent
- increase of anger and aggressiveness in social interactions
- growing intolerance and inflexibility
- lack of willpower and self-motivation, at the same time increasing greed and the drive to manipulate
- deliberate undercutting of the sense of awe and wonder, religion will be dismissed as just "fantasy"
- music will be reduced to mainly rhythm
- dance will become solipsistic rather than communal

---

12   See McGilchrist, *The Master and His Emissary,* 428–434.

- the human body will be viewed as a machine
- the natural world will be seen as something to exploit
- language will become "woolly" and abstract

Thus, we come to the role of theology and the church, that – together with the fine arts – might be among the last bulwarks against the omnipresent hegemony of the left-brain approach. McGilchrist sees a role for the western church, but observes that the church often acted in a contraproductive way by joining the opinions of those who apply material answers to spiritual problems. Instead, the church, in his opinion, should have the confidence to stick to its own values and agenda. He insists that we need metaphor and *mythos* as a way to understand the world. These myths are not optional or a kind of luxury, we have no option *not* to choose a myth: if we discard one myth, another will impose itself on us. It is like the famous saying attributed to G. K. Chesterton, that "When men choose not to believe in God, they do not thereafter believe in nothing, they then become capable of believing in anything."[13] John Calvin similarly observed that humans are a "factory of idols."[14] This is what the Old Testament already had been emphasizing: who turns away from the Creator-God, automatically awakens the idols. Moreover, any idol will ir-

---

[13] The quote is widely attributed to Gilbert Keith Chesterton, yet cannot be found in his works. Its first mention is most probably in Emile Cammaerts, *Chesterton. The Laughing Prophet* (1937). See Dale Ahlquist in his foreword to a newer edition of Cammaerts's book, "'The first effect of not believing in God is to believe in anything.' G. K. Chesterton's most famous quotation, right? Well, yes and no. Chesterton is certainly famous for saying it, but the trouble is that he never quite said it. The line above comes from Emile Cammaerts in this book, *The Laughing Prophet*. He is making a reference to ideas expressed by Chesterton in some Father Brown stories, ideas which even contain fragments of the famous quotation, but it may, in fact, be Cammaerts who actually said the most well known saying that Chesterton did not say." Emile Cammaerts, *The Laughing Prophet. The Seven Virtues and G. K. Chesterton,* Hopkins, MN (no date, originally published 1937), 1. The quotation can be found on page 230, and, indeed, seems to be Cammaerts's conclusion rather than a quotation from any of Chesterton's works. Cammaerts gives this famous summary before quoting Chesterton, "And a dog is an omen and a cat is a mystery, and a pig is a mascot and a beetle is a scarab, calling up all the menagerie of polytheism from Egypt and old India, ... and all because you are frightened of four words: 'He was made Man'."

[14] *Inst.* I.11.8, "[T]he human mind is, so to speak, a perpetual forge of idols." John Calvin, *The Institutes of the Christian Religion*, trans. Henry Beveridge, New York 2011.

resistibly de-humanize its human worshiper.[15] By lack of any better, and induced by its machine-building culture, the western world has chosen the metaphor of the machine to understand reality, but this will not bring us too far.[16]

In order to rediscover a right hemisphere approach, McGilchrist suggests that we can learn from oriental culture. East-Asian ways of thinking are less marked by rationality. Oriental cultures also appreciate the fact that everything is fleeting. Japanese temples are rebuilt every 20 years, giving every new generation the possibility to acquire the techniques of temple building. Yet the new building is seen as the same temple! Thus, the classical philosophical question about how much of Theseus's ship can be replaced during restoration without losing its identity, would have posed no problem for Japanese philosophers.[17] It appears, thus, that East-Asians have a more holistic approach of reality. Moreover, they ground self-esteem or self-worth not upon – unearned – thinking highly of yourself, but on being a good citizen and member of your society. Therefore, experiencing failure leads within the western culture for many people to giving up and to depression, while in East-Asian cultures failure results in the determination to do better. In short, in McGilchrist's view, the interplay between right and left-brain is still more balanced in oriental cultures than in western culture.[18]

The Bible as Antidote to Cultural Disaster

If we would more or less accept McGilchrist's analysis, the question arises whether theology might have an antidote to this situation. My answer to that question is positive, perhaps with a few restrictions. The cultural situation described by McGilchrist consists of both reduction of our humanity,

---

[15] See Ps 115:4–8; 135:15–18, stating that those who make or worship idols will become equal to them, having eyes, but not seeing, having ears, but not hearing, etc.
[16] McGilchrist, *The Master and His Emissary*, 441.
[17] In fact, the situation is a little bit more complicated than indicated by McGilchrist. As it turns out, Japanese conservation and restauration of wooden buildings usually retains as much of the original timber as possible. See Alejandro Martínez de Arbulo, "The Ship of Theseus: A Misleading Paradox? The Authenticity of Wooden Built Heritage in Japanese Conservation Practice," *Journal of Architectural Conservation* 29 (2023) 2, 151–167.
[18] McGilchrist, *The Master and His Emissary*, 452–459.

and of a reduction of reality. Theology may provide answers for both of these reductions.

I suggest starting with the biblical antidote to the reduction of our humanity. If a left-brain oriented world produces self-propagating parodies of life, this touches upon what the Bible states about humans being created in the image of God. Among other things, this being created in the image of God means that humans have the task to represent God's good rule on earth. This way of acting on behalf of the Creator must by definition include making room for all the multicolored aspects of created reality. Creating parodies of life, as it were mechanistic images of humans themselves, not only tends to reduce reality to its mechanistic and materialistic part, but also brings into existence a new kind of idolatry. Idolatry is basically worshiping creation instead of the Creator. The new aspect to this would be that, now, humans are not only worshiping creation, but also their own creations consisting of a left-brain determined parody of life.

The Old Testament has a striking observation about worshiping idols. Idols have mouths, but do not speak; eyes, but do not see; they have ears, but do not hear; noses, but do not smell; they have hands, but do not feel; feet, but do not walk. Nothing really disturbing – but then comes the scary part: Those who make them and worship them will become like them.[19] Having still a mouth, but neither be able to speak of God's glory, nor in defense of their fellow humans. Having eyes, but being blind for injustice. Their ears become deaf for the cry of the disenfranchised. Their hands and feet do not hurry to help. In short, worshiping idols dehumanizes, making people sub-human and never super-human. Moreover, its effects are progressive. In the end, it can even eradicate our humanity in such a way, that – but for the grace of the Creator-God – we may end up not only as sub-human, but also as someone who changed into a *former* human being.

The left-brain driven activity can fill the world with parodies of life. Looking clear-cut, well-designed, and flawless. Seemingly apt for worship. Yet they are much more inferior compared to humans with all their flaws and imperfections. This is, for example, the reason why Artificial Intelligence will never be able to keep up with God-given "natural" intelligence. Exactly because of the fact that Artificial Intelligence in contrast to Natural Intelligence misses embodiment. Embodied intelligence always becomes aware of the utter complexity of the world, which can never be grasped in

---

[19] Ps 115:4–8; 135:15–18.

a "left-brain-only" way of looking to and dealing with the world. Biblical narrative, poetry, wisdom, and apocalyptic may call western civilization back to the multicolored nature of reality. And by doing so may stimulate us to worship the real Creator for this complexity of the created reality. It seems that reflecting God's wise rule towards the world and reflecting back to God the praise of creation – which only humans can articulate in words – will make visible again the image of God in humans.[20]

I think we should still add a caveat, here, given the functioning of mostly western theology. After all, western post-enlightenment theology has been deeply influenced by the rise of the left-brain dominance of our present culture.

The Bible, however, by contrast, is a book that allows for all kind of differences, not being a copy of something else. Psalms abound with both praise and doubt, experiences of both being lost as well as being found. The book of Job answers the problem of suffering by not giving an answer. The Bible contains and depicts a multifaceted real world. It does not provide a low resolution map of reality, but displays reality itself with all its jagged edges, colorfulness, joy, humor, pain, transience, deceit and sin, being lost and being saved, eventually finding peace, even within suffering. There is an overarching narrative, but that overarching view is not established by left-brain logical constructions. However, for biblical scholarship to play a constitutional part in the formation of a more balanced view of human beings within the world, it should leave behind the more left hemisphere driven methods that can be found in both the liberal and the fundamentalist reading of the Bible. Otherwise biblical theology, too, runs the risk of putting a map of reality over reality itself as its substitute.

As an example of this too much left-brain oriented approach may serve the so called historical critical method, which is neither "historical" nor, for that matter, "critical." After all, this method is based on a mainly philosophical – and not an historical – reconstruction of "religion" in Ancient Israel. Therefore, the method should be critical towards itself as well and adapt to new historical data. Similarly, a "fundamentalist" reading of the Bible uses the same rational methods to interpret these ancient texts, e.g. in the debate about creation or evolution. In that debate, evolutionists state – based on their scientific method – that the Bible does not give trustworthy historical information about creation, while fundamentalist exegesis uses the same scientific methodological approaches to defend

---

[20]   See also the quotation from N. T. Wright in note 23.

that the Bible does so. Yet this might not quite be the right approach to understand the biblical creation narratives in their own literary and historical contexts. The historical critical method with its "assured scholarly results" – perhaps unsurprisingly – has a high "so what?"-character and therefore makes itself boringly superfluous. The fundamentalist approach with its so-called "biblical" answers to scientific challenges will eventually lose the debate, and, far worse, lose gullible believers, thus making itself superfluous as well. Both of these approaches apply a left-brain hemisphere approach above listening in a way that is in tune with the texts.

Only then, when tuning in to texts, new understandings of ancient narratives may – almost in the literal sense of the word – "pop up" through sensing the metaphors, intuitions, implicitness, intertextuality, cross-references, bottomlessness, and multi-layered presence of these texts. These are all phenomena that simply cannot be grasped by the left-brain. Therefore, they tend to be neglected or even scorned upon; they only can play their important part when the left-brain gives the results of its ordering and synthesizing activities back to its "master," the right hemisphere. Only then can these texts begin to contribute again something indispensable to shaping our world in a wholesome way. They may even give us back some sanity, and may keep humanity human.

Till We Have Faces

One of C. S. Lewis's greatest novels has the title *Till We Have Faces.*[21] It is a remake of the ancient story of Eros and Psyche. The protagonist of the book is a queen who always hides her face, in the first place because people thought she was very ugly. Yet, upon covering her face with a veil, she discovered that by not showing her face she could throw people she met off balance, and as a result, she could easily dominate them. It is only at the end of the tale when, in a dream, she meets the gods whom she continuously insulted of injustice. In this encounter with the divine, she discovers that we cannot meet the gods face-to-face, and the gods cannot communicate with us face-to-face, as long as we have no faces.

This might be an impressive metaphor for what it means to be the image of God. It means that functioning as an image of God is never something static, something we inherently possess, but is either diminishing or

---

[21] C. S. Lewis, *Till We Have Faces. A Myth Retold,* New York 1957.

evermore becoming real. Being the image of God is a dynamic process, never a "fact" we can take for granted and put away on one of our theological or philosophical shelves. In fact, the question of *imago Dei* may turn out to be a question of life or death. Therefore, it is not indifferent whether we are left to a rational left-brain theology, and even boringly so, or that we receive a hope-giving, life-renewing, inspiring theology, in which the right brain – called the "master" in McGilchrist's idiom – receives back the results of its "emissary's" efforts in order to pay attention to the overarching narrative lines, to metaphor and intertextuality. I think it is no exaggeration to call being the image of God a question of life or death. Especially if this is not an inborn quality, but a *vocation*. Qualities are things someone has or does not have. But a *vocation* is a call we have to respond to. Or not. Just to quote here N. T. Wright: "If we can study Genesis and human origins without hearing *the call to be an image-bearing human being renewed in Jesus,* we are massively missing the point, perhaps pursuing our own dream of an otherworldly salvation that merely colludes with the forces of evil."[22] Biblical studies solely left to a left-brain approach may result exactly in something like that. With as a result that we create many things in our own image – and by doing so, we ourselves will become less and less human.[23] We might, therefore, meditate on the words of St Paul: "And we all, with unveiled face, reflecting the glory of the Lord, are being changed into his likeness from one degree of glory to another; for this comes from the Lord who is the Spirit."[24]

[22]   N. T. Wright, in: John H. Walton, *The Lost World of Adam and Eve. Genesis 2–3 and the Human Origins Debate,* Downers Grove, IL 2015, 179.

[23]   Cf. N. T. Wright, *For All the Saints. Remembering the Christian Departed,* Harrisburg, PA 2004, 44, "The central fact about humans in the Bible is that they bear the image of God (Genesis 1.26–28, etc.). I understand this as a vocation as much as an innate character. Humans are summoned to worship and love their creator, and to reflect his image into the world. When, however, instead of worshipping and loving him, they worship and love that which is not him – in other words, something within the order of creation, whether spiritual or material – they turn away from him. But they can only be maintained in his image, as genuine humans, by worshipping him; they depend on him for their life and character. The rest of creation, by contrast, is subject to decay and death. If we worship it, or some part of it, instead of the life-giving God, we are invoking death upon ourselves instead of life."

[24]   2 Cor 3:18, "ἡμεῖς δὲ πάντες ἀνακεκαλυμμένῳ προσώπῳ τὴν δόξαν κυρίου κατοπτριζόμενοι τὴν αὐτὴν εἰκόνα μεταμορφούμεθα ἀπὸ δόξης εἰς δόξαν καθάπερ ἀπὸ κυρίου πνεύματος."

List of contributors

Ibolya Balla, Associate professor, Biblical Institute, Pápa Reformed Theological Seminary, Pápa, Hungary

Zoltán Balikó, Associate professor, Institute of Systematic Theology, Pápa Reformed Theological Seminary, Pápa, Hungary

Jacob J. T. Doedens, Associate professor, Biblical Institute, Pápa Reformed Theological Seminary, Pápa, Hungary

Gyopárka Köves, PhD student, Károli Gáspár Reformed University, Budapest, Hungary

Bernhard Kaiser, Professor, János Selye University, Faculty of Reformed Theology, Komarno, Slovakia

György Kustár, Assistant professor, Sárospatak Reformed Theological University, Sárospatak, Hungary

Francis M. Macatangay, Adjunct Professor of Sacred Scripture, School of Theology of the University of St. Thomas, Houston, USA

József Nagy, Associate professor, Biblical Institute, Pápa Reformed Theological Seminary, Pápa, Hungary

Áron Németh, Associate professor, Debrecen Reformed Theological University, Debrecen, Hungary

Mirjam Piplica, PhD student, John Paul II Catholic University, Lublin, Poland

Theo Pleizier, Assistant professor, Protestant Theological University, Groningen, The Netherlands

Enoh Šeba, Assistant professor, University Centre for Protestant Theology Matthias Flacius Illyricus, University of Zagreb, Croatia

Marcin Zieliński, Assistant professor, John Paul II Catholic University, Lublin, Poland